Discovering the
OUTLAW TRAIL

Routes, Hideouts & Stories
from the Wild West

Mike Bezemek

MOUNTAINEERS
BOOKS

MOUNTAINEERS BOOKS is dedicated to the exploration, preservation, and enjoyment of outdoor and wilderness areas.

1001 SW Klickitat Way, Suite 201, Seattle, WA 98134
800-553-4453, mountaineersbooks.org

Printed in China
Distributed in the United Kingdom by Cordee, cordee.co.uk

First edition, 2023

Cover design: McKenzie Long
Interior design & layout: Melissa McFeeters
Cartographer: Lohnes + Wright
All photographs by the author unless credited otherwise
Photos: Cover (from top, left to right), *The Wind River Range is aptly named atop Whiskey Mountain (Adventure 70); Sunset at Paria Townsite (Adventure 39); The Fort Worth Five, including Butch Cassidy—key members of the Wild Bunch; Overlanding in Robbers Roost (Adventures 19–21); Mountain bikers at the Little Grand Canyon in the San Rafael Swell (Adventure 22)*; page 3, *Highway 95 in Utah, not far from Hite Marina (Adventure 29, but practically a million miles from everywhere else*; page 4, *An outlaw adventurer—if there ever was one—jumps across boulders at Vedauwoo Recreation Area in Wyoming (Adventure 60).*; page 304, *Bald eagles are SO dramatic about everything.*
Page 49 photo courtesy of History Colorado (Accession #93.499.13)

Library of Congress Cataloging-in-Publication Data is available at https://lccn.loc.gov/2023004083. The e-book record is available at https://lccn.loc.gov/2023004084.

Disclaimer: Please employ common sense when using this guide. Before embarking, make sure you realistically assess your own skills, experience, fitness, and equipment. Be sure to recognize the inherent dangers found in desert, canyon, and mountain settings. Assume responsibility for your own actions and safety, including awareness of changing or unfavorable conditions and navigation of dangerous or unmaintained roads and trails. Ultimately, this book contains only the personal opinions and experiences of the author. The publisher and author are expressly not responsible for any adverse consequences resulting directly or indirectly from information contained in this book.

Mountaineers Books titles may be purchased for corporate, educational, or other promotional sales, and our authors are available for a wide range of events. For information on special discounts or booking an author, contact our customer service at 800-553-4453 or mbooks@mountaineersbooks.org.

Printed on FSC®-certified materials

ISBN (paperback): 978-1-68051-523-7
ISBN (ebook): 978-1-68051-524-4

An independent nonprofit publisher since 1960

For all the adventurers who keep the spirit of rebellion alive on the outlaw trail

Contents

PART I Discovering the Outlaw Trail

PART II Stories from the Outlaw Trail

PART III Traveling the Outlaw Trail

PART IV The Ends of the Outlaw Trail— Stories Conclude

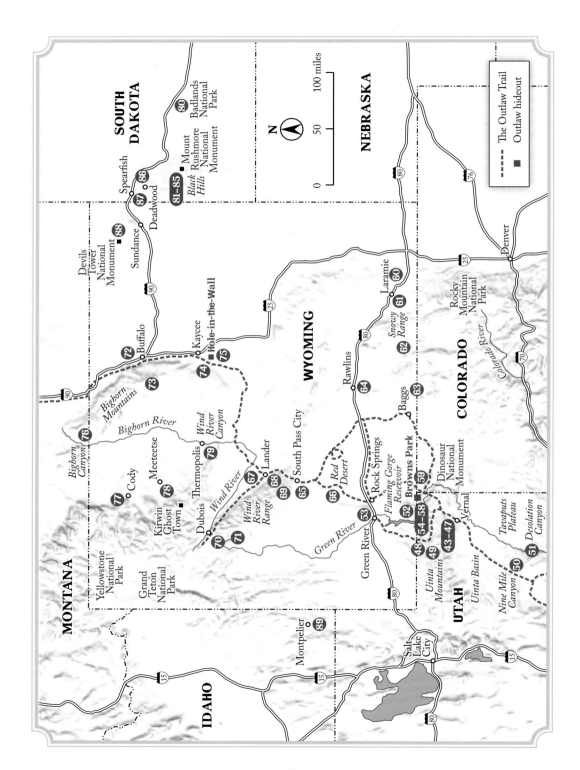

SOUTH DAKOTA

NEBRASKA

100 miles

50

0

N

The Outlaw Trail
Outlaw hideout

Badlands National Park

Spearfish
Mount Rushmore National Monument

Black Hills

Deadwood

80

81–85

87
86
80

Denver

25

Devils Tower National Monument

Sundance

90

Buffalo

Hole-in-the-Wall

Kaycee

83

72

73

74

75

90

Bigborn Mountains

25

WYOMING

Laramie

60

Snowy Range

61

62

Rocky Mountain National Park

COLORADO

Colorado River

70

Bigborn River

76

Rawlins

64

Baggs

63

Bigborn Canyon

Wind River Canyon

Thermopolis

79

Lander

South Pass City

Red Desert

Rock Springs

59

Dinosaur National Monument

Cody

Meeteetse

78

Dubois

67

63
69

65

66

53

Flaming Gorge Reservoir

Browns Park

52

54–58

Vernal

77

Kirwin Ghost Town

Wind River

Wind River Range

70
71

Green River

Green River

80

48
49

43–47

Uinta Mountains

Uinta Basin

UTAH

Tavaputs Plateau

Desolation Canyon

51

50

Nine Mile Canyon

MONTANA

Yellowstone National Park

Grand Teton National Park

IDAHO

Montpelier

88

15

15

Salt Lake City

15

80

15

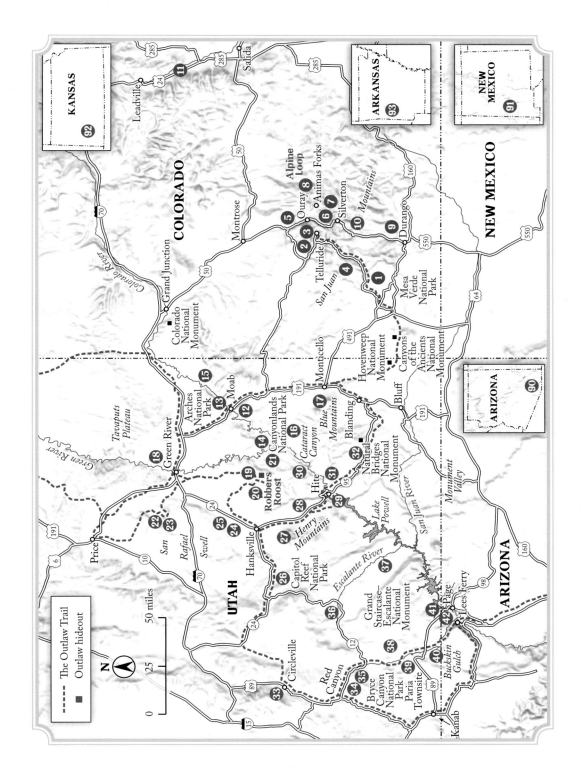

KANSAS
92

ARKANSAS
93

NEW MEXICO
91

ARIZONA
90

COLORADO

NEW MEXICO

UTAH

ARIZONA

The Outlaw Trail
Outlaw hideout

N

50 miles

0   25

285

285

Salida

24

Leadville

11

50

Montrose

Grand Junction

Colorado River

70

Colorado National Monument

Alpine Loop

Animas Forks

Ouray 8
5
2 3
6 7
Silverton
San Juan Mountains
10
9
Durango

Telluride

4

1

Mesa Verde National Park

550

550

160

64

San Juan Mountains

Monticello

491

Hovenweep National Monument

Canyons of the Ancients National Monument

Bluff

191

191

15

Moab

Arches National Park
13

12

Canyonlands National Park

17

Blue Mountains

Blanding

16

Cataract Canyon

14

21

Natural Bridges National Monument
32

30

Hite

31

95

29

Lake Powell

San Juan River

Monument Valley

160

Green River

18

19

Robbers Roost

20

28

27

Henry Mountains

Hanksville

24

25

24

26

Capitol Reef National Park

Tavaputs Plateau

Green River

Price

191

6

10

70

San Rafael Swell

22
23

Escalante River

37

Grand Staircase–Escalante National Monument

Page
41
42
Lees Ferry

98

36

38

Circleville

12

Red Canyon

35

34

Bryce Canyon National Park

39

40

Paria Townsite

Buckskin Gulch

89

89

Kanab

33

89

The road to Hole-in-the-Wall hideout (Adventure 75) snakes through Red Wall Country.

PART I

DISCOVERING THE

OUTLAW TRAIL

Rugged Routes ★ **Remote Hideouts**

INTRODUCTION

Welcome to the Outlaw Trail!

IN THE DAYS of the Wild West, the outlaw trail was a series of rugged routes linking remote hideouts across the American territories west of the Mississippi. Winding over mountain ranges and across desert mesas, into river valleys and through slot canyons, these interwoven trails were frequented by livestock rustlers and bank robbers, including Butch Cassidy and the Wild Bunch gang.

As the American frontier came to an end in the early twentieth century, the law closed in, the outlaws scattered, and the hideouts were abandoned. Eventually, the actual outlaw trails became faint traces from a legendary era—remembered in film and literature, but mostly forgotten by the travelers who speed through these remarkable landscapes on modern highways between the best-known spots, like famous national parks.

Today, due to the same impenetrable terrain where lawmen once feared to tread, the outlaw trail offers some of the best outdoor adventures in the US. You can hike and bike on old sections of trail once used by bandits on horseback. Visit sites that were home to some

of the most dramatic episodes during the Wild West, including historic ranches, frontier settlements, ghost towns, and infamous hideouts. Travel to the summit of mountain ranges where bandits kept watch for hired posses and descend into stunning rock formations where rustlers hid stolen livestock. Scramble through remote slot canyons that once saw dramatic chases. Paddle through high mountain valleys with mysterious histories. Camp at remote hideouts that are little changed since outlaws bedded down for the night.

Most outlaw adventures featured in this book are located in Utah and Wyoming, clustered around key hideouts like Robbers Roost in the Canyonlands area, Browns Park in the Uinta Mountains near Flaming Gorge, and

> This book combines outdoor adventures and historic sites from the outlaw trail, clustered into ninety-three trips, with stories from the Wild West era about Butch Cassidy, Queen Ann Bassett, Browns Park, and the Wild Bunch.

From the trailhead it's just a 3-mile hike to the famous Hole-in-the-Wall hideout (Adventure 75).

Hole-in-the-Wall in the Red Wall Country south of the Bighorn Mountains. Other adventures follow connecting routes into adjacent areas across the Colorado Plateau and Western Rockies, including the San Juan Mountains of Colorado, the Paria River area of Arizona, and the Black Hills of South Dakota.

Along the way, this book brings the past to life with stories from the Old West and a multi-episode narrative that follows the exploits of Butch Cassidy, the Wild Bunch, and Queen Ann Bassett in Browns Park. Plus, this book will deepen your experiences with listings for relevant museums, books, and films.

Whether you want to skip town for the occasional weekend excursion or hit the road on a multisport expedition of a week to a month or more, *Discovering the Outlaw Trail* will take you to some of the most exhilarating spots in the West while you discover stories from one of the most iconic and dangerous periods in American history.

MODERN EXPLORATIONS: BECOMING AN OUTLAW ADVENTURER

Another Red Canyon like any other? • This pile of boards is pretty cool when you think about it • Lees Ferry is more than a boat launch • Why so many books (and murders) for Browns Park? • Hot damn, there's a trail to follow!

When I first encountered the guided horse trip, I was mountain biking down some sandy switchbacks on the Rich Trail. This was in Red Canyon, Utah. One of the many, many Red Canyons in Utah, where red canyons are sort of like Clear Lakes or Main Streets.

In this particular Red Canyon, go figure: it's mostly dramatic *orange* hoodoos sharing eroded ridge space with stubby cedars. Makes you wonder why they didn't call it Orange Canyon. Regardless, it's gorgeous country, so why split hair colors?

Hoodoos pop up like prairie dogs from sand-draped talus slopes. Cedars tuck into tiered drainages, then sweep across open basins toward the shadowy hulk of Flat Top Mountain. Yep, there are also a lot of Flat Top Mountains too. Out in Utah, they're sort of like Bald Peaks or Bear Creeks.

As I dismounted my bike and moved off trail so the horses wouldn't spook, the lead wrangler drawled to his guests, "He just might be one of the good ones."

Mountain bikers aren't some evil cult with sore butts and nice calves, I considered saying. Instead, I just laughed along with this jovial

The Thunder Mountain Trail in Red Canyon is about as Wild-Westy as it gets (Adventure 34).

cowboy who had the ruddy features and demeanor of John Wayne crossed with hints of something modern, like he'd worked in finance before retiring to a part-time life of wrangling city slickers around the high desert.

After chatting a few minutes, I continued on my way, exploring the intersecting Red Canyon trail system while scouting out a potential bike-packing loop through the heart of the Paunsaugunt Plateau. This is one of the best regions in Utah, with one of the most badass names you've never heard of, despite the fact you've probably been there. Thing is, most of the plateau seems forgotten, being overshadowed by its most famous attraction, Bryce Canyon.

An hour later, I was riding the Cassidy Trail, where I encountered the same group again, this time reunited with the other half of their party, led by a young wrangler about my age. Unlike the brimmed hat, flannel shirt, and belt buckle of his older compatriot, the young wrangler wore a T-shirt, ball cap, and jeans.

"I'll tell you what," said the lead wrangler, pointing into the distance. "There's a cabin Butch Cassidy lived in at the top of Casto." He claimed Butch occupied the cabin in the 1880s.

As the lead wrangler led his guests away, the younger wrangler rolled his eyes and glanced wistfully at my bike, like he wanted to swap conveyances.

"He doesn't know," whispered the young wrangler with a chuckle. "We ride the same damn trail every day."

"The future's all yours, you lousy bicycle."

—BUTCH CASSIDY (A.K.A. PAUL NEWMAN IN *BUTCH CASSIDY AND THE SUNDANCE KID*, AS WRITTEN BY WILLIAM GOLDMAN)

I didn't find the cabin that day, riding up and down the double-track all-terrain vehicle (ATV) trail through this scenic canyon: Hopping off my bike. Scrambling over ridges. Looking behind stacks of hoodoos. It was like hunting for a living outlaw, not an abandoned hideout. I saw more cows than folks. At one point during my ride, some grazing cattle mistook me for a cowboy and herded along for a hectic half mile.

Before driving out of Red Canyon, I stopped by the visitor center to ask. I'd become acquaintances with a friendly staffer—he was a lanky six feet five and maybe twenty-one with a fake ID—who pointed out an old-timer, a ranger who moved around the visitor center in a rolling desk chair.

"He might know," said the young staffer before leaning in. "But he tends to get off topic."

A half hour later, I'd learned a lot from this genial fella. He'd been on every road and trail on the plateau, circa 1975. I also learned it was CastO Canyon, not CastRo—a common mistake. Plus, the famous tunnel through Red Fin Rock? Completed in 1925—to celebrate the opening of what was then called Utah National Park, later renamed Bryce Canyon National Park. Not-so-fun fact: every season, a few oncoming cars collide after swerving over the double line to get away from the arched tunnel ceiling—which is plenty high, being thirteen feet six inches tall at the corners, just like the sign says. And what about that Butch Cassidy cabin?

"There's no Butch Cassidy cabin up there," said the ranger, shaking his head skeptically and rolling away in his chair.

I found the collapsed cabin on a terrace above Casto Creek when I returned a few months later.

Sure, it wasn't the most impressive site. A pile of stones that might have been a fireplace and some boards splayed out like the structure had bored itself to death. But the search was an absolute blast.

I wondered, maybe this was Butch Cassidy's cabin? Suddenly, that pile of boards in a remote desert canyon seemed a lot more interesting. But the West is filled with sites supposedly related to America's most famous outlaw. *Butch drank at this bar! Cassidy robbed this old bank! Man, that dude ate a sandwich here!*

I wanted to learn more, but after driving off to the next adventure, I didn't think much more about that collapsed cabin. Being a big fan of the film *Butch Cassidy and the Sundance Kid*, I knew the memorable characters played by Paul Newman and Robert Redford were based on real-life outlaws. But, like a lot of people, I'd come to think of the infamous outlaw era as more a part of American fiction and western mythology. A Butch Cassidy cabin on an actual outlaw trail—one that could still be followed? That seemed no more real to me than a sand-worn movie set near Kanab.

· · · · · ·

I next stumbled onto the outlaw trail at Lees Ferry, while preparing for a springtime river trip down the Colorado through the Grand Canyon. To be honest, when we paddlers are setting out on this multiweek trip of a lifetime, we're usually not thinking about much more than what's downstream. But instead of dashing off down the river like I'd done before, this time I arrived a few days early to explore Lees Ferry and search for a pack-rafting route into the final flowing 15 miles of Glen Canyon upstream.

While I read about John D. Lee, the outlaw connection surfaced again. Lee established the ferry in the early 1870s while hiding from federal investigators seeking to arrest him for his leading role in the Mountain Meadows

Massacre. At that time, Lees Ferry was the only place to cross the Colorado River within a hundred miles, the typical route to and from Kanab, Utah, and a common spot for outlaws just passing through.

But what really spurred my interest to explore the outlaw trail happened in Browns Park. While visiting a pair of restored graves at the John Jarvie Historic Ranch, I read about the violent history in this otherwise empty valley, and my curiosity was more than piqued. I spoke to the ranger, who rattled off a list of books about what was then called Browns Hole—the list had more entries than the valley today has residents. What had happened here?

· · · · · ·

That winter, I started to read about Butch Cassidy, the Sundance Kid, the rowdy Wild Bunch, gritty Ann and Josie Bassett, the vicious Harvey Logan, and ruthless assassin Tom Horn. I read about famous hideouts, like Hole-in-the-Wall and Robbers Roost. These were names I'd heard before, names I'd spotted on the occasional information sign, but I'd never spent much time placing the corresponding stories in the physical world.

As I studied maps showing the overlapping routes that linked up hideouts and roughly formed a north-to-south grid of outlaw trails, I realized I'd already explored many of these places. I'd stood at the Black Dragon Canyon View Area on I-70 and seen the narrow slots of the San Rafael Swell, which served as corridors for several of Butch's most daring escapes. I'd explored canyons around the Roost, where cattle rustlers hid their stolen herds. I'd floated down the Colorado River to Dandy Crossing, even been inside Josie Bassett's cabin at Cub

Creek, where she moved after growing up in Browns Park.

But the reason I'd been to these places wasn't because of the outlaw trail—not directly, at least. The same rugged topography that once made this country inaccessible to lawmen and ideal for hardy outlaws to hide makes it one of the greatest adventure-sports corridors in the United States today. Old sections of the outlaw trail that once saw bandits on horseback can now be hiked, biked, and backpacked. Old water crossings have become access points for premier paddling trips. By combining the stories of the past with outdoor adventures of today, it wasn't just possible to follow the outlaw trail but to discover it anew—not through motion pictures and novels but on the ground, in person—and have a ton of fun the entire time.

So that's what I did. Sometimes with a bike, other times with a boat or a backpack. Sometimes I went alone, other times my wife and friends came with. I followed the outlaw trail in hopes of experiencing the same rugged country that was home to one of the wildest periods in American history. Along the way, I found I had a few questions about the Old West era. Who were the outlaws? And why do we celebrate them? Was it ever as simple as good guys and bad guys? Was Butch Cassidy actually the heroic gentleman bandit he's made out to be? Of course, which are the best adventures along the outlaw trail, both for fun and for connecting with the past? Oh, also, where can I find a decent beer in Utah?

This was my path to becoming an outlaw adventurer. I hope this book will help you explore this uniquely American region—and discover a remarkable period in US history—for yourself.

All of Western History before the Outlaw Era, with Apologies, like a Shotgun Blast to the Page

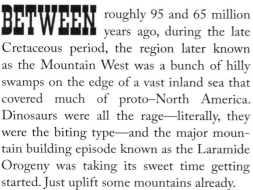

BETWEEN roughly 95 and 65 million years ago, during the late Cretaceous period, the region later known as the Mountain West was a bunch of hilly swamps on the edge of a vast inland sea that covered much of proto–North America. Dinosaurs were all the rage—literally, they were the biting type—and the major mountain building episode known as the Laramide Orogeny was taking its sweet time getting started. Just uplift some mountains already.

The biggest result is the Rocky Mountains, which run north-south throughout outlaw trail country. Subranges include the Bighorn Mountains, Grand Tetons, Wind River Range, and Snowy Mountains in Wyoming; the San Juan Mountains in Colorado; and the Uinta Mountains and Henry Mountains in Utah. (For more, see the "geology" FAQ at the end of the How to Use This Book chapter.)

Um . . . let's flash forward so that we can wrap up this little history before the universe collapses in on itself. Anyhoo . . . about 15,000 years ago, it wasn't unshaven cowboys but woolly mammoths that romantically ruled the West. The vast herds were stalked by Native tribes who originally came from Eurasia when the two continents were bumping uglies for an impressive fifteen centuries of low sea level.

This was all happening during the last major glaciation in North America, and not to get all dramatic, but it was majorly cold. Dense ice caps covered the Rocky Mountains, and *powder for days* meant if you're a nomadic hunter, you dead.

During the following 14.5 millennia, the Native peoples progressed from primitive hunter-gatherers to a complex network of interwoven tribes and civilizations. In the Four Corners region (where Arizona, Utah, Colorado, and New Mexico meet), the ancestral people built stone structures, pueblos, and ceremonial centers. They decorated sandstone cliffs with intricate pictographs and petroglyphs. And, yeah, they smoked some stuff.

· · · · · ·

Meanwhile, in the eastern part of North America, white Europeans established a series of thirteen colonies starting in the seventeenth century. The colonists were escaping religious persecution, pervasive poverty, and overbearing nobility. They were pretty pleased that, for once, they'd be out of earshot of those preachy kings and queens. Particularly in the southern colonies, the newcomers enslaved Africans on large plantations to pick tobacco and cotton and build the wealth for a new country.

A revolution fought in the late eighteenth century led to a rapid westward expansion that, through a series of treaties and military campaigns, forced the Native populations farther west on what became known as the Trail of Tears. Moving with them were mountain men, who trapped beaver pelts for fancy top hats that were all the craze in eastern and European industrial cities. Next came a cross-country message service called the Pony Express, and later electric wires were strung between poles for something called a telegraph.

In the 1860s, these somewhat-united states fought a massive civil war related to the question of how and where slavery could continue. But as the conflict dragged on into its fourth bloody year, President Abraham Lincoln decided to link the outcome to abolishing slavery. The war was a total disaster, with 650,000 deaths. Afterward, the eastern US was in ruins.

Many surviving white Americans began to ascribe to a belief called Manifest Destiny—essentially, God wanted them to populate the entire continental area, from the Atlantic to the Pacific, later called the Lower 48. For some reason, God decided to send them west in covered wagons with terrible suspension and excessive ventilation that were pulled by oxen and took months to get anywhere. They followed all kinds of trails and routes across the Great Plains and over the passes of the Rocky Mountains.

But then! A few years after the war came the iron horses, a.k.a. steam trains. An intercontinental railroad was completed at Promontory Summit in 1869, which ushered in the Gilded Age, basically a period of ruthless postwar greed. Suddenly, it seemed like everyone and their brother was fighting for market share in barbed wire, potent potions, and handguns. It was sell, baby, sell.

Which, naturally, led to a series of gold and silver rushes. Several of these rushes happened on lands previously ceded to Native Americans, who soon found their treaties broken. The wide-open prairies, once home to massive herds of roaming bison hunted by Plains Indians, were cleared by mass extermination. And a series of military campaigns pushed the remaining tribes onto reservations.

A herd of American bison crosses the high plains in Badlands National Park (Adventure 80).

To feed the massive mining camps and insta-towns, huge cattle drives brought long-horn cattle up from Texas, following trails like the Chisholm, the Western, and the Goodnight-Loving. Large corporations, like the railroads, began establishing monopolies over regional commerce. Cattle companies grew bigger by the day. Small-time ranchers and family homesteaders found themselves increasingly pushed off public land by range bullies. It grew harder and harder to make ends meet. This was clearly not the manifest destiny they'd been promised.

It became common for rural cowboys to just, you know, pluck a few loose cows or horses from the larger herds. It was all open country, and who would notice if a few went missing? The people were hungry and poor, and those big-biz folks were getting fatter by the year.

At first, these young cowboys stuck to mostly rustling. But as more money came to the area and the early white arrivals were pinched by rising prices and big-city invasions, speculators, land grabbers, and the like, a new type of cowboy emerged called the outlaw. They especially loved robbing travelers in stagecoaches. But if said dudes were standing in the deposit line at banks or riding in trains, that worked too.

The friendlier outlaws kept their robbery to the rich businessmen in top hats, while cozying up to the poor townsfolk along the way—offering them cold hard cash, typically gold coins, in exchange for their silence. This generosity earned the best of them a Robin Hood kind of rep from some of these people, even though the worst of the outlaws were violent murderers and thieves.

By the 1880s and into the 1890s, a newer and younger generation arose who didn't carry the baggage of the Civil War. This was a time when townsfolk were growing increasingly intolerant of the crime and risky behavior, the drinking and prostitution, that followed the loot. They begged for more lawmen and sheriffs and marshals to rid their towns of the outlaw element. And, thus, the stage was set for the Wild West.

Stories from the outlaw trail begin in Part II with *Wild Bunch Stories: Episode 1, Escape from Telluride, 1889.*

THE WHAT AND WHERE OF THE OUTLAW TRAIL

More than anything, it was the completion of the transcontinental railroad in 1869 that created the so-called outlaw trail. Along with the trains carrying gold and cash came the population booms and busts, the false-front mining towns, the frontier banks, the massive cattle

Check out an Old West newspaper office at Museum of the American West in Lander (Adventure 67).

Originally, the term *outlaw trail* referred to an individual who had gone bad, committed a crime, and then had to run from the law. After robbing a bank or committing a murder, the newly turned bandit "had to take to the outlaw trail."

drives, and the corporate ranches. For the last three decades of the 1800s, the outlaws used Native American trails and pioneer routes to escape after robberies. Eventually, a semi-secretive network of overlapping trails stretched from Montana to Mexico, linking up outlaw-friendly ranches and remote hideouts.

After the Wild West passed from haphazard reality to romanticized and embellished myth, some researchers and historians attempted to document the actual routes frequented by the outlaws. During the twentieth century, writers like Charles Kelly in *The Outlaw Trail*, Pearl Baker in *The Wild Bunch at Robbers Roost*, and Richard Patterson in *Historical Atlas of the Outlaw West* paid particular attention to the geography surrounding outlaw tales. Some writers and researchers began to use the term *outlaw trail* to generally describe the routes that linked up major hideouts, ranches, robbery sites, and frontier towns frequented by outlaws.

From the Little Rocky Mountains of Montana, one trail went southeast into Wyoming on the east side of the Bighorn Mountains, through towns like Sheridan, Buffalo, and Kaycee, before turning west through Red Wall Country near the famous Hole-in-the-Wall hideout. (For all these places, see the overview map at the start of this book.)

From the Bighorn Mountains region, several routes crossed the Bighorn Basin, passing through towns like Thermopolis and Cody.

The Lowdown on the "Owl Hoot" Trail

In the Wild West, some referred to the outlaw trail, and the concept of going bad, as the Owl Hoot Trail. Individual outlaws would be called *owlhoots*. The origin of this term is uncertain, with some suggesting it came from the practice of Native Americans mimicking owl hoots to signal danger—a practice adopted by American cowboys and outlaws.

Another possibility is that *owl hoot* is an example of metathesis (geekout alert—don't shoot!), in which two sounds are swapped, sometimes for humorous effect. In this case, the hard 't' sound in the word 'out' switches to the second word 'hoot," and the soft 'l' sound in the word 'law' switches to the first word, "owl." And perhaps *owl hoot* was a way to discuss illegal activities and alleged outlaws while being somewhat more discreet—possibly even challenging the notion that outlaws were on the wrong side of the law or that there was a good and bad side of the law to begin with.

A few north-south routes through the basin connected to towns like Meeteetse, at the foot of the Absaroka Mountains. Eventually, the trail joined another route along the eastern side of the Wind River Range. This trail passed through towns like Dubois, Lander, and Atlantic City. From South Pass, the trail crossed the desolate Red Desert on the way to towns like Rock Springs and Green River, Wyoming, before continuing south into Utah.

Another Wyoming spur of the outlaw trail went south from Hole-in-the-Wall toward towns like Baggs, Grand Encampment, and Laramie, passing around and sometimes through the Snowy Range and Sierra Madre mountains. From there, the trail continued southwest through the Little Snake River valley and down into Colorado, including the town of Craig and the Powder Wash region.

Near the three-state border of Wyoming, Utah, and Colorado, several spurs of the outlaw trail converged in one of the most famous hideouts, Browns Hole. Today called Browns Park, the trail next crossed the eastern Uinta Mountains in the Diamond Mountain region and passed through the town of Vernal, Utah.

Several north-south routes ran through the Uinta Basin, including a stagecoach and military road through Nine Mile Canyon. Another path followed the Green River through Desolation and Gray Canyons. A third route followed the eastern side of the Tavaputs Plateau.

In Utah's Canyonlands region, these several routes emerged from the Roan and Book Cliffs, passing through the San Rafael Swell in the west; the town of Green River, Utah, in the north; and Moab in the east. Several routes converged at the infamous hideout of Robbers Roost, a nearly impenetrable 2,000-square-mile region filled with entrenched canyons and dizzying slots that repelled lawmen for decades.

From Hanksville, the trail skirted the foothills of the Henry Mountains and descended through North Wash and Trachyte Canyon to cross the Colorado River at Dandy Crossing, near present-day Hite Marina. Heading east, one route followed White Canyon into Colorado and the San Juan Mountains. Another route continued south of the Colorado River toward Arizona.

Meanwhile, farther north, another route led west from Robbers Roost through the geologic formation called the Grand Staircase. Around Kanab, Utah, this trail turned south and crossed the Colorado River at Lees Ferry, Arizona.

At the southern ends of the outlaw trail, one spur is typically located on the western side of New Mexico passing through the Gila Mountains, and another spur is on the eastern side of the state, near Cimarron and Las Cruces, continuing into the heart of Texas cattle country. In Arizona, the trail passed through the notorious town of Tombstone and continued by way of Skeleton Canyon into Old Mexico. Of course, there were countless other trails used by outlaws on the run, with the trails just described being some of the more widely discussed routes.

While key hideouts like Hole-in-the-Wall, Browns Hole, and Robbers Roost were used by outlaws since at least the 1860s, many of the most famous exploits happened during the 1890s, plus a few years on either side. Butch Cassidy, a leading figure in the Wild Bunch gang during that time, became one of the best-known outlaws—especially after being immortalized by Paul Newman in the award-winning 1969 film *Butch Cassidy and the Sundance Kid* (see next section). Cassidy participated in some of the biggest bank and train robberies during the era before fleeing to South America as the Wild West era came to a violent end.

RESOURCES: BOOKS AND MOVIES

This section gives you a taste of some favorite books that can help acquaint you with the outlaw trail. One of the most fascinating aspects of the Wild West is sorting the facts from the myths. Although figuring out what actually happened can be quite tricky, one way is to simply read every single book on the topic a few times and then compare and contrast. Bring your reading glasses! For a full list of every book and article used in the creation of this book, check out the bibliography at the back of the book.

A book on display at the Museum of the American West in Lander, Wyoming (Adventure 67)

The Outlaw Trail: A History of Butch Cassidy and His Wild Bunch by Charles Kelly is a beloved classic, one of the early books attempting to sort facts from myths surrounding the exploits of Butch Cassidy and many other outlaws who rode between major hideouts around the Mountain West. During the 1930s, Kelly interviewed and corresponded with still-living figures and relatives from the Wild West era, including Matt Warner and Ann Bassett. The book was originally self-published in 1938 after commercial publishers rejected the manuscript, with at least one editor deeming it poorly organized. This was a fair concern, given that many chapters present material geographically. Those looking for a straightforward chronological story about Cassidy and company may find Kelly's meandering, tangential approach tedious. Still, the book is a fun read filled with countless anecdotes about outlaws, both big and small, even while adding new inconsistencies and errors along the way. Due to its early success, the book was rereleased commercially in 1959, the same year Kelly retired as the first superintendent of Capitol Reef National Monument.

Butch Cassidy: A Biography by Richard Patterson is an excellent tome about the most famous rider on the outlaw trail. In addition to telling the story, Patterson weighs the evidence for various historical accounts and later theories. He's also interested in the geography and topography of outlaw trail exploits, an approach that readers who are familiar with the regions involved may particularly appreciate.

Another book by Patterson, which is out of print but can be found used, is *Historical Atlas of the Outlaw West*. The book presents many popular outlaw tales, both historical and mythological, by state and location. It's not exactly a guidebook, being focused on stories more than sites, but it can still lead motivated readers to plenty of excellent places from Wild West history.

The Outlaw Trail: A Journey Through Time by Robert Redford tells the story of the actor's horse riding and rafting trip along the outlaw trail, a few years after he became world famous from his film role as the Sundance Kid. The remarkable journey was part of a National Geographic documentary, and the book includes stunning landscape photography by Jonathan Blair. Redford's story is well written and humorous, demonstrating an enthusiastic interest in the history and including many encounters with important figures and places along the trail, especially a meeting with Lula Parker Betenson. Another highlight: a raft trip with the cantankerous author Edward Abbey, who was also a seasonal ranger at Arches National Park.

Butch Cassidy, My Brother by Lula Parker Betenson was told to Dora Flack when Butch's sister Lula (born 1886) was in her eighties. After the hit 1969 film, Lula was invited on national talk shows to discuss her brother, and the reignited interest led to her own book, in which she claims to tell the story as the family knew it. Lula was born two years after Butch left home, so her version is probably based on family and regional lore, with her most startling claim being that Butch didn't die in a shootout in South America but came to visit the family in Circleville, Utah, during the 1920s. Modern observers tend to have split opinions about Lula's claim, with some suggesting her story was designed to sell books. Others, including Bill Betenson (see next paragraph), say that while Lula was the only family member to report Butch alive, she wasn't the only person in the region who shared such stories. Regardless of any controversy, Lula was a pretty funny lady.

> "During the filming of *Butch Cassidy and the Sundance Kid*, I visited the set in Saint George, Utah. Paul Newman approached me and grinned, 'Hi, I'm Butch.' I replied, 'Hi, I'm your sister.'
>
> —Lula Parker Betenson,
> *Butch Cassidy, My Brother*

Butch Cassidy, My Uncle: A Family Portrait by Bill Betenson is one of the most recent books to examine the life of Butch Cassidy, in this case written by Lula Parker Betenson's great-grandson. This excellent biography fills many gaps in the historic record with a mix of research and family lore, while adding further context to Lula's account. The result is an intimate story about not just Robert LeRoy (a.k.a. Butch) but other Parker family members, including his brother Dan, a short-term outlaw who also spent time in prison before going straight.

The Wild Bunch at Robbers Roost by Pearl Baker is a detailed and entertaining book that collects many stories and legends surrounding the Robbers Roost hideout and its use by the Wild Bunch and other lesser-known outlaws. Baker, who ran the Robbers Roost Ranch as a young woman during the 1930s, is an excellent storyteller, and her chapters are filled with colorful anecdotes and humor.

If you want to get the story straight from the horse rider's mouth, then consider checking out these books written or cowritten by two actual outlaws and a lawman: *The Last of the Bandit Riders* by Matt Warner, *Tom McCarty's Own Story: Autobiography of an Outlaw* by Tom McCarty, and *A Cowboy Detective: A True Story of Twenty-Two Years with a World-Famous Detective Agency* by Pinkerton agent Charles A. Siringo.

Outlaw Trail Sacred Text?
Butch Cassidy and the Sundance Kid

"Slow and disappointing." "Cinematic schizophrenia." "A gnawing emptiness." "Could have been lifted from a Batman and Robin episode."

Man, some of the initial reviews were not kind to *Butch Cassidy and the Sundance Kid*. Yet this classic outlaw movie stole the hearts of audiences (sorry, couldn't help it) and was

Butch and Sundance are beloved to this day in Deadwood, South Dakota, and other towns across the west (Adventure 86).

the top-grossing film of 1969. Starring Paul Newman, Robert Redford, and Katharine Ross, the film was nominated for seven Oscars and won four—including best screenplay for William Goldman.

With endless comic banter and quotable one-liners, it's regularly placed on lists of greatest Westerns of all time. For many viewers, it will be their first encounter with the infamous exploits of the Wild Bunch (called the Hole-in-the-Wall Gang in the film). And, like the screenwriter says, it gets more of the story right than wrong.

"Much of what follows is true."

—WILLIAM GOLDMAN,
SCREENWRITER FOR *BUTCH CASSIDY AND THE SUNDANCE KID*

To summarize: In the fading, sometimes sepia-toned days of the Wild West, an affable Butch Cassidy and grizzled gunfighter Sundance Kid crack a ton of jokes while (a) blowing up two train cars and one E. C. Woodcock, (b) getting chased across some of the West's most beautiful landscapes for twenty-four minutes by a dude whose hat somehow always stays white, (c) partying in New York City with Etta Place, (d) escaping to Bolivia, (e) robbing a ton of banks and always getting chased by the exact same policemen, and (f) finally meeting their match.

Filming locations were mostly around Utah and Colorado, and curious film pilgrims can visit many of the sites featured in the film. The ghost town of Grafton, on the Virgin River off UT 9, served as Etta Place's town. The scenes set at Hole-in-the-Wall, Wyoming, were shot in Cave Valley in the Kolob Canyons area of Zion National Park, Utah.

The train robberies were filmed on the Durango-Silverton Railroad in the San Juan Mountains of Colorado (Adventure 10). The epic chase sequence was filmed in Snow Canyon near Saint George, Utah. When the two outlaws leap from a cliff, they land in the Animas River upstream of Durango, Colorado. And when they go to Bolivia, it's actually Mexico—mostly Taxco, Tlayacapan, and Cuernavaca.

Butch Cassidy and the Sundance Kid is definitely a great film, and one that only gets better the more you know about the actual events the story is based on.

Rob Yourself of Two More Hours

I feel obligated to mention a follow-up prequel, *Butch and Sundance: The Early Days* (1979). If you make it through the trailer, you're halfway to being an outlaw. Watch the whole film, which has little basis in fact, and you have the persistence to become president of the entire outlaw trail.

The Wild Bunch (1969), directed by Sam Peckinpah and starring William Holden, is not actually related to the historical Wild Bunch. Though the film was produced by Warner Brothers to compete with *Butch Cassidy and the Sundance Kid* from 20th Century Fox, it only borrows the gang's name and a few basic themes from the time period. The film follows an aging gang of outlaws operating around the US-Mexico border in 1913, looking for one final heist as the Wild West era comes to an end. In the process, they become entangled with the Mexican Revolution. The film was acclaimed for innovative cinematography and criticized for graphic depictions of violence, including one of the first to simulate bullet exit wounds. The scenery is remarkable, shot in Mexico along the Rio Nazas and other locations in the state of Coahuila on the Texas border.

Since we're discussing Westerns with references to the outlaw trail that skirt that whole basis-in-fact part, perhaps I should mention *Cat Ballou* (1965). Starring Jane Fonda in the title role, this dark drama follows an 1894 college graduate swept up in a violent rampage of train robbery and murder. Nah, I'm just messing. It's a musical-comedy spoof about train robbery and murder. Lee Marvin won only a single Academy Award for best actor despite portraying two characters in the film, only one of whom beats late-stage alcoholism for an afternoon jaunt as some kind of rhinestone bullfighter. (You'll see.) Nat King Cole, in his final role, is part of a banjo-playing Greek chorus. At one point, the outlaws stop by Hole-in-the-Wall hideout, which looks more like a ghost town in Southern California. For some reason, the saloon is filled with patrons in their eighties and the bartender is a downtrodden fifty-five-year-old named Butch Cassidy. There are definitely some fun moments in this silly film, and at least they gave the best line to Butch. When Marvin suggests they share a round, Butch replies, "Old times' sake? That means you have no cash."

Finally, and lacking any direct connections to the stories in this book, I am pleased to mention the great Sergio Leone's "spaghetti Westerns." Shot in Italy, set in the American West, and with the dialogue recorded in your cousin's basement, these are some of the greatest films ever made, with musical scores by the remarkable Ennio Morricone, who basically created the soundtrack for the outlaw trail. The "Dollars Trilogy" stars Clint Eastwood as the man with no name, with films including *A Fistful of Dollars* (1964), *For a Few Dollars More* (1965), and *The Good, the Bad, and the Ugly* (1966).

Another classic is *Once Upon a Time in the West* (1968). And don't forget the oddly named *Duck, You Sucker!* (1971). Basically, buy a popcorn machine.

How to Use This Book

IS THIS BOOK a storytelling guide? A narrated guidebook? However you describe it, *Discovering the Outlaw Trail* is not your typical guidebook.

Around half the book tells a seventeen-episode story—a narrative meant to be read in order, just like a Wild West paperback novel—about the outlaw trail's most famous riders, including Butch Cassidy, Queen Ann Bassett, Elzy Lay, and the Sundance Kid. Here and there, other Old West stories stand alone in some of the travel-and-adventure chapters, outside the larger narrative.

Meanwhile, the other half of the book is a trip guide that helps you get out there and explore the outlaw trail for yourself. Sure, things are a bit different these days. Modern infrastructure now allows much easier access to many classic sites from the era; highways and interstates often follow railways and rivers. I-80 from Salt Lake City, Utah, through Laramie, Wyoming, more or less follows the route of the Union Pacific Railroad. I-70 from Green River, Utah, follows the Denver and Rio Grande Railroad east into Colorado, where the tracks made a dramatic turn south

along the Arkansas River. Today many rivers are dammed, wiping out some historic sites and impounding large bodies of water like Flaming Gorge Reservoir in southern Wyoming and Lake Powell in southern Utah.

HOW TO USE THIS BOOK

☞ Use this book to learn about the outlaw trail and the Wild West.

☞ Use this book to plan fun and amazing road trips with outlaw-themed adventures, like visiting historic sites, hideouts, museums, and campgrounds.

☞ Use this book to plan some outdoor adventures, from hiking to camping, biking to paddling to whitewater rafting.

☞ Use this book to read some dramatic stories from the outlaw trail, including the exploits of Butch Cassidy, the Wild Bunch, and Queen Ann Bassett in Browns Park.

But despite such changes, the region retains the ruggedness and essence of the Wild West.

Put the Wild Bunch stories and the trip guide together, and the result is a hybrid between a historical narrative nonfiction book and a traditional guidebook. Organizing a book of this nature is a bit complex, so let's all go ahead and make ourselves a big pot of cowboy coffee. Alright, ready? Drink half the pot as quick as you can. And here we go.

The book is divided into four parts. Part 1, Discovering the Outlaw Trail, includes mostly informational chapters. There's an introduction to the outlaw trail, including some hopefully entertaining stories about my own modern explorations of how I first encountered the outlaw trail.

Part 2, Stories from the Outlaw Trail, combines two interwoven narratives. Wild Bunch Stories follow the exploits of Butch Cassidy and the famous gang of many names, sometimes called the Wild Bunch or the Hole-in-the-Wall Gang. Browns Park Stories follow the life of Ann Bassett and the happenings in the famous hideout valley of Browns Park during the Wild West era. While you can

A historical sign at the Wyoming Territorial Prison in Laramie (Adventure 61) reminds us about the outlaws' infamous love for rules.

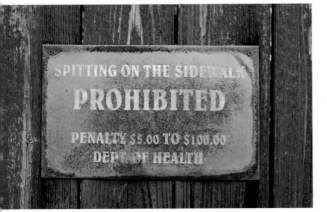

HOW NOT TO USE THIS BOOK

☞ Don't use this book for adventures on non-outlaw trails, like the Appalachian Trail or Pacific Crest Trail, where banditry is not only frowned on but, as of the time of this writing, very illegal.

☞ Don't use this book to rob a bank, like writing threatening notes inside the cover, passing it to a teller, and expecting them to just hand over a bag of cash that's not coming from your own account.

☞ Don't expect this book to stop a bullet. That said, if the situation arises and the book is all you have, it's worth a shot.

certainly read one of these two storylines or skip around, the two sets of interwoven stories are meant to be read in chronological order. The twelve episodes in Part II span roughly the 1860s to around the turn of the twentieth century.

Part 3, Traveling the Outlaw Trail, is where you'll find the trip guide to the many activities and sites, organized into just over ninety adventures and divided into twelve chapters by region, from southwestern Colorado west into Utah, then north into Wyoming and east into a corner of South Dakota, with the last chapter branching out into the nearby states of Idaho, Arizona, New Mexico, Kansas, and Arkansas. These adventures and activities include historic sites and outlaw hideouts, hiking and biking trails, paddling and rafting trips, four-wheel-drive road trips and scenic drives, and museums and walking tours. In most cases, the adventures include a Wild

West connection—but occasionally these are just really great adventure-travel spots that happen to fall into the outlaw-relevant regions.

Adventures span a wide range of difficulties. There are many easy-to-access sites, like historic ranches, museums, and viewpoints. You'll also find tons of mellower activities, like scenic drives, walking tours, easy trails, and hot springs. In other cases, and sometimes within the same adventure, I offer options for much more challenging exploits: long-distance hiking and backpacking trips, mountain biking trails, remote hideouts in rugged landscapes, 4x4 driving routes, whitewater paddling, high-elevation summit hikes, and the occasional good ol' fashioned suffer-fest. There's room for all kinds of trips along the outlaw trail, and you can go as easy or as hard as you want. On that note, many adventure listings offer enough information to fully explore the featured activity or site. But in other cases, especially when an activity is particularly challenging, you'll need to do supplementary research and/or obtain more detailed topographic maps or road maps for proper safety and navigation. Finally, interspersed throughout the travel chapters are some Old West stories and a couple more of my modern explorations, including photography and mishaps along the trail.

Finally, Part 4, The Ends of the Outlaw Trail—Stories Conclude, wraps everything up with five more episodes about the Wild Bunch and Browns Park, an epilogue, and resources and a bibliography. In this section you'll learn about the end of the Wild West era as the American frontier came to a close. Yes, we'll be following Butch Cassidy to South America, where he allegedly died. But we also follow him back to the United States and the outlaw trail. Cough, cough. What?!

Now would be a great time to down that other half of the coffeepot. Because, pardner, we got two hundred–plus pages to go.

TYPES OF TRIPS ON THE OUTLAW TRAIL

Historically, most folks took to the outlaw trail out of necessity. After robbing their first stagecoach, general store, or frontier bank, they were chased out of town by sheriffs and armed posses. Luckily, today there are many casual (and mostly legal) ways to hit the outlaw trail.

As I mentioned, there's a wide variety of adventures in this book, from easy to more challenging. The overview map at the start of the book gives you a general idea of what's where, from historic sites to towns and highways. Each adventure includes icons following its title to help you quickly identify what kinds of activities and sites that adventure includes. Once you know which types of activities interest you, proceed to Suggested Trips later in this chapter and Ask an Outlaw (FAQ) at the end of this chapter to start planning!

Scenic drives, four-wheel-drive road trips, and viewpoints. A primary purpose of this book is to offer plenty of customizable road trips with a Wild West theme. Depending on your point of origin, outlaw-themed road trips can range from just a weekend to a full week and even a month or longer. How challenging you make your road trip depends on which types of adventures you choose. More than half the sites and adventures in this book can be reached via paved roads. Around a quarter of the sites are reached by well-maintained dirt and gravel roads that can be traveled by most two-wheel-drive vehicles when the road is dry and in good condition. The remaining sites require a high-clearance, and typically four-wheel-drive, vehicle at all times—though in some cases you can join a guided trip. The road trip icon 🚗 lets you know which adventures include a scenic drive, and the 4x4 icon 🚙 signals the rugged four-wheel-drive road trips. Also included are some dramatic roadside Old West-y viewpoints 🔔.

Historic sites, museums, and walking tours. In addition to reading the stories in this book (and other suggested reading), visiting relevant museums, hideouts, and historic sites really brings the outlaw trail to life. Some museums and sites are specifically focused on outlaws, while others are generally western- or mining-themed but have exhibits or elements relevant to understanding the outlaw era, including walking tours in a few preserved historic towns from the time period plus a few historic railroads. Look for the museum icon 🏛 for indoor museums and the historic sites icon 🏚 for outlaw hideouts, ghost towns, and other outdoor sites. Walking tours, which mostly pass through towns and historic districts, are denoted by 👢.

Hiking and backpacking. One of the best ways to experience the outlaw trail is to lace up your boots and start walking. Some trails are short and easy, while others are longer or harder due to backcountry terrain, steepness, or elevation gain. Many trails highlighted in this book are found along or near routes once used by actual outlaws, while others just happen to be great trails in regions with outlaw history. Either way, you'll experience at ground level the same dramatic landscapes that remain little changed since the days of the Wild West. Look for the hiking icon 👟 to find on-trail adventures.

Mountain biking and road cycling. Some of the trails and roads winding through outlaw country have in recent times become popular mountain-bike trails, paved road-biking or gravel cycling rides, and even bike-packing/bike-touring routes. While biking is not the primary focus of this book, several of the outlaw adventures involve bicycling—look for the biking icon 🚲 for road cycling and the mountain biking icon 🚵 for off-road cycling.

QUICK GUIDE TO THE ICONS

 Camping

 Canoe, kayak, or paddleboarding

 Hiking

 Historic sites

 Mountain biking

 Museums

 Old West-y viewpoint

 Road cycling

 Road trip

 Rugged 4x4 trip

 Walking Tour

 Whitewater rafting

How many types of adventures can you have at the Island in the Sky District of Canyonlands National Park (Adventure 14)? Yes, this is a direct challenge.

paddling icon ; for whitewater rafting, it will be the icon. Next, please note that I am not a fisherman, but I do come across some great fishing areas in my travels. Since I don't want to leave your hook hanging, I make brief mentions of fishing spots throughout the book.

Camping. There are some great campgrounds, dispersed camping areas, and backcountry campsites along the outlaw trail. While there are too many to list, I do mention some options throughout each region—especially those with explicit outlaw connections. Look for the camping icon .

Types of Trips *Not* Included

I wish this book could cover every possible adventure you might dream up—but there are a few activities I chose not to include.

Climbing, canyoneering, and mountaineering. Due to the rugged nature of the outlaw trail, many regions in this book have become world renowned for technical adventure sports. These advanced activities are beyond the scope of this book's travels and adventures, so they receive only brief mentions throughout the chapters—you'll have to dig elsewhere for the details on these kinds of activities.

Horseback riding. It might seem strange that a book about the outlaw trail doesn't cover horse trips. Many trails included in this book do allow horseback riding, and some outfitters offer guided horse trips, but you'll need to do your own research to wrangle a horseback ride. The contemporary explorer of the outlaw trails in this book will probably encounter more day hikers, backpackers, and mountain bikers (typically, in that order) than they will horseback riders. As the outlaws would say, the times, they are a-changing.

Other times, I mention nearby biking options, but you'll need to seek out more information and maps to fully plan those biking trips.

Paddling and rafting trips, with minor shout-outs to fishing. Outlaws had to frequently cross rivers, by ford or ferry, and sometimes they even went downstream via rafts—or fell in by accident. I have included a number of great paddling trips in stunning canyons and landscapes along the outlaw trail, including lakes, reservoirs, and flatwater or whitewater river trips. For many of these trips, you can either join a guide company or do it yourself (DIY). When the trip involves a canoe, kayak, or paddleboard, look for the

THE LOWDOWN ON THE DETAILS

The twelve chapters in Part 3 each have a more-detailed map of their area. Please note that these maps are for planning and overview purposes and not for navigation. You'll want to carry current road and trail maps during your adventures. Following the chapter title, the subtitle describes the chapter's general region, such as southwest Colorado. Within each chapter, each adventure's title is followed by activity icons (described in Types of Trips on the Outlaw Trail, above), and the text description gives details for heading out on your own.

The information in each adventure is organized by the headings listed below to help you find what you want to know. Not every heading is used in every adventure, the exact order varies depending on the situation, and occasionally I adjust the headings just for kicks. But, hey, this is a book about having fun outlaw adventures, not a librarian's guide to the Dewey Decimal System.

THE WHOLE KIT AND CABOODLE: Each chapter starts with an overview to the region to help get you oriented.

THE LOWDOWN: Each adventure starts with a shorter, more specific introduction to that adventure, with a summary of what to expect and what's noteworthy.

THE LOOT: This heading tells about stuff you mostly look at, such as museums, historic sites, preserved ranches, ghost towns, rock art, ruins, monuments, natural arches, railroad rides, and scenic drives. Many of these attractions have Old West significance, and they are highlighted in **boldface** so they're easy to spot. (Note that when these types of places require physical effort to reach, they may be discussed under the next heading.)

THE ACTION: This heading covers more-active adventures, such as hiking trails, mountain biking, cycling, whitewater rafting, flatwater paddling, challenging 4x4 routes, summiting mountains, and the like. The names of trails and sites are also highlighted in **boldface**.

Map Legend

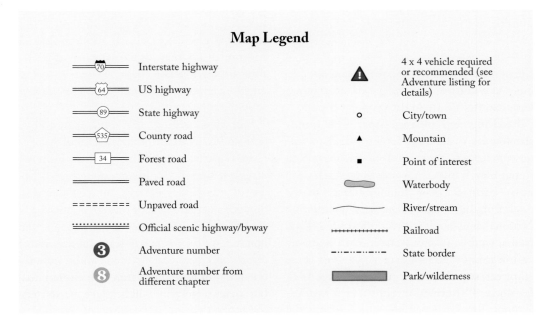

70 ═══ Interstate highway	⚠ 4 x 4 vehicle required or recommended (see Adventure listing for details)
64 ═══ US highway	
89 ═══ State highway	○ City/town
535 ═══ County road	▲ Mountain
34 ═══ Forest road	▪ Point of interest
═══ Paved road	▭ Waterbody
========= Unpaved road	River/stream
·············· Official scenic highway/byway	++++++++ Railroad
❸ Adventure number	─·─·─·─ State border
❽ Adventure number from different chapter	▭ Park/wilderness

RIDE ONWARD: Here you'll find suggestions for more activities and sites near the featured adventure, so you can go farther or keep on exploring the area.

THE HARDSHIPS: This listing tells you about any particular challenges associated with an activity, including hazards such as rough terrain, area wildlife, flash-flood potential, and more. (On these topics, also review the FAQ at the end of this chapter, specially the sections on "slot canyons and flash floods," "flora and fauna," and "physical fitness."

THE GIDDYUP: Here you'll find the driving directions to reach a specific attraction, whether it's in a town or at a trailhead. In the case of some road trip adventures, sites and activities along the way may be folded into the driving directions to keep things simple.

THE LAW: If permits are required, that information is listed here, along with the rules or regulations of the managing agencies.

THE SUSPECTS: This listing describes the land manager, agency, or business responsible for an attraction and also gives their phone number and/or web address. Longer URLs are listed in Resources at the end of the book.

THE SCENE OF THE CRIME: Here you'll find the address and/or GPS coordinates for specific attractions. The GPS information is based on the WGS 84 datum.

X MARKS THE SPOT: This listing provides the names of relevant maps for each adventure. If a map is available online, short URLs will be found here. Longer map URLs will be found at the back of the book in Resources. In the case of physical maps, I mostly use waterproof National Geographic Trails Illustrated Topo Maps, which are listed both in the chapters and in Resources. However, these don't cover all places, so I also point out a few maps from Latitude 40° Recreation Topo Maps and one

from the US Forest Service—all listed in Resources.

THE TICKING CLOCK: Here you'll find the common seasons to visit (for more on this topic, see the "weather" FAQ at the end of this chapter). Also under this heading are the typical days an attraction is open and other timing-related information. Please note that due to the COVID-19 pandemic, many attractions' open hours and days were frequently changing during the time of research—check with the site to confirm!

THE TAKE: If there's a fee required, that's noted under this heading, though costs are ballpark estimates, and you'll want to view the attraction's website for specifics.

THE DIGS: If an area has noteworthy lodgings or camping nearby, this listing provides that information—the name of the place, the phone number and/or website (THE SUSPECTS), its address and/or GPS coordinates (THE SCENE OF THE CRIME), and other similar information.

THE SNORT: I might even mention a brewery or ten.

THE JIG: Look here for the game, the catch, the fine print—basically, anything else you might need to know before you go.

THE YARNS: This listing makes connections between the sites and stories, typically listing which of the book's Wild Bunch, Browns Park, or Old West episodes relate to this particular place. That way, during your adventure, you can imagine the outlaws on the trail with you.

SUGGESTED TRIPS

If you're looking for something specific, use the handy trip finder below to learn about some of the top options. Keep in mind these are only a handful of adventures from the entire book, but these suggestions will help get you started.

Famous Hideouts

20. Robbers Roost Spring, Cabin, and Caves: Used by rustlers and outlaws on the run.

59. Eastern Browns Park: An empty valley with a wild past.

75. Hole-in-the-Wall Hideout: Perhaps the most remote and dramatic of the famous Wild Bunch hideouts.

Dramatic Escape Routes

4. Escape from Telluride Unofficial Outlaw Byway: Scenic drive following the route from the bank robbery that turned Bob Parker into Butch Cassidy.

23. Buckhorn Wash: Sheer-walled canyon that was the scene of fleeing outlaws and a determined posse.

39. Paria Townsite and Paria Box and 42, Lees Ferry and Glen Canyon: Before the Wild Bunch, Tom McCarty and company made a daring crossing of the Colorado River at Lees Ferry and a mad dash up Paria Canyon.

Top Historic Sites

33. Butch Cassidy's Boyhood Home: The cabin in Circleville, Utah, where the saga of the Wild Bunch arguably began.

45. Dinosaur National Monument (Utah Side): Site of Josie Bassett Morris Cabin, homestead of a famous Browns Park figure.

58. John Jarvie Historic Ranch: One of the best-preserved Old West ranches on the outlaw trail.

61. Wyoming Territorial Prison: Butch Cassidy served his one and only prison term here.

93. Fort Smith, Arkansas: Preserved 11-acre Fort Smith National Historic Site includes restored courtroom of "Hanging Judge" Parker and a replica gallows.

Ghost Towns

7. Animas Forks Ghost Town: One of the highest-elevation ghost towns in the US.

39. Paria Townsite and Paria Box: Stone ruins in a geologically stunning valley.

65. South Pass City State Historic Site: An entire Old West mining town preserved south of the Wind River Range.

78. Meeteetse and Kirwin Ghost Town: A picturesque mining ghost town in the Absaroka Mountains.

Restored Frontier Towns

63. Medicine Bow Mountains Museums: Little Snake River Museum and Grand Encampment Museum offer a big picture of Old West life in Wyoming.

67. Lander: Turn-of-the-twentieth-century village preserved at Museum of the American West.

77. Cody: Original Hole-in-the-Wall cabin now rests at Old Trail Town, a quintessential Wild West street.

92. Dodge City, Kansas: Boot Hill Museum is a replica frontier town, while Fort Larned National Historic Site preserves an 1858–1878 military outpost on the Santa Fe Trail.

Museums

63. Medicine Bow Mountains Museums: Six—count 'em—regional museums tell the stories of two little-known Wyoming subranges of the Rockies.

77. Cody: Comprehensive exhibits at the Buffalo Bill Museum about the life of Buffalo Bill Cody and the Wild West Show, plus Plains Indians, western art, natural history, and historical firearms.

86. Deadwood and Lead: History of South Dakota's Black Hills is displayed in the Deadwood and Lead Museums.

Another view, looking down on the Thunder Mountain Trail (Adventure 34), provides a strong, implicit suggestion that, yes, you should check this thing out.

Old West Railroads

10. Durango and Silverton Railroad: A historic ride along Colorado's Animas River.

11. Upper Arkansas River Valley: A dramatic ride on the Royal Gorge Railroad through a sheer-walled Colorado canyon.

84. The 1880 Train: A scenic ride through South Dakota's Black Hills.

Scenic Drives—Paved

1. San Juan Skyway: 235 miles through high mountain passes, alpine scenery, and plenty of highlights.

28. North Wash: UT 95 features stunning landscapes in plunging North Wash and above White Canyon.

36. Million Dollar Highway and Calf Creek: Don't miss Scenic Byway 12 from Red Canyon past Bryce Canyon and Grand Staircase–Escalante to Capitol Reef.

47. Flaming Gorge–Uintas Scenic Byway: Scenic route in eastern Uinta Mountains.

62. Snowy Range and Scenic Byway: Drive through a hidden Wyoming mountain range.

79. Thermopolis and Wind River Canyon: 34-mile scenic byway in a dramatic gorge.

81. Needles Highway and Cathedral Spires Trail: 14-mile drive through impressive rock spires in South Dakota's Black Hills.

Scenic Drives—Unpaved

8. Alpine Loop 4x4 Trail: It doesn't get much higher than this rugged and very challenging 4x4 trail through the San Juan Mountains.

14. Island in the Sky District: The rough White Rim Road circles Canyonlands National Park between the Green and Colorado Rivers.

38. Cottonwood Canyon Road: 46 miles of sandy road through the Grand Staircase, including dramatic Cockscomb Ridge.

Easier and/or Shorter Hikes

22. Little Grand Canyon: Mostly flat Good Water Rim Trail can be hiked as far as you want, up to 16 miles one-way, above a startling chasm.

25. San Rafael Reef: Fairly easy hike through flat-bottomed Chute Canyon.

45. Dinosaur National Monument (Utah Side): Two short trails depart from Josie Bassett Morris Cabin to Box Canyon and Hog Canyon.

57. Canyon Rim Trail: Scenic trail perched high above the reservoir in Red Canyon.

70. Dubois and Lake Louise Trail: Short but very steep Lake Louise Trail climbs to the lake's granite basin.

81. Needles Highway and Cathedral Spires Trail: Hike through dramatic granite spires at Custer State Park in South Dakota's Black Hills.

Longer and Harder Hikes

16. Needles District: 11-mile Chesler Park–Joint Trail Loop leads to narrow slots that feel like an outlaw hideout.

19. Horseshoe Canyon: 7-mile roundtrip hike near former outlaw hideout in Robbers Roost ends at unreal Great Gallery petroglyph site.

25. San Rafael Reef: Awesome nontechnical canyoneering route through the dizzying slots of Crack Canyon.

26. Capitol Reef National Park: Combine Grand Wash Trail's impressive narrows with Cassidy Arch Trail for an 8-mile out-and-back with 670 feet of elevation gain.

31. Sundance Trail: Challenging only begins to describe the landslide descent into Dark Canyon, leading to a creek with waterfalls in a remote desert canyon.

34. Red Canyon: Combine 9-mile one-way Cassidy Trail with Losee Canyon Trail for a 12-mile loop through hoodoos.

40. Wire Pass to Buckskin Gulch: Hike inside the twisty labyrinth of the Southwest's longest slot canyon.

62. Snowy Range and Scenic Byway: A few trails lead to the summit of Medicine Bow Peak, the Snowy Range's tallest.

73. Cloud Peak Wilderness: Spend up to a week of backpacking on the Solitude Loop through the Bighorn Mountains.

Road and Gravel Biking

28. North Wash: Day trips on quiet UT 95 or self- or van-supported multiday tours out of Moab.

34. Red Canyon: Paved, shared-use 18-mile Red Canyon Bicycle Trail is popular for road cycling and connects to UT 63 in Bryce Canyon.

35. Bryce Canyon National Park: 15 miles of UT 63 in Bryce Canyon National Park, from Inspiration Point to Rainbow Point, with 1,600 feet of climbing, is excellent.

85. Mickelson Rail Trail: 109-mile one-way gravel cycling and walking path through the Black Hills starts from Deadwood, South Dakota.

Mountain Biking

12. Moab: It's all world-class here, especially Slick Rock and the Whole Enchilada.

22. Little Grand Canyon: 16-mile one-way Good Water Rim Trail overlooks a surprising chasm in Utah.

34. Thunder Mountain Trail: Ride downhill through endless hoodoos near Bryce Canyon.

44. McCoy Flats Trail System: An up-and-coming cross-country trail system in the Uinta Basin.

Rafting and Paddling Trips

11. Upper Arkansas River Valley: A ton of whitewater rafting opportunities in a high Colorado valley.

15. Colorado River Trips: A variety of canyon trips, from flatwater to whitewater, near Moab.

18. Green River, Utah: More (and quieter) river opportunities near Moab and Canyonlands National Park.

30. Cataract Canyon River Trip: Some of the biggest rapids in North America, on the Colorado in Canyonlands National Park.

41. Southern Lake Powell: Several trips on the reservoir worth checking out.

51. Desolation and Gray Canyons River Trip: Two remote Green River canyons on 85 miles that mix floating with whitewater.

54. Green River through Red Canyon: A stunning section of easy whitewater on the Green River below Flaming Gorge Dam.

79. Thermopolis and Wind River Canyon: Whitewater rafting through a dramatic Wyoming canyon.

LEAVE NO TRACE— LIKE AN OUTLAW

If we overlook a few behaviors—like haphazardly firing a six-shooter in the general direction of an overzealous deputy while riding a galloping horse through a pristine meadow—well, then, weren't outlaws early practitioners of the outdoor ethic called Leave No Trace (LNT)? Bear with me.

Basically, when modern adventurers travel through backcountry and wilderness settings, the goal is to minimize the impact and damage from the visit. The outlaws' goal was to minimize any evidence of their presence—so, different objectives but a similar approach. Here are the seven principles of LNT, with an outlaw spin.

Plan and prepare for your trip. Research all the regulations, hazards, and conditions for where you're traveling. Know about elevation, wildlife concerns (e.g., are there black or grizzly bears in the area?), poison ivy presence, weather forecast, and the like. **The maps in this book give just a general overview and are most emphatically not intended to be used for navigation; obtain a suitable map and use a compass to properly orient yourself** (see The Ten Essentials sidebar). I mean, an outlaw wouldn't rely on passersby for directions after robbing a bank. So just plan out your trip like you're running from the law and hopefully no authorities will be needed for a rescue.

Travel and camp on durable surfaces. Limit the signs of your presence by sticking to the trail and camping on sand. Outlaws did this to throw the law off their tracks, but modern adventurers do it to maintain the natural qualities of the wilderness for future visitors. There is also a benefit to the flora and fauna if you avoid stomping down tall grass

Outlaws didn't drop energy-bar wrappers during their escapades, so why should we? This pristine spot is Chute Canyon in the San Rafael Reef (Adventure 25). With a little effort, we can keep it pristine.

and reducing animal habitat. Stepping on wildflowers isn't the same as robbing a bank, sure. But if you can complete your hike without doing either, then why not?

Dispose of waste properly. In other words, *pack it in, pack it out.* Nothing says "amateur" more than a wad of used toilet paper behind a tree or a trail of energy-bar wrappers leading to an outlaw camp. Keep track of your trash when hiking and camping—not just for aesthetic reasons, but because food and odors can attract a posse of wild animals. Watch out for high winds blowing away empty bags and other litter. Perform a "sweep" for trash before leaving your campsite. Use established backcountry toilets when they're available, but if you need to bury human waste, dig a cathole about six to eight inches deep, at least two hundred feet from rivers, creeks, camps, and trails—and don't bury the TP; pack it out.

Leave what you find. Especially in wilderness areas or spots with historic artifacts, like Native American pottery or old mining equipment, leave flowers, rocks, and other natural features undisturbed. Think of these wild places as living museums. The people who will visit after you hope to experience them intact too. I mean, you wouldn't steal an 1880s revolver from a museum display case, right? ('Cause then you'd become an actual outlaw, and these days all the good hideouts have hikers in them.)

Minimize campfire hazards. Follow current regulations, typically found as updates on the websites of the local managing agency. At certain times of year, due to risk of wildfire, campfires may be banned. In places where open fires are allowed, use existing fire rings and keep fires manageable. Only gather wood when allowed by the managing agency, and in areas where wood is scarce consider substituting a propane fire ring or campstove. Put fires out at night so that a stiff wind doesn't create a massive blaze that alerts authorities to your location. And remember: they have satellites these days for hunting down outlaws who start wildfires.

Respect wildlife. I'm not saying you need to salute a moose, but at least keep enough distance so it doesn't charge. Who wants to be that guy in a viral video who tried to pet a bison and got "pet" by its horns? In camp, secure your food, trash, and any scented items so that bears and other animals don't become habituated to stealing snacks: hang food four feet from a tree trunk and ten feet off the ground, or use a bear canister. If a campground has bear-proof food and/ or trash containers, use them (hint: your car isn't critter-proof). Once a bear goes down the outlaw trail of visiting campgrounds, it often has to be relocated or, in some sad cases, euthanized.

Be considerate of other visitors. Observe quiet hours in campgrounds as a courtesy to fellow campers. Earphones for trail tunes are a bit better than forcing other hikers to listen to your dub-step mix. When hiking or biking on a single-track trail, it is customary for descending hikers or bikers to stop and let ascending hikers or riders pass. And when families and young kids are nearby, what about holding back the F-bombs? I mean, even most outlaws were polite around children.

A Note about Safety

The Ten Essentials

The point of the Ten Essentials, originated by The Mountaineers, has always been to answer two basic questions: Can you prevent emergencies and respond positively should one occur (items 1–5)? And can you safely spend a night—or more—outside if necessary (items 6–10)? Use this list as a guide and tailor it to the needs of your outing.

1. Navigation: map and compass
2. Headlamp (don't forget the batteries)
3. Sun protection
4. First-aid kit
5. Knife
6. Fire starter, matches, or lighter
7. Shelter: emergency blanket or poncho, even for day hikes
8. Extra food
9. Extra water
10. Extra clothes

ASK AN OUTLAW (FAQ)

Before you begin your own adventures, here are some common questions and answers about **what to expect** and **how to plan** for the outlaw trail.

As folks like to say out West, the most accurate info comes straight from the horse's mouth. Or, in this case, how about the mouth of a crotchety outlaw who answers your questions with a blend of practical and Old West-y advice?

Listed below are the topics the FAQs cover because they're the most relevant, while other less important topics are distributed throughout the How to Use This Book chapter.

- geology and landscape
- weather
- slot canyons and flash floods
- flora and fauna
- physical fitness
- gear and clothes
- coolers
- emergency supplies
- road trips
- hideouts
- brunch
- millennials

Gentle reader: So, what kind of role did **geology and landscape** play in shaping the outlaw trail?

Outlaw: A big role . . .What, you need a bigger answer than that? Well, let me just peruse this newfangled internet for a moment . . . OK. So the two things most relevant to how so many outlaws successfully evaded capture around Utah and Wyoming during the late nineteenth century relates to two major geologic events. The creation of the Rocky Mountains and the uplifting of the Colorado Plateau.

Both events were caused by the Laramide Orogeny, which occurred, oh, about 75 to 45 million years ago. The Rockies sprung up big and tall and the Colorado Plateau lifted upward as mostly one giant block of horizontally layered rock. This created all kinds of mountain ranges, big and small, plus deep canyons, river gorges, abrupt mesas, and steep cliffs. This jumbled and rugged landscape caused a real challenge for settlements and the building of roads and trains. Mining brought in a few routes and plenty of money, and so off we went with our loot and hid out where townsfolk hadn't arrived yet.

Gentle reader: What's the **weather** like on the outlaw trail?

Outlaw: Well, with all them darn mountains all over the place, it's a lot like mountain weather. Expect sudden wind gusts and temperature swings. Nights are cold, even in summer and especially during spring and fall. A lot of the outlaw trail ranges from 4,000 to 10,000 feet in elevation, and according to big-city scientists, temperatures drop about 3 degrees Fahrenheit for every 1,000 feet of elevation. So just because your newfangled weather app forecasts 65 degrees for the nearest town, if that town is 3,000 feet below your trailhead, you'll probably get temps in the 50s when you begin your hike.

Another thing you need to figure is that even though there's so much gosh-darn desert, there's still a chance for precipitation at any time of year, including heavy thunderstorms and even snowstorms at higher elevations. When those occasional storms do hit, they're often powerful, violent bursts, where the sky opens up like a vault and instead of dumping loot, it's dropping bullet-sized raindrops or hail. That's especially the case during monsoon season in the southern half of the trail, which happens during mid- to late summer.

Heat and sun exposure can also be extreme in summer. If you plan on hiking, biking, or paddling, watch the thermometer to avoid heat exhaustion or heat stroke. Tackle more-strenuous activities during early morning, late afternoon, or early evening if midday temps are too hot. Bring plenty of water and use lots of sunscreen (also see the "gear and clothes" FAQ below).

Gentle reader: What's the danger with **slot canyons and flash floods**?

Outlaw: Well, in short, put those two things together and they punch your ticket to the pearly gates. Basically, if there's ever a chance of thunderstorms in the area—even if we're talking 10 miles away—don't go into

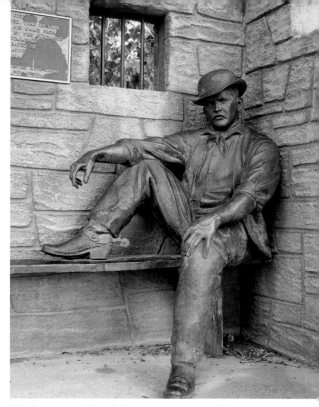

No, this statue doesn't depict some super chill outlaw therapist. It's the Sundance Kid himself, in the Wyoming town where he earned his nickname (Adventure 88).

a slot canyon. Flash floods can come from far away, and if they catch you off guard, it's worse—way worse—than a posse charging around the corner. See, these flash floods are more like a galloping wall of mud and rocks that will knock you flat before you know what hit you. When in doubt, stay out.

Gentle reader: What's the **flora and fauna** like on the outlaw trail?

Outlaw: Flora's a great gal. I'm not too familiar with Fauna. But wait. You're not talking about Hell's Half Acre in Fort Worth, are you? Plants and animals, you say? Boy, did I step in it there.

Plant life can be pretty sparse along the outlaw trail—just another reason why it remained so unpopulated that we were able to run amok. At higher elevations and in the north, it's greener, with plenty of pine forests and abundant wildlife like deer, elk, moose, and bear. As you head downhill and to the south, it's more desert-like, with succulents, cactuses, and scrub brush. In the canyons, you may see bighorn sheep, rabbits, and ravens. And, almost forgot, poison ivy at elevations lower than about 4,000 to 5,000 feet.

One thing that's surprising about desert areas is how fragile they are, even though they seem tough as old saddle leather. Plants grow slower than molasses, and even the soil takes decades to rebuild if it's damaged. If you toss an apple core or orange peel, it takes years to break down. Tread softly (see Leave No Trace—Like an Outlaw, earlier in this chapter).

A final item worth discussing is the sand. It's gonna get into everything, so you might as well start preparing now. Head to your nearest beach, and just sort of roll around until you've made your peace with it.

Gentle reader: What level of **physical fitness** do I need for adventuring on the outlaw trail?

Outlaw: Well, we outlaws usually just robbed and rustled our way into shape. But generally, most anyone can explore the historic sites on the outlaw trail by vehicle. That said, if you want to lasso some of the harder adventures and more-physical activities, like longer hikes, you'll want to be in good physical condition. Basically, if you plan to day hike, say, 10 miles with 2,000 feet of elevation gain (i.e., about 2,000 steps per mile, plus add thirty to sixty minutes for ascending every 1,000 feet), then before your trip make sure to work your way up (from shorter to longer mileage) by completing several practice hikes of that same length and steepness. Partner, you got any poorly guarded hilltop banks about 20,000 steps away from your home?

Gentle reader: What kind of **gear and clothes** do I need for the outlaw trail?

Outlaw: The days are long gone when all you needed was a horse and a hat, mostly due to public decency laws. These days, it's all nylon this and polyester that. Anyhoo, you don't need to have the best and most expensive gear, but you do need to be prepared for the outlaw trail.

Bring enough layers and types of clothes for both hot and cold weather in the same trip, no matter the season. Be prepared for rain and especially wind. A cheap tent might collapse in a storm, so use something sturdy that you can tie down with guy lines. Prepare for plenty of sun and little shade—so sun hat, long sleeves, and lightweight and cool clothing.

Have good footwear too, given that much of the terrain is rocky and loose. Or for slickrock, you'll want shoes with good grippy traction. Cowboy boots are for saloons these days.

A pair of lightweight hiking pants are a good idea, given the chance for bugs near rivers or water sources. Oh, and also the prickly cactuses out in the desert.

And, of course, if you do any specialty activities like mountain biking or paddling, you'll have a whole bunch of technical equipment for those as well.

Gentle reader: What kind of **cooler** is best for those hot desert trips along the outlaw trail? On one hand, a rotomolded cooler, like a Yeti, seems better for long-term ice retention. But the thicker sidewalls sacrifice interior volume, as compared to your more standard insulated cooler, like an Igloo marine, which offers more storage space but with thinner side walls. But! If you're going to be opening the lid so often anyway and making frequent fuel stops, is it that big a deal to frequently drain the cooler and spend a few more dollars on ice every day or two? I guess that can add up. Ultimately, I just have to pick one, but I have a major case of buyer paralysis. Help! Am I overthinking this?

Outlaw: Yep.

Gentle reader: What kind of **emergency supplies** should I carry on the outlaw trail?

Outlaw: Well, I wouldn't go anywhere without a first-aid kit. Next, consider getting a large water jug for your vehicle in case you break down in the middle of nowhere. Five gallons ought to do it. Something similar for gasoline—a few extra gallons in an airtight fuel container. Carry extra food in case you get stuck somewhere unexpected. And plenty of clothes and blankets or sleeping bags. Plus all the gadgets: A few headlamps or flashlights. Extra batteries. And, these days, emergency satellite communicators are sure popular—just figure that these aren't a substitute for sound judgment. Also see The Ten Essentials sidebar earlier in this chapter.

Gentle reader: I want to tackle the entire outlaw trail in one glorious three-month **road trip**. Where should I start?

Outlaw: Make like the old cattle drives and follow the weather. If you start in the spring, go south to north and stick to lower elevations first. Let those higher latitudes and taller mountains thaw out, melt off the snow, warm up some. If you start, let's say, late summer or early fall, do the opposite. Go north to south, start high, move to lower elevations

and latitudes as they cool down. And if you start in, say, July? Then pardner, may God have mercy on your soul.

Gentle reader: How did outlaws first discover **hideouts** like Hole-in-the-Wall, when so many people these days can barely follow a trail to Hole-in-the-Wall?

Outlaw: There are those folks who follow trails and those folks who blaze 'em. Say, fella, why are you rolling your eyes like that? Alright, alright. I'll level with you. Sometimes we just got the horse drunk to see where we'd end up.

Gentle reader: Are there any good **brunch** places on the outlaw trail?

Outlaw: Hey, why don't you go ahead and explain this whole brunch thing to me. So you just wait around hungry for five hours after the sun comes up? Plan your whole day around mixing breakfast flapjacks with suppertime roasted potatoes? Fruit the sparkling wine? I think I'd hang myself before doing that once a week.

Gentle reader: Hey, what do outlaws think about **millennials**?

Outlaw: Back in our day, around the turn of the twentieth century, we actually called millennials the Lost Generation. And what with their newfangled locomotives and horseless buggies, they killed all kinds of great things: cattle rustling, robbing wagon trains, trial-free hangings, murderous frontier raids . . .

At Old Trail Town in Cody, Wyoming (Adventure 77), a collection of boardwalks and wagons helps recreate an exceptional Wild West street.

PART II

STORIES

from the

OUTLAW TRAIL

The Wild Bunch

Browns Park

WILD BUNCH STORIES

Escape from Telluride, 1889

A shoebox or a bank? • Bob is the alias of a true rookie • Who needs hats for a getaway? • Those branches are charging us! • Not quite a homecoming via the outlaw trail

FROM THE OUTSIDE,
the San Miguel Valley Bank didn't look like much of a target. Even with a false front, the single-story wooden building resembled a shoebox wedged between the two-story brick McCormick Hardware Company on one side and a large drugstore on the other.

It was noon on a Monday in late June 1889. The San Juan Mountains loomed jagged and snowcapped above Colorado Avenue. Marked by overlapping wheel ruts and horse hooves, it was the dirt main street running through the mining boomtown of Telluride. A few doors away from the bank, the saloon already had customers inside.

Three sharply dressed cowboys sat around a table, having drinks and occasionally glancing out the windows at passersby. They'd ridden into town a few days before and passed the weekend spending their pay and flirting with local girls. Two of the cowboys were in their early to mid-twenties—jovial young men who joked often and smiled when they talked. The other man was stern and older, maybe mid-thirties, and went by the name Tom McCarty. Short and thin, he had a lean, weathered face from years working on the range.

"There he goes," said one of the younger cowboys, nodding toward the street.

An employee in a suit exited the bank with a satchel, mounted a horse, and rode off. He was the bank cashier making his daily collection rounds. Soon the three cowboys paid and left.

Outside the saloon, they untied their horses and saddled up, then rode across the street and, oddly, stopped. The two younger men casually dismounted, stepped onto the creaky plank walkway, and disappeared inside the bank.

Unlike its plain exterior, the bank's interior was richly appointed with polished wood and brass furnishings. The lone teller, sitting inside the cage, asked how he could help them. The reply was a revolver pointed under his nose.

"Keep quiet now," said the robber. "Or suffer the pain of instant death."

Holding the revolver was a stocky young man with black hair who went by the alias Matt Warner. Only twenty-five years old, Warner was Tom McCarty's brother-in-law and had already accompanied him on many rustling raids and robberies. Warner nodded to his friend that the vault was open.

The accomplice was also stocky but with dirty-blond hair and a strikingly square face. At twenty-three years old, the young man had rustled plenty of

Colorado Avenue in Telluride as photographed by W.J. Carpenter around 1889 (History Colorado)

livestock, but this was his first major robbery. He went by the alias Bob. Like a true rookie, this was short for his real name, Robert LeRoy Parker.

Bob hopped behind the cage and nervously filled a sack with stacks of cash. No one in the room—including himself, though he sometimes made dreamy comments around the campfire about making his mark in the world—knew that someday he would become the Wild West's most accomplished outlaw, the infamous Butch Cassidy.

But for now, it was just young Bob collecting all the greenbacks and gold he could find. Once finished, the two friends warned the teller to stay put and walked outside.

> ## "With the Telluride robbery, [Bob] Parker crossed the line from small-time rustler to a full-fledged outlaw."
>
> —BILL BETENSON, *BUTCH CASSIDY, MY UNCLE*

Bystanders seemed unconcerned as the outlaws rode west on Colorado Avenue, but eventually a commotion arose behind the bandits. Word had spread. At the edge of town, the outlaws fired their guns randomly to discourage pursuit. Startled by the shots, Bob's horse bucked, nearly throwing him, but instead he only lost his hat.

"Hy-ah!" shouted the bandits, spurring their horses and galloping away.

For 4 miles, their route from Telluride followed the San Miguel River through a deep glacial valley, bright green and colored by spring wildflowers. At Keystone Hill, they met a hired man holding a relay of fresh horses. After swapping mounts, they were about to divide up the $20,000 haul when a familiar face rode up.

It was rancher Harry Adsit passing by with a friend on his way to town. Bob and Matt had worked for the past year at his Prospector Ranch on Lone Cone Mountain. A few weeks before, the young men had abruptly quit, saying they were heading back to Utah to visit their families. The two parties exchanged brief pleasantries and went their respective ways.

$20,000 in 1889 would be worth over a half million dollars today.

As Adsit approached Telluride, he encountered a quickly formed posse of shop clerks and townsfolk, led by the county sheriff. Learning about the robbery, Adsit explained he'd seen the suspects—though he didn't identify them by name or mention they were former employees. The sheriff asked the rancher to lead the way. The posse followed the bandits' tracks up into the mountains along the steep South Fork San Miguel River, running high

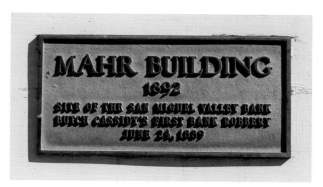

All that remains of the first bank Butch robbed is this plaque commemorating the location, but the historic downtown of Telluride (Adventure 2) retains much of its Old West charm.

from snowmelt. Whether due to hesitance or inexperience, the posse moved slowly and fell farther behind, especially once the fresh hoofprints deviated from the main trail into the woods.

By now, the outlaws had passed the mountain outpost of Ames, where the next summer one of the world's first hydroelectric plants would be commissioned. From there they turned south, following Lake Fork into a narrow alpine valley, past Trout Lake, and over Lizard Head Pass into the Dolores River headwaters. Around Coal Creek, they turned northwest away from the river, ascending steep cliffs before dropping down to the West Fork Dolores. After riding about 25 miles, waiting for them in a mining camp they called Hot Spring was their second relay of horses.

With fresh horses, they pushed the pace through this narrow river valley for about 20 miles to a third relay, near where the West Fork joined the main Dolores River. By following this roundabout route, the outlaws had avoided the main road through Rico—where local authorities had received notice of the heist and were organizing for pursuit. Meanwhile, another posse was forming near Durango. Near the headwaters of the West Fork Dolores, one of the posses found wrappers from stacks of $500 and $1,000 bills.

In the foothills of the San Juans, the outlaws turned southeast across Haycamp Mesa, reaching their fourth relay point around sunset. They continued onward through dusk to a fifth and final change of horses, around ten o'clock near Mud Springs. By now, they had traveled 80 miles from Telluride, and after continuing a short way, they made a fireless camp in the forest.

They dashed off early the next morning, only to discover the Telluride posse had ridden through the night and was hot on their trail. The outlaws spent much of the second day eluding these pursuers in the brushy hills between the Dolores and Mancos Rivers. That evening, they lassoed an abandoned pony near the summit of a small mountain. After tying branches to its tail, they whipped its rear, sending it galloping downhill. The snapping of dry timber caused the confused posse to think the outlaws were making a charge, and they turned and chased the pony. Later that night, they called off the search and returned home.

The outlaws spent a few days lying low near the La Plata Mountains, north of Mancos. But a letter sent by one of their relay accomplices, asking for supplies, was intercepted by the sheriff. A new posse was formed, except when it reached the area mentioned in the letter, the trail had grown cold.

Already, back in Telluride, the legend of the robbery and the daring bandits was growing—possibly as a way for the failed pursuers to deflect blame and save face. Some items were true, some embellished, and others plain made up. Posse members told newspapers the outlaws had placed gunnysacks on their horses' feet and rode across slickrock. The posse claimed they'd found a note from the outlaws warning them to quit the chase or risk getting shot. Searchers kept the spent horses, left behind by the outlaws—partly as souvenirs and partly as compensation for their efforts.

A few months later, when the carcasses of four horses were found hitched to a tree along the escape route, they were attributed to a relay station the outlaws had skipped. And years later, when the name Butch Cassidy was known throughout the West, Adsit even claimed to have received a letter from Bob Parker, only ten days after the robbery, regarding a horse Adsit had given his departing ranch hand.

"Dear Harry, I understand the sheriff of San Miguel County is riding the dappled brown colt you gave me," Bob allegedly wrote, explaining that the horse had packed him 110 miles in ten hours across broken country. "Please send him over to me at Moab, Utah, at the first opportunity."

It's doubtful the fleeing outlaws had much time for letter writing.

During the days after the robbery, the three outlaws worked their way through rough terrain, past the northern slopes of Mesa Verde and the Ute Mountains. At the base of Cannonball Mesa, they followed McElmo Canyon away from the Rockies, across the state border, and into southeastern Utah's desert of burnt-orange rocks and sunken canyons, a region familiar to each of them since childhood.

Given the circumstances, it wasn't exactly a homecoming. Especially for Bob, who, after several years away, was finally returning to Utah—this time by way of the outlaw trail.

Explore the Outlaw Trail!

To bring the story of Butch Cassidy's first robbery to life, start by checking out the old bank site on Colorado Avenue in **Adventure 2: Telluride Historic District**. Next, you can roughly drive the outlaws' escape route in **Adventure 4: Escape from Telluride Unofficial Outlaw Byway**.

WILD BUNCH STORIES

The Beginnings of Bob Parker, 1866–1889

They sure love the number 13 • Mike Cassidy, did you say? • Bryce Canyon connections • Jail cell can't lock up that personality • The money went faster than the horse • A trio is formed • The devilment is in the details

PLENTY OF chance events and random luck—whether good or bad is open to debate—went into placing those three outlaws in the sandy desert of eastern Utah during the summer of 1889.

On Friday the thirteenth of April 1866, the future Butch Cassidy was born Robert LeRoy Parker, the eldest of eventually thirteen children, to Maximillian and Ann Parker in Beaver, Utah. Bob's mom and dad were second-generation Mormons, and the entire family was accustomed to hard life on the western frontier.

In 1856, when Maxi was thirteen (OK, that number is popping up a lot, but let's move on), he helped his parents pull a handcart from Iowa across the Great Plains. The family had recently immigrated from England, answering Brigham Young's call, and the journey was an absolute nightmare. One child went missing on the plains and was found by the father after four days of searching. Eventually, the father's feet became so bad he couldn't walk, after which mom and kids pulled the cart by themselves to Utah.

When Bob was thirteen (man, did this family just plan things around the number thirteen?!), the Parkers moved to a ranch south of Circleville, Utah, on a mountainous plateau near the top step of the Grand Staircase. Bob's

Butch Cassidy's boyhood home in Circleville, Utah (Adventure 33)

brother Dan, a year younger, tended to follow in the footsteps of the elder brother, who went to work at area ranches at a young age.

At around age sixteen, Bob went to work on the Marshall Ranch. Not only did the owner have his own issues with following the law, but one day a real-life outlaw hired on with the operation. His name was Mike Cassidy, and he was said to hide stolen livestock amid the breaks and hoodoos of nearby Bryce Canyon.

From Mike Cassidy, Bob learned all kinds of skills that would later come in handy, like shooting, riding, and rustling—a.k.a. stealing—horse and cattle, then using a hot iron to doctor the brand. Massive herds of cattle were being driven across the West to feed the American migration underway. Who would notice when a few went missing?

This was not Bob's first experience with the law. A story is told that when young Bob needed a new pair of overalls for work one day, he found the shop in town closed. He let himself inside and found what he needed. He left an IOU, with his name, promising to return and pay. The unimpressed shopkeeper filed charges for theft, which led to a warrant and arrest that Bob did not appreciate, feeling that his word was good.

When Bob was eighteen, he left home in a hurry, after an ambiguous incident involving some stolen cattle that never fully came to light. Some said Bob was framed or accepted responsibility for someone else's crime. But given that he rolled with Mike Cassidy, who fled the Circleville area a year later under similar circumstances, it's anyone's guess. Regardless, according to some accounts, this would be the last time Bob, a.k.a. Butch Cassidy, stepped foot in the family home in Circleville until twenty years *after* his death (long story, but we'll get there, promise!).

For the next few years, Bob drifted around the Mountain West working various jobs. His first stop was bustling Telluride, Colorado, where he earned good money mule-packing ore down from the mines. That winter he roamed into Wyoming and Nebraska before returning to Telluride for the summer of '85, when he had his next brush with the law.

While in town, Bob kept his horse on a ranch near the San Miguel River. The rancher really liked this horse, which led to a disagreement. When Bob took the horse, the rancher reported it stolen. So Bob rode southwest along the same escape route he'd later take after the San Miguel Bank robbery. He was arrested near Montrose, Colorado.

When Bob's concerned father, Maxi, came from Utah, he found the cell door unlocked.

"Dad!" shouted Bob. "What in hell are you doing here?"

"By gum, young man," said Maxi, eyeing his son on a jail cell cot, "I might ask you the same question."

"They're not afraid I'll escape," said Bob, grinning. "I plan to stay right here until I get my horse."

This was the first in a string of reports about the powers of Bob's charismatic personality. He had convinced the jailers he was innocent. The issue was sorted in Bob's favor, and he was free to go. His father tried to convince him to return to Utah, but twenty-year-old Bob was on the lookout for more adventures.

Another Bryce Canyon Connection?

The outlaw origin story of Matt Warner is eerily similar to a legend attributed to Butch Cassidy around the Panguitch, Utah, area where it's claimed that Butch beat up a competitor over a girl in town and fled to hide at a cabin in Red Canyon. Visit the area in **Adventure 34: Red Canyon and Thunder Mountain Trail** and **Adventure 35: Bryce Canyon National Park**, in Chapter 5, Grand Staircase and South Lake Powell.

"Bob was always up to some outlandish devilment."

—Lula Parker Betenson, *Butch Cassidy, My Brother*

During 1886, he roamed into Wyoming, likely working as a cowboy, and was back in Telluride by 1887. One day at a bar, he met a young fella named Willard Erastus Christianson, who went by the much simpler handle of

Matt Warner. Both were born and raised Mormon in Utah, though not necessarily practitioners.

At the age of fourteen (luckier number), Matt had run away from his home of Levan, Utah—100 miles north of Circleville—after beating up a rival over a girl. Fearing he had killed the other boy, the teenage Matt took to rustling on the outlaw trail and never looked back.

When Bob met him, Matt was taking a hiatus from the outlaw life to race horses—one of the biggest wagering sports in Colorado. Their friendship began with one such wager over drinks. For his upcoming race in Telluride, Matt was riding his champion mare, Betty, against a local colt.

"I know the Mulcahy colt," said Bob. "It has never been beat. You are going to lose."

Matt told Bob to put his money where his mouth was, so Bob bet the colt and lost his entire ride—horse, saddle, and spurs. Matt felt bad, but Bob insisted: "A bet's a bet and I never squawk when I lose."

The Fairyland Loop Trail in Bryce Canyon National Park (Adventure 35) winds through hoodoo terrain that young Butch Cassidy may have explored.

So Matt insisted Bob go partners with him in the racing business.

At first, the racing went well. They set up matches for Betty across southwestern Colorado. The mare usually won, and the prize money went faster than the mare. They were running out of locals willing to race, when one day at a bar in Cortez, Matt introduced Bob to his brother-in-law, Tom McCarty.

Around ten years older than Matt, Tom was already an infamous outlaw known throughout the West for his rustling and robberies. Rumors said he was the leader of the Blue Mountain Gang, a.k.a. the McCarty Gang, given his younger brother Bill and brother-in-law Matt were also members.

While holdups of stagecoaches, trains, and banks were common in the frontier West, most robbers came away with little loot due to drunken planning and sloppy execution. Alleged McCarty Gang exploits were more successful, and unsolved crimes were often attributed to them regardless of evidence: Ransacking a peddler's wagon near Browns Hole. Raiding cattle herds in Old Mexico. A train holdup near Grand Junction. Even the First National Bank of Denver, where Tom supposedly approached the bank president with a warning that the bank was about to be robbed. The banker thanked Tom for the tip and asked how he knew.

"I am the man who is going to rob your bank," answered Tom. Then he produced a vial of clear liquid, claiming it was the explosive nitroglycerine.

Running low on money, Bob and Matt went to work for Harry Adsit up on Lone Cone Mountain. But they kept in touch with Tom, visiting him over the winter. At some point during a conversation, lamenting how they spent better than they earned, a logical solution came out. Some kind of robbery. Maybe the bank in Telluride? Bob knew the town and bank from his work on the mule team. They'd need more men. McCarty would organize a team of relays. Bob suggested his younger brother Dan could man one of them.

Explore the Outlaw Trail!

See where Bob Parker grew up in **Adventure 33: Butch Cassidy's Boyhood Home** and check out his old stomping grounds with the adventures listed above under Another Bryce Canyon Connection?

Soon, Tom and Matt struck out for Utah to scout the route. And Bob rode into Telluride to study the payroll delivery schedules from the mines, where he was spotted trying to teach his horse to stay put as he ran and jumped into the saddle.

It was late May 1889. A month later, they rode out of Telluride, into the history books, and across that hot Utah desert—where we now rejoin their escape.

WILD BUNCH STORIES

EPISODE 3

On the Outlaw Trail, 1889

No time to visit, bro • 4:00 a.m. business issues • A final stand? • This robbery is weighing on us, literally • Sweating in the shade • Do you want water or pants?

ONCE IN UTAH, the three outlaws left McElmo Canyon and passed through squat tablelands before turning northwest and navigating through a labyrinth of drainages that connect to Montezuma Canyon. Hopefully, by following this lesser-known route, they would avoid any posses searching around the main road running through Blanding and Monticello.

After more than 50 miles of hard riding, they reached the Carlisle Ranch at the head of Montezuma Canyon, in the northeastern foothills of the Blue Mountains. They changed horses at the outlaw-friendly ranch, and the trio continued north through Dry Valley. They passed an iconic landmark, a three-tiered dome of sandstone rising from the desert floor, later called Church Rock. As they rode beneath the conical La Sal Mountains, it's likely they skipped a visit to Bill McCarty, who owned a ranch on the southern slopes. Instead, the three pushed through the night.

> "They made one of the wildest rides in their history."
>
> —CHARLES KELLY, THE OUTLAW TRAIL

Continuing through the boxy Spanish Valley, they reached the ferry at Moab around four in the morning, having traveled another 50 miles. They crawled around on their bellies, scouting the riverbank for signs of deputies, but the coast seemed clear. The ferry operators were asleep on a hillside above the Grand River (now the Colorado River), avoiding the ferry house on this hot summer night.

Rousing one man by whispering for him to rise with his hands up, Matt discovered he was acquainted with all five. The river was running high from spring runoff, and another employee explained it was dangerous to cross in the dark.

"Our business lies rolling," replied Matt. "We've got to get across the river."

"Come on," said ferry owner Lester Taylor. "We'll put them across."

After crossing, they paid Taylor with a ten-dollar gold piece and rode north. The outlaws took a circuitous route through an upland region filled with bizarre sandstone formations—rock pillars, sheer-walled buttes, and improbable arches. In the early morning light, it was nerve-racking trying not to get lost in this dizzying landscape. Reaching the brush-covered flats of Salt Valley, they rode into open country again. Feeling uneasy, Matt trained a pair of field glasses behind them. Three miles back, and gaining, were six men on horseback.

The Henry Mountains as seen from Robbers Roost (chapters 3 and 4)

At the northern end of Salt Valley, the outlaws made a mad dash across Whipsaw Flats toward the Book Cliffs, the abrupt southern edge of the Tavaputs Plateau that features a series of knife-edge ridges resembling hardback spines on a bookshelf. As the outlaws approached the cliffs, a second posse appeared in the distance to their left, closing off any chance at a western route onto the plateau. An eastern route went through Thompson Springs, a stop on the Denver and Rio Grande Railroad, but the town might very well have more lawmen waiting.

Making a split-second decision, the outlaws took a risky entrance through a narrow opening in the cliffs, hoping they could find an exit. Instead, they soon stared up at sheer cliffs and a dry waterfall. The men turned around, pulled out their Winchester rifles, and placed their fingers on the triggers. After a frantic ride of nearly 300 miles across two states, they prepared to make what might be their final stand.

But no one came. After a few minutes, they cautiously retraced their tracks, expecting to be met with rifle fire. Outside the canyon, there was no sign of the lawmen. They had continued riding across the sandy basin. With this second chance, the outlaws picked a new route up through the Book Cliffs and continued higher into the reddish-and-beige-banded Roan Cliffs, the Tavaputs' second tier of cliffs.

As they followed a creek canyon up through the mountainous plateau, the physical toll of their endeavor began to weigh on them—literally. Given the relay changes and the fear their horses might be shot out from under them, they'd strapped the cash and coins from the robbery to their bodies with leather money belts, which constantly rubbed and bounced as the outlaws bounded over rough terrain. During brief rest stops, the men would start dancing around, swearing and clawing at the belts, threatening to tear them off and ride away.

Instead, they continued north over a pass and descended another creek drainage into sandy, desolate country. After crossing the shallow and silty White River, they traded away their spent horses, plus some robbery money, for fresh mounts from local Native Americans.

Soon afterward, another posse picked up their trail, so they scooted through Coyote Basin, passing just west of Cliff Ridge, and lost the party after crossing the Green River below the upthrust Split Mountain. Following the curve of Red Wash, they turned northwest onto the flanks of Diamond Mountain and followed Crouse Canyon into the infamous Browns Hole, a remote valley where the borders of Utah, Colorado, and Wyoming meet.

Under normal circumstances, their arrival might have been cause for a celebratory reunion with friends like Charlie Crouse, the Bassett family, and fellow rustlers who called this remote valley and regular hideout home.

Instead, they were whisked away at Crouse's suggestion to a secluded cabin the hard-drinking rancher kept in dense forest on Diamond Mountain.

At the cabin, the men finally got their first rest after the hard days on the outlaw trail. They lounged around. Slept. Played cards. Ate food Crouse provided. Drank from a nearby spring. Drank whiskey with Crouse. In the days when they were simple rustlers, they might have stayed in Browns Park for weeks or months. But the scope of the Telluride robbery was way more than some missing livestock. After a few days, one of Crouse's ranch hands burst into the cabin to warn them. A posse was at the ranch.

And so off they went, over the Diamond Mountain crest and back south through the dusty Uinta Basin. They rode at night and hid during the day, this time working their way through the western side of the Tavaputs and coming down through the Roan and Book Cliffs into an entirely different region: the San Rafael Swell, with sweeping dunes, tortuous canyonlands, and bulging sandstone uplifts. They'd previously avoided this area given the intense heat in July, but now the Robbers Roost area was their last chance at escape.

In the San Rafael Swell, they followed a twisting trail through pink, peach, and cream-colored formations of stacked sedimentary rocks. They made camp in a spring-fed side canyon of the San Rafael River, not far from a plunging chasm that some claimed resembled a miniature version of the Big Canyon—a place they'd never seen but heard about, an increasingly famous spot in Arizona Territory. It's now called the Grand Canyon, ever since a one-armed Civil War major passed through in rowboats.

The trio spent the summer sweating in the shade. When supplies ran low, they decided the young newcomer, least likely to be spotted

A sketch of Matt Warner from a Salt Lake Herald article in 1896 (Library of Congress)

by lawmen, should go to town. Hanksville was closer but too small to risk a visit. So Bob rode 50 miles to Green River, Utah, a stop on the Colorado and Rio Grande Railroad, where he might blend into the crowds coming and going. He did not blend in, being spotted by his own uncle, Dan Gilles.

Bob hightailed it back to the Swell and warned the others. What if someone had noticed the encounter with a young man fitting the description of the now-infamous Telluride robbers? There was a reward for their capture, after all.

From that day forward, the outlaws took turns keeping watch. Patrolling the area for horse hoofprints—which, one day, Matt spotted in nearby open desert. As Warner later told the story (see *The Last of the Bandit Riders* in the bibliography), the three outlaws hid in rocks above and watched.

Three lawmen appeared, riding toward their camp. After continuing for a way, they stopped and took a fork in a different direction. The trio breathed a sigh of relief but then realized what was happening. The lawmen were riding deeper into the Swell in late summer. The outlaws knew there was no water that way, and the three riders seemed unprepared for what was to come. If they became stranded or worse, more posses would convene to search the region. They'd be hellbent on finding the lawmen and, next, the outlaws.

A few minutes later, a rifle shot erupted through the canyon. The lawmen looked up and saw an outlaw waving. As they rode toward him, they spotted a stick with a note attached. *You're heading for death in that direction*, read the note. *If you want water, follow me.*

The thirsty lawmen followed horse tracks to a spring and collected water. Then the outlaws surrounded them, rifles drawn, and disarmed them. They took the lawmen's pants and sent them riding across the desert back toward Green River. After a few miles, their legs were so roughed up, they were forced to walk.

More likely, Matt was embellishing. Shortly after Bob returned from Green River, the three outlaws turned north once more, heading for Wyoming and whatever came next.

Explore the Outlaw Trail!

This wild escape passed through some pretty stunning places, listed below in the order they appear in the story, starting with the little-visited **Adventure 17: Blue Mountains**. Next came a now-famous outdoor town, **Adventure 12: Moab**. And that improbable landscape across the river? It later became **Adventure 13: Arches National Park**. There are limited ways to explore the Tavaputs, with two being **Adventure 50: Nine Mile Canyon** and **Adventure 51: Desolation and Gray Canyons River Trip**. See the bizarre Split Mountain in **Adventure 45: Dinosaur National Monument (Utah Side)** and continue into the infamous Browns Park hideout with **Adventure 58: John Jarvie Historic Ranch** and **Adventure 59: Eastern Browns Park**. After returning south, the outlaws' hideout camp was possibly near **Adventure 22: Little Grand Canyon**, based on the limited descriptions, and the supply run took Butch to **Adventure 18: Green River, Utah**, where you can also access the Book Cliffs. Enjoy!

Early Days in Browns Hole, 1878–1884

And an organ? • *Idyllic wilderness to outlaw haven* • *A coming cattle boom* • *Isom Dart and Matt Rash* • *Range wars rising* • *Ann Bassett's brush with rustling*

SNOW WAS MELTING in the mountains when the Bassett family passed through Irish Canyon into Browns Hole in the spring of 1878. They had come from Arkansas by rail to Green River, Wyoming, where they switched to a pair of wagons.

For frontier settlers, they were an unlikely bunch. The matriarch, Elizabeth, was only twenty-two years old and seven months pregnant with her third child. The patriarch was a mild-mannered clerk named Herb, twenty-one years older than his wife. Four-year-old Josie and two-year-old Samuel perched atop the wagons, which were packed with furniture. Bed frames and feather mattresses. Walnut bureaus. An iron cookstove. Boxes filled with china, glassware, and books. They even had an organ.

Leading the way was Herb's younger half brother Sam, who had a small ranch in Browns Hole, an isolated valley about 25 miles long and surrounded by mountains, with the calm Green River running through it. Sam had been a young prospector, guide, and trapper when he came to Browns Hole in the 1850s and decided to stay.

During the previous twenty-four years, Sam had watched the valley grow from an idyllic wilderness, where Native Americans mingled with white trappers and early homesteaders, to a patchwork of small family ranches that shared the open range. One homestead was owned by Jose and Pablo Herrera, brothers who had fled the unrest along the border of New and Old Mexico. The Hoys, four brothers and an uncle, occupied the fertile bottomlands by the river and mostly kept to themselves, somewhat miffed that the entire valley wasn't theirs. John and Nellie Jarvie were a married couple who ran the trading post at the west end of the valley. And the hard-drinking and nefarious Charlie Crouse operated a ranch at the foot of Diamond Mountain, the southern border of Browns Hole.

By the late 1870s, newer settlers were following the lead of John Wesley Powell. The American explorer had come down the Green River on his expedition to the Grand Canyon in 1869 and renamed the valley Browns Park. To Elizabeth, this softer term better captured the beauty of red rock mountains draped in pine and cedar. She not only enthusiastically adopted the convention but encouraged others to do the same.

While their own home was being built, the Bassett family squeezed into Sam's two-room log cabin, which had neither windows nor flooring. Two months later, Elizabeth gave birth to Ann. As the first white child born in the valley, her life would witness the series of drastic changes across the West during the late nineteenth century—a time of livestock rustling, increasingly powerful cattle barons, and expanding range wars.

Books on display at the Little Snake River Museum in Savery, Wyoming (Adventure 63)

Many challenges arose during the Bassetts' early years. Unable to nurse Ann, Elizabeth arranged for a wet nurse, a Ute woman who camped with her tribe nearby. When the Bassetts moved into a cabin on their new ranch, the next challenge was figuring out how to ranch. Their first winter was a hungry one, with mostly frontier rations—canned beans, flour, and salted pork. Luckily, other families occasionally brought them things like bread and eggs. By 1879, they had planted a vegetable garden and acquired several head of livestock.

That fall, word of the Meeker Massacre reached Browns Hole. It was one of the last atrocities of the Indian Wars, a string of violent military actions by the US Army and murderous retaliations from Native tribes. The result would be the forced relocation of all Ute persons to a reservation in the nearby Uinta Basin. Immediately following the massacre, many white settlers fled in a panic from Browns Hole.

The Bassetts went to Green River, Wyoming. City convenience may have appealed to docile Herb, but the energetic Elizabeth hopelessly missed life in the mountain-ringed valley. While in town, she became acutely aware of the economic potential of a coming cattle boom, which would follow the wave of western settlement.

In the spring of 1881, the Bassetts returned to Browns Park, moving to a new spread. Located at the foot of Cold Springs Mountain, they were a few miles north of the Gates of Lodore, a pair of sheer cliffs rising on either side of the Green River where it plunged out of the valley and into the eastern Uinta Mountains.

The Bassetts hewed logs and built a new cabin, chicken coop, and bunkhouse. They piped the spring for irrigation, cleared hay fields, and planted a vegetable garden and orchard. In a new corral, they raised horses and cattle, which they branded with a connected "UP" and set loose on the open range. Given that the Bassett Ranch was on the main road leading into the valley from the east, they became something of a country inn, often hosting strangers at their dinner table and in their bunkhouse. An expanding ranch needed hands, so in 1883 Elizabeth hired the first.

His name was Isom Dart, an African American cowboy who was born enslaved in 1849 in Arkansas. He had come from Texas on a cattle drive for the Middlesex Land and Cattle Company, located 25 miles northwest of the Bassett Ranch. Afterward, Isom drifted into Browns Park, looking for work. Isom soon became an essential ranch hand and family friend, playing with the kids and riding the range with Bassett cattle while building his own herd. He was particularly known for an ability to break broncs without the use of spurs, and he also crafted leather lariats and lassos.

Soon, Isom was joined in the Bassett bunkhouse by his young cowboy friend from Texas, Matt Rash. After running as trail boss on a cattle drive, eighteen-year-old Matt had gone northwest of Flaming Gorge and worked for the Circle K until it was bought out by Middlesex. Matt came into Browns Park pushing his own herd of cattle and soon signed on with

Explore the Outlaw Trail!

Given how little the valley has changed since the outlaw days, traveling back in time is quite possible in Browns Park, with **Adventure 59: Eastern Browns Park** and **Adventure 58: John Jarvie Historic Ranch**. You can check out two towns with Old West origins in **Adventure 53: Green River and Rock Springs (Wyoming)**. And while in the area, make sure to check out the modern highlights, including **Adventure 52: Flaming Gorge Dam and Reservoir**.

Elizabeth as her ranch manager. The third hand was Jim McKnight, a few years younger than Matt, from Scotland by way of Rock Springs, Wyoming.

By this time, tensions between small ranchers and large cattle companies were heating up. In recent years, Middlesex had tried to buy up land in Browns Park, but the valley's independent ranchers refused to sell. Owned by Boston businessmen, Middlesex's managers knew that when its cattle strayed into Browns Park, they could expect around 20 percent "leakage" from rustling, compared with the normal 10 percent losses elsewhere. In general, the valley inhabitants looked at company cattle as invaders, and they had no problem with appropriating the occasional stray, often with some creative rebranding. Meanwhile, Middlesex cowboys would patrol the region, looking to retake their lost and stolen cattle.

When Ann was five, she found a sickly stray calf with Middlesex's "Flying VD" brand. A company manager gave Ann the animal, and she took it home to the Bassett Ranch. Three years later, a Middlesex cowboy on a roundup spotted the cow and plucked it from the Bassett herd. When eight-year-old Ann found out, she demanded the manager return her cow. As soon as Ann had it back, she asked one of the family's ranch hands to alter the brand. Thus, young Ann had her first of many brushes with rustling.

> ## "The war between the large cattlemen and the small ranchers had already begun. That war would continue for twenty-five more years."
> —Grace McClure, *The Bassett Women*

In September 1884, Browns Park was surveyed. Previously, all homesteaders had been squatters. Now they could file for clear titles to their ranches. Herb Bassett immediately went to the county seat in September, but not all valley residents moved so quickly. In an underhanded move, Valentine Hoy—one of the four Hoy brothers—hired some men and took them to the county seat in a scheme to obtain the lands of several homesteaders who had not filed. Valley residents were outraged, but the titles were ironclad, and the homesteaders were forced to leave. Browns Park had its first cattle baron, with more on the way.

Thirty miles east of the park, another operator named Ora Haley from Laramie had established the Two Bar Ranch. For now, he caused no trouble for valley ranchers, but in time, Two Bar would become one of the largest cattle companies in the West—a path that would eventually lead right to Ann Bassett.

WILD BUNCH STORIES

EPISODE 5

Wyoming Rambles, or Becoming Butch Cassidy, 1889–1896

Front-porch days and back-porch nights • A big dumb kid who liked to joke • Causing trouble in Lander • A nickname is born • Range wars rising • An unfair trial • Honor among thieves

IT WAS EARLY fall in 1889 when the young man christened Robert LeRoy Parker decided his own name was a liability—both for him, having been spotted by his former employer Harry Adsit, and for his family, who might soon bear the shame of his new profession. His new last name came in honor of his rustling mentor, Mike Cassidy, back home. The reason for the new first name he kept under his hat.

With this new alias, George Cassidy was soon on his own again. After the trio arrived in Wyoming, Matt and Tom veered west to winter in Star Valley. Meanwhile, Cassidy pressed north along the east side of the Wind River Range toward Lander.

The years following the Telluride robbery would be a rambling and enigmatic time in Cassidy's life. To those Wyoming folks watching from

The Wyoming Territorial Prison, in Laramie, Wyoming (Adventure 61), still looks much like it did during Butch's stint.

front porches during the day, George Cassidy might have appeared to be a friendly and law-abiding citizen trying to make a go at cowboying and ranching. To those looking closer, shadier dealings seemed to be happening off back porches under cover of darkness.

Cassidy's first stop was at a ranch owned by a man named Brown. This mysterious fifty-year-old was rumored to be Cap Brown, a notorious live-stock rustler who had fled Utah, having been among the first to operate in Robbers Roost. Through mentor Mike Cassidy, a teenaged Bob Parker had met Cap Brown in the mid-1880s, picking up a few jobs moving stolen cattle through Roost country and onward for sale in Telluride—Bob's first introduction to the riches that awaited far from home.

That fall in '89, Cassidy was spotted in Browns Park on the Bassett Ranch. He worked as a ranch hand for matriarch Elizabeth Bassett while reading books and articles from husband Herb's library. When the day was done, daughter Josie Bassett said he'd ride through the gate, wring the necks of a few chickens, and invite himself to dinner.

"A big dumb kid who liked to joke," observed Josie, who joined Cassidy at a few valley dances when she was fifteen. Often her eleven-year-old sister, Ann, would tag along behind.

Next, Cassidy was going partners with a new friend, Al Hainer, on a small ranch near Dubois, Wyoming, in the Upper Wind River valley, between the mountains and desolate red-gray badlands. It was a rough winter, with more than a few nights keeping warm in the saloon. The following spring, they went looking for new interests.

One that caught their eye was causing trouble in Lander. One time they hitched four unbroken horses to a stagecoach, filled it with laughing young women, and went careening down Main Street. Another time they stole buddy John Lee's buckboard, crashing it into a hitching rail in front of Coalter's Saloon and flying off of the destroyed buckboard.

"John," called out Cassidy, lying on the sidewalk. "Come get your buckboard."

Another winter, Cassidy took a brief job as a butcher in Rock Springs, where he met Douglas A. Preston, saving the life of his future lawyer during a saloon brawl. A chance meeting that would soon come in handy.

When Cassidy visited Matt Warner and Tom McCarty over in Star Valley, Matt learned about Cassidy's part-time job. He laughingly called him "Butch," and the famous alias was born.

At various times Butch Cassidy was spotted in Johnson County, Wyoming, where the range wars were heating up between powerful cattle barons and small independent ranchers. Expressing contempt for the actions of wealthy ranchers

> # Explore the Outlaw Trail!
>
> Cassidy sure did like to ramble, so why not join him across Wyoming? (Warning, unless you are also taking a seven-year trip, consider plotting a more efficient course.) Butch's ranch was near **Adventure 70: Dubois and Lake Louise Trail**, and you can still party on the same streets (well, sidewalks) of **Adventure 67: Lander**. There are now more breweries than butcher shops in the latter town of **Adventure 53: Green River and Rock Springs (Wyoming)**. In Johnson County, at the very least check out **Adventure 72: Buffalo** and **Adventure 75: Hole-in-the-Wall Hideout**. See the Bighorn Basin while traveling to **Adventure 77: Cody, Adventure 78: Meeteetse and Kirwin Ghost Town**, or **Adventure 79: Thermopolis and Wind River Canyon**. Finally, Butch did his time in Laramie at **Adventure 61: Wyoming Territorial Prison**.

waging an increasingly brutal war against small-time rustlers just trying to survive, Butch convinced Matt and Tom to reunite for a risky cattle raid around the Bighorn Mountains.

They collected strays and mavericks—unbranded calves—throughout the Powder River country, including the area near Hole-in-the-Wall. This

Butch Cassidy's mug shot from the Territorial Prison in Laramie (Library of Congress)

famous outlaw hideout in Red Wall Country had been in use since the 1860s or 1870s. A precipitous trail wound up through a notch in the Red Wall, which was hard to traverse and easy to defend, leading to a tight V-shaped valley open to the west. A cabin in the valley would later serve as a perfect rendezvous spot for later capers. But for now, they were sticking with rustling.

After gathering fifty head, the outlaws were riding across the Bighorn Basin when one of the cattle baron's patrols came up behind. The trio abandoned their stolen cattle and made a dash west across high plains, dodging the occasional rifle shot from their pursuers. The chase lasted hours, until they reached a wooded cliff bank above the Wind River, which was running high and swift from spring runoff.

Realizing they were trapped, Matt rode his horse straight down the cliff and into the river. He and his horse were swept away. The remaining two watched Matt flailing in the current, glanced at each other, then back at the cautiously approaching posse, rifles at the ready. Then Butch and Tom followed Matt into the river.

In late spring 1892, Butch's luck ran out at a ranch near Star Valley. He was lying in the bunkhouse when unfamiliar footsteps approached. A voice declared he had a warrant for arrest.

"Well, get to shooting," said Butch, reaching for his Colt 45.

In dashed County Deputy Bob Calverly, aiming a revolver and pulling the trigger. The gun misfired several times while more lawmen rushed the room. Butch never got a shot off, but he received a few knocks to the head from the capturing posse. Outside, he discovered ranch partner Al Hainer had been arrested as well.

The two were taken to Fremont County Jail in Lander, where they learned the charges related to purchasing stolen horses the summer before. Butch and Al had been swept up in the same antirustler campaigns currently unfolding in Johnson County and across the state of Wyoming. The men spent two sweltering summer months in jail before making bail.

A year later, the trial convened. Douglas Preston served as Butch's defense attorney. That trial ended with a verdict of not guilty, so area ranchers arranged another charge for stealing a different horse, this one valued at only five dollars. The second trial resulted in a split verdict in the summer of 1894. Al was acquitted, but Butch was found guilty and sentenced to two years. Even the judge admitted the trial may have been unfair.

On July 15, 1894, Cassidy arrived by train at the Wyoming Territorial Prison in Laramie, an imposing fort-like structure. When the warden noticed this burly new prisoner hadn't been required to wear leg irons, he demanded the sheriff explain.

"Honor among thieves, I guess," joked Butch.

George Cassidy was listed as prisoner number 187 and issued a prison uniform. During the customary inspection, the intake officer noted a scar under Cassidy's left eye from being pistol-whipped by Deputy Calverly during his arrest. Throughout Cassidy's incarceration, other inmates attempted numerous prison breaks and some even succeeded. But Butch was a model prisoner, reading books and working various jobs in the prison garden and ranch.

> "Cassidy is . . . a brave, daring fellow and a man well calculated to be a leader, and should his inclinations run that way, I do not doubt but that he would be capable of organizing and leading a lot of desperate men to desperate deeds."
>
> —JUDGE JESSE KNIGHT, 1895, QUOTED BY BILL BETENSON IN *BUTCH CASSIDY, MY UNCLE*

Butch made friends with the guards as well as fellow prisoners, including his cell mate, a rustler named Rocky Stoner. Due to a physical resemblance, another inmate might very well have been Cassidy's brother had his name not been William T. Wilcox. Another friend was Joe Nutcher, whose brother just happened to be the thief who sold Butch the stolen horses that put him prison. Other times, former coworkers arrived to serve time.

The governor granted Butch's request for a full pardon for being a model prisoner, on the condition that he swear to never commit another crime in the young state of Wyoming. Butch agreed and, after serving eighteen months, he walked through the prison gates in mid-January 1896. But secretly, he was embittered by his sham trial and already plotting his next steps.

A Most Desperate Plot, 1896

Browns Park happenings • Enter Elzy Lay • Matt Warner's bodyguard days • A real high wheeler • An uneventful escape • There may be a battle • The fake of the century

ON HIS RELEASE from prison in January 1896, Butch went straight to Browns Park to stay with Matt Warner, who had built a cabin and ranch on Diamond Mountain. While Butch was locked up, Matt had married an eighteen-year-old Mormon girl from Star Valley named Rose. When Rose learned about Matt's outlaw life, she took their newborn and left. To win her back, Matt tried to go straight by working his new ranch. But no sooner had she returned than Rose developed a cancerous tumor and her leg was amputated. She moved to Vernal to recover, where Matt would frequently visit.

Butch discovered plenty more had happened during the past four years in Browns Park. In December 1892, matriarch Elizabeth Bassett had been taken with a mysterious illness. While bedridden, her favorite milk cow was caught in a roundup by a cattle company. Furious, Elizabeth saddled her horse and rode into the valley. She retrieved her cow, but after returning, her condition took a turn for the worse. She died early the next morning, at age thirty-seven. Now the passive Herb was left to deal with two wild daughters, eighteen-year-old Josie and fourteen-year-old Ann.

A year later, Josie dropped out of college in Salt Lake City and returned to the valley with some abrupt news. She was pregnant by Bassett Ranch manager Jim McKnight. They married in the spring of 1893 and moved up to Beaver Creek to take over operation of Uncle Sam Bassett's ranch. More recently, Charlie Crouse had sold his valley ranch and opened a saloon in Vernal.

While staying at Matt's ranch on Diamond Mountain, Butch had the company of another friend and occasional accomplice, Elzy Lay, a charming outlaw with a reputation as a lady's man. At one time, Elzy was a part owner of the Gambling-Hell Saloon along a wild strip of bars and brothels near Fort Duchesne, Utah, in the Uinta Basin. But the feds had shut down the operation for moving counterfeit cash. One of Elzy's law-abiding skills was breaking horses, which he was doing for Matt. Another of Elzy's skills was

Buckskin Gulch (Adventure 40) on the Utah-Arizona state line

robbery, and soon he and Butch would embark on their first joint venture on the outlaw trail.

> ## "Most of the episodes in [*Butch Cassidy and the Sundance Kid*] involved Elzy Lay instead of the Sundance Kid, but who would go to a movie entitled Butch Cassidy and Elzy Lay?"
>
> —LULA PARKER BETENSON, *BUTCH CASSIDY, MY BROTHER*

When Butch was roaming around Wyoming in the early 1890s, Elzy had become a frequent sighting in the valley, where he began to court Josie Bassett. But by 1896, Elzy had taken up with a girl named Maude Davis from Vernal. These arrangements allowed Elzy and Matt to take turns tending the ranch and visiting their ladies in town.

In May of that year, Matt was drinking in Crouse's saloon, where he met a local prospector who was searching for the source of a gold deposit in the high Uintas. Complicating the search were three other miners looking for the same deposit. The prospector hired Matt and his drinking buddy for

Old Trail Town in Cody, Wyoming (Adventure 77), combines twenty-six historic buildings—including the original Hole-in-the-Wall cabin—into a preserved Old West town.

protection, in hopes they would scare off his competitors. But when the three men rode up into the mountains, a gunfight broke out and two of the competitors were killed.

Matt, his friend, and the prospector were arrested and locked up in the Uintah County Jail in Vernal. Soon, the townsfolk tried to lynch them but were stopped by the sheriff. To prevent another attack, the three suspects were transported by the less-traveled Carter Military Road through the Uinta Mountains to stand trial in Ogden. Without the money to hire a lawyer, Matt was looking at a life sentence.

In late July, three strangers arrived in Montpelier, Idaho, and took jobs on a nearby ranch harvesting hay. Going by new aliases, these men were actually Butch, Elzy, and Bub Meeks. Butch had insisted they take the job as cover. Their real purpose came after work, with long rides into the surrounding country planning an escape route with spots to stash horses for a relay. After a few weeks laboring under the hot sun, they quit their jobs, saddled up, and rode into town.

After dismounting outside the bank, Bub tended the horses. Butch and Elzy pulled bandannas over their faces and unholstered their revolvers. A few men standing on the boardwalk were herded inside the bank, where they joined three employees and some surprised

Explore the Outlaw Trail!

Those outlaws sure did get around, and so can you. Explore the High Uintas with, at minimum, **Adventure 47: Flaming Gorge–Uintas Scenic Byway**. A good base for discovering the area is **Adventure 43: Vernal**. Plus, consider a side trip to the scene of the crime, **Adventure 89: Butch Cassidy Bank Robbery Museum, Montpelier, Idaho.**

customers. Butch covered the crowd, who were ordered to line up facing the wall. Elzy went behind the cage and demanded bills. The teller said there were none, while casually reaching down with one hand toward what appeared to be a rifle.

"Goddamn liar," said Elzy, clubbing the teller's head with his gun.

Butch shouted at him to lay off.

Elzy used a large sack to collect bills from the cage before moving to the unlocked vault and gathering gold and silver coins. After taking the teller's rifle, he casually walked outside and secured the haul to their horses. When Elzy was ready to ride, Butch warned the captives to stay inside for ten minutes. After a seven-year hiatus, he walked outside from his second bank robbery. The trio slowly rode their horses out of town before digging in their spurs and galloping up Montpelier Canyon, through hills covered in dry golden grass.

Back in town, the bank cashier waited until he couldn't hear the robbers' horses. Then he ran for the town deputy, a part-time official who didn't have a horse or gun. He'd never needed such things in the sleepy town. Instead, the deputy hopped on the only conveyance available—a high-wheel bicycle. He pedaled atop the teetering thing down the main street, hoping to get a glimpse of the outlaws' direction out of town.

Eventually, the sheriff and another deputy arrived and formed a posse of townsfolk. But as they rode up Montpelier Canyon, the inexperienced townsfolk developed second thoughts and reared up. They were small-town citizens, not gunmen. The sheriff and deputy rode onward, and when the townsfolk heard gunfire in the distance, they returned to Montpelier. A rumor spread that the two missing lawmen had been killed. This sad news was immediately printed in the local newspaper, and the sheriff and deputy read about their own demise when they returned from their failed pursuit.

For the outlaws, the escape was mostly uneventful. They made their relays. Turned south along Smiths Fork and rode over rocky ridges. Hid their tracks with a Native American trick: placing homemade leather moccasins over their horses' hooves. A second posse never got close.

Newspapers reported a wide range in the amount stolen, from $5,000 to more than $15,000. Whatever the exact amount, it was enough to cover Matt Warner's legal fees. Butch and Elzy put the stolen loot on retainer with Douglas A. Preston of Rock Springs, Wyoming, who hired two of Utah's finest defense attorneys in the matter, including Orlando S. Powers.

During the September trial, a front-page article in the *Salt Lake Herald* caused a stir. "Most Desperate Plot Unearthed," read the headline. "Connection of the Montpelier Bank Robber with Murders Near Vernal Last Spring. There may be a battle. How Cassady [*sic*] and His Gang Proposed to Liberate Their Pals . . . Looted the Bank to Get Defense Money."

Basically, the article laid out the entire caper and then some. Not only had Cassidy and gang robbed the Montpelier Bank to pay for Matt Warner's defense but the article also claimed they were camped north of Ogden, ready to break him out if necessary.

Douglas Preston and Orlando Powers replied with a series of counter-claims and accusations: Cassidy wasn't wanted for any crimes, anywhere. He had an alibi. The article was the work of an overzealous reporter willing to lie for readers. Riffing off these denials, a rival editor at the *Ogden Standard* called the *Herald* story the fake of the century.

When the jury returned a verdict, Matt Warner was acquitted of first-degree murder but found guilty of voluntary manslaughter. The sentence was five years in the Utah State Penitentiary. Right after Butch had gotten out, his best friend from the outlaw trail was going inside.

WILD BUNCH STORIES

Desperadoes at Castle Gate, 1896–1897

Shifting situations • Bloodcurdling coffee • A new kid called Sundance • Camping in canyon country • We're horse racers, swear • Can't ride? Run!

AFTER THE Montpelier robbery, Butch and Elzy needed a place to lie low, so they rented a cabin north of Vernal, Utah. Elzy had recently married Maude, who came to stay. Butch was joined by Ann Bassett, now eighteen and looking for adventure. The couples strung a wire between two beds and draped blankets over it for privacy. This make-shift living situation didn't last long: in late October a warrant was issued for the outlaws' arrest. They just dodged a posse by riding up to the Bassett Ranch in Browns Park.

To show appreciation for their valley hosts, Butch, Elzy, and a few outlaw pals paid for a huge Thanksgiving dinner. The women wore fashionable dresses with leg-of-mutton sleeves and boned collars. The men wore suits with bow ties and served the table.

"Just shows how etiquette can put fear into a brave man's heart," observed Ann.

She found it hilarious watching Butch, a cowboy accustomed to robbing banks, struggle with what she called the bloodcurdling job of pouring coffee. After he kept reaching across guests' faces to grab a cup, a meeting was held in the kitchen to instruct the now-famous outlaw on the finer points of dining etiquette.

Scenic Wind River Canyon near Thermopolis, Wyoming (Adventure 79)

Another outlaw turned waiter for the evening was a newer face around Browns Park. His name was Harry Longabaugh, but folks called him the Sundance Kid, given that he had been jailed in the Wyoming town of the same name during his early twenties. Four years before, he helped rob the Great Northern Railroad near Malta, Montana—a botched job that netted him and two accomplices just seventy dollars, with only Sundance escaping arrest.

> "As the train gathered speed one of the men crawled over the tender and, about a mile out of town, ordered the engineer to apply the brakes. . . . The robbery was hardly profitable, but, worse than that, the robbers had difficulty keeping their handkerchiefs in place."
>
> —RICHARD PATTERSON, DESCRIBING (IN *BUTCH CASSIDY: A BIOGRAPHY*) THE SUNDANCE KID'S FIRST TRAIN ROBBERY, IN 1892, SEVERAL YEARS BEFORE HE PARTNERED UP WITH BUTCH CASSIDY

The Thanksgiving feast shifted to a nearby ranch house for a dance party until sunup. But soon after the holiday, Butch and Elzy decided Browns Park wasn't safe, so they headed south for Robbers Roost.

On the eastern rim of Horseshoe Canyon, they set up three canvas tents in cedar trees. Throughout the winter, many people came and went. One long-term visitor was Elzy's wife, Maude. Another was a mysterious young woman named Etta Place, who stayed with Butch. The two women became friends, often walking through a startling landscape of slickrock formations and sand flats.

Meanwhile, other familiar faces included Bub Meeks, the third bandit from the Montpelier heist. Another was Joe Walker, a horse thief and hard case known for drunken rampages and fighting who was a Roost regular. And Blue John Griffith, who was a Rooster known more for his skill with boats than horses, having come from Grand Junction, Colorado, via the Westwater area on the Grand River (today the Colorado River). The men spent much time inside a tent, clearly planning something. Made famous by the Montpelier robbery, Butch and Elzy were now more committed than ever to a life on the outlaw trail. They might as well make the most of it.

In March, Blue John took the ladies to catch a train at Green River, Utah. And the boys rode about 90 miles north, through the sand dunes and rugged terrain of the San Rafael Swell toward Castle Gate.

Home to the Pleasant Valley Coal Company, Castle Gate was a small mining town named for a pair of rock towers rising on either side of the tumbling Price River. Leading through this narrow canyon was a single dirt road, which Butch and Elzy followed into town in mid-April 1897.

This time, they didn't arrive looking like hay harvesters. Instead, they rode their horses bareback with racing rigs. Castle Gate wasn't a ranching town filled with drifting cowboys, but it was on the regional horse racing circuit, and the outlaws came prepared. They spent the next few days milling around the company store, claiming to be training their horses for an upcoming race in Salt Lake City. Meanwhile, they kept an eye and ear out for a delivery by the Denver and Rio Grande Railroad.

The train arrived at noon on Wednesday, signaled by a shrill whistle blast. The precise delivery day and time was purposely randomized to discourage theft, but once the payroll

Visit!

Today the mining company and town of Castle Gate are gone. One of the rock tower "gates" collapsed from dynamiting the road cut for US 6, which runs through the canyon. All that remains are the in-use railroad tracks, some clearings where the town once stood, and coal seams running through the cliffs. A commemorative plaque on the north side of US 6, a half mile west of the junction with US 191, marks the townsite.

arrived, the paymaster, E. L. Carpenter, and his clerk had a standard routine: Retrieve a leather satchel and some sacks from the express-car agent. Carry them across the yard past the store. Climb the stairs to the payroll office.

This time, when Carpenter reached the base of the stairs, a man stepped out and pointed a revolver in his face.

"Drop the sacks," said Butch.

The paymaster complied, dropping two sacks and the satchel. But the clerk carrying a third sack panicked and ran inside the company store. A curious miner stuck his head outside.

"Get back in there, you son of a bitch," shouted Elzy, aiming a gun from atop his horse, "or I'll fill your belly with hot lead."

Things got chaotic from there. Butch grabbed the three fallen bags and handed two of them to Elzy, who dropped the reins for Butch's horse during the exchange. The horse spooked and took off down the road.

"Desperadoes at Castle Gate . . . A crime that may be classed with the most daring exploits of the James Gang."

—SALT LAKE HERALD, APRIL 22, 1897

"Don't anybody make a mistake," said Butch to the gathering crowd. He watched his horse escaping without him, while Elzy galloped after in pursuit. "Everything's going to be alright."

Then Butch ran.

Down the road, Elzy corralled the spooked horse. A few rifle shots came their way from the second floor of the company building. Butch hopped on, and they rode out from Castle Gate into the desert basin beyond.

Explore the Outlaw Trail!

The Sundance Kid earned his nickname doing jail time in **Adventure 88: Wyoming Black Hills.** In Robbers Roost, the fleeing bandits camped near **Adventure 19: Horseshoe Canyon.** Blue John ran boats on some of the same sections popular today in **Adventure 15: Colorado River Trips.**

WILD BUNCH STORIES

Into the Roost, 1897

Wire cutting • All posses converge • The persistent paymaster of Castle Gate •
Spring at the Orange Cliffs • Cowardly lawmen • Blue John in relief

THE TWO outlaws fled out of Price Canyon, bypassing west of Helper on a trail through Spring Canyon. Ten miles from the robbery, they reached their first horse relay, at Gordon Creek. Continuing south for another 20 miles, they cut telegraph wires outside the town of Cleveland. Soon after, a US Mail carrier saw in the distance two determined riders, noticing that one wore riding goggles while the other wore a slouch hat and squinted through the dust.

Behind them, a hasty pursuit had commenced at Castle Gate. Only moments after the robbery, paymaster Carpenter had tried to telegraph the sheriff. But when he tapped the key, the line was dead. On hearing the whistle blast of the arriving train, Joe Walker had climbed a pole south of town and cut the wire.

Next, Carpenter ran for the steam engine, demanding the engineer cut loose from the train cars and head back to Price. A miner soon followed the outlaws in a horse-drawn buggy, discovering one stolen sack and the satchel abandoned by the roadside. The sack was full of silver. The leather satchel had some checks, but the cash was gone.

When Carpenter reached Price, the sheriff telegraphed towns along the outlaws' escape route, getting his messages in just before Butch and Elzy cut the lines. Two towns heeded the call, with residents in Huntington and Castle Dale forming posses along the western edges of the San Rafael Swell.

The sheriff of Price led his own posse south. During the late afternoon, each posse proceeded into the northern Swell.

By now the outlaws had reached Buckhorn Wash, where they'd stashed a second horse relay, about 35 miles from the first. Butch and Elzy followed the muddy stream bed downhill between stands of cottonwoods and rising walls of Navajo sandstone, in places decorated with ancient pictographs from a lost culture. This tributary canyon joined the San Rafael River at the downstream end of the Little Grand Canyon, familiar to Butch from the days when he was still Bob Parker. Here, the men turned east and followed a rugged plateau as the river dropped out of sight into a series of box canyons.

Up on the plateau, the posses were suffering setbacks. The one from Price lost the outlaws' trail near Cleveland and wasted time while circling. As darkness descended, the posses from Huntington and Castle Dale converged near the head of Buckhorn Wash and fired on each other. Two horses died and one member took a bullet in the leg. Eventually, everyone turned back except for five determined men—one of whom was E. L. Carpenter, the persistent paymaster from Castle Gate.

A waning moon rose around midnight as the outlaws pushed onward toward Mexican Mountain, where a final horse relay was stationed. From there, they followed the bending San Rafael River south and passed through a slot canyon of the San Rafael Reef and entered open desert country.

The five trailing men caught up to Butch and Elzy in the open desert near Wildcat Butte, and shots were exchanged. But as the outlaws passed Little Flat Top, this lingering posse had second thoughts about following them into the canyon country of Robbers Roost. The outlaws were game for a fight, plus they might soon have reinforcements.

One of the many unnamed side canyons in North Wash (Adventure 28)

Rumors said dozens, if not hundreds, of outlaws might lurk within. The five men turned around.

"The robbers acted with the utmost coolness, and the affair was evidently well planned."

—*Salt Lake Herald*, April 22, 1897

The outlaws eventually reached Horseshoe Canyon and continued another 10 miles east to the Orange Cliffs, making their camp in a hidden shady spot. They counted the take, about $8,000. Watched for lawmen and waited. Played cards, drank whiskey, and sent out friends to Green River for supplies.

Within days of the Castle Gate robbery, local news articles blamed outlaws from Robbers Roost. Butch Cassidy was identified as one of the robbers, with articles claiming he'd retreated into a stronghold deep within the dizzying region. Despite this knowledge, authorities on the periphery of the Roost were unwilling to move in. Citizens throughout the region grumbled about their ineffective and cowardly lawmen.

Finally, in June, a deputy US Marshal from Salt Lake City named Joe Bush, who was known for carrying a sawed-off shotgun, took up the challenge. Funded by a regional cattle company, Bush led eight heavily armed men on a circuit of Roost country during mid-June. After two days of searching, all they found was Blue John.

They caught the man with his pants down. Kind of. Standing outside of a ranch house in the Henry Mountains around dawn, Blue John was relieving himself. Surprised, he instinctively pulled his sidearm but didn't fire. Still, the action allowed Deputy Bush to accuse Blue John of resisting arrest. He was taken to Wayne County, where he was soon released without charges.

News articles were not kind to yet another failure by regional law officers. The Roost, as

Explore the Outlaw Trail!

This mad dash took the outlaws through some of the most rugged and remote landscapes in canyon country. To explore the Swell like they fled across it, check out **Adventure 23: Buckhorn Wash** (near **Adventure 22: Little Grand Canyon**) and **Adventure 25: San Rafael Reef**. From there, the bandits entered the Robbers Roost region. Though uncertain, perhaps they stopped at **Adventure 20: Robbers Roost Spring, Cabin, and Caves** on their way back to a hideout camp near **Adventure 19: Horseshoe Canyon**. A great way to see the Henry Mountains up close is **Adventure 27: Mount Ellen Summit Hike**, or, from afar, on the way to **Adventure 28: North Wash**.

A cartoon from an 1898 article in the San Francisco Call *(Library of Congress)*

far as outside observers were concerned, was impenetrable. The outlaws were too familiar with the topography, too prepared, and too savvy to ever be caught within its depths. Rewards offered by E. L. Carpenter—$1,000 per robber and $1,000 for the return of the Castle Gate payroll—might as well be given directly to Butch and Elzy. Where they were now was anyone's guess.

A few weeks before Blue John's embarrassing capture, Butch and Elzy had broken camp in the rising summer heat and ridden the outlaw trail north over the Tavaputs Plateau and through the Uinta Basin to Browns Park. They were still at large and looking for their next score.

EPISODE 9

A Gang by Any Name, 1897–1898

Flat Nose Currie and Harvey Logan • That Wild Bunch from Browns Park • The battle of Belle Fourche • Another botched bank robbery • Fencepost shooting and rattlesnake throwing • The most notorious outlaw the West ever saw • The burial of Butch Cassidy • Writing on the wall

IN BROWNS PARK during the summer of 1897, the semblance of a gang began to appear. Butch Cassidy. Elzy Lay. Bub Meeks. The Sundance Kid. All were claimed to be seen coming and going. There were newer faces too.

One was George "Flat Nose" Currie, about a decade older than the others, who looked like he'd spent his extra years taking too many strikes to the face. Another newcomer was a vicious outlaw named Harvey Logan. He went by the nickname Kid Curry, after his partner and mentor Flat Nose. Harvey dressed sloppily and was on the smaller side, but he never backed down from a fight and won most. A few years before, he'd been mostly a livestock rustler. Then he killed a man named Landusky in the eponymous town he founded—a wild hideout in the Little Rocky Mountains of Montana. After that, Logan was a regular on the outlaw trail.

A crime wave of rustling and robbing was in progress throughout the tristate area of Utah, Colorado, and Wyoming. Increasingly, observers and reporters on the periphery of the various hideouts placed blame on what they described as a well-organized criminal syndicate. Some called it the

Robbers Roost Gang, the Hole-in-the-Wall Gang, the Red Desert Gang, the Powder Springs Gang, or that Wild Bunch from Browns Park.

It seemed that almost any remote region where an outlaw was spotted was fair game for the naming of a new gang. Whether there even was such an organization is questionable. For the most part, the outlaws were acquaintances who partnered up for jobs out of necessity and increasingly became friends when celebrating in town. Butch was credited as the leader of many heists, which was often news to not just readers but Butch himself. Meanwhile, the cattle companies, banks, and railroad companies were offering rewards and hiring lawmen in hopes of wiping away the outlaw threat.

In mid-June, Bub Meeks got careless in Fort Bridger, Wyoming. Arousing suspicion after a saloon robbery, Bub was picked up by the local sheriff, who called for the Montpelier cashier to come to town. The cashier identified him as the unmasked man who had held the horses during that robbery. Soon Bub was on his way to the Idaho penitentiary.

Meanwhile, a few states east, the Sundance Kid, Harvey Logan, and Flat Nose Currie rode into Belle Fourche, north of the Black Hills in South Dakota. It was the third weekend in June, and the town was holding a reunion for Civil War veterans. The outlaws waited until Saturday morning so the bank could fill up with deposits from the festival.

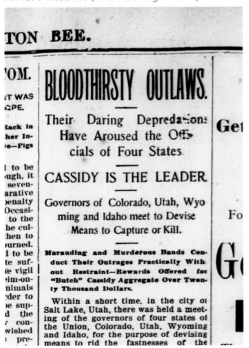

An 1899 headline (The Washington Bee)

With three accomplices waiting outside, the trio entered the bank, pulled their guns, and began collecting cash from the depositors in line. From outside, a passerby saw what was happening and began shouting. Harvey shot out the window glass, and the three outlaws in the street began firing into the air. The outlaws scattered into the streets of Belle Fourche as Civil War veterans regained the form of their youth and rained a storm of bullets toward the outlaws.

During the chaos, one of the accomplices, Tom O'Day, was stranded when his horse spooked. He tried to hide in plain sight inside a nearby saloon, but a witness spotted him, and he was arrested. The other outlaws rode furiously for the state line, splitting up in Wyoming.

Sundance went south and hid in the attic of a small-town newspaper. Eventually, he reunited with Logan, and they went north to Red Lodge, Montana, where they botched yet another bank robbery. This time they approached the town marshal and offered a bribe for him to be conveniently out of town. The marshal wasn't interested in the vacation offer. Instead, he informed the sheriff, who chased the boys 100 miles across Montana before they surrendered during a gunfight.

"Don't tell me how to rob a bank. I know how to rob a bank."

—THE SUNDANCE KID, A.K.A. ROBERT REDFORD IN *BUTCH CASSIDY AND THE SUNDANCE KID*, AS WRITTEN BY WILLIAM GOLDMAN

The captured outlaws gave their names as brothers, Tom and Frank Jones. Convinced these Jones boys were the same hard cases from Belle Fourche, the sheriff took them to South Dakota. They were locked in the Deadwood jail, where they reunited with Tom O'Day. Together, the three of them overpowered the guard on the night of All Hallows' Eve, October 31. O'Day was recaptured near Spearfish, but Logan and Sundance escaped.

The saga of the Belle Fourche bank robbery became a much-publicized exploit of the Wild Bunch. But other than offering notoriety, it was a total failure, netting only ninety-seven dollars.

. . . .

Butch Cassidy didn't participate in the robbery. He was still being cautious after the escape from Castle Gate. Instead, he'd left Browns Park and taken a real job on a ranch near Sheridan, Wyoming, just east of the Bighorn Mountains. There he did his best to blend in with the surroundings and not attract much notice.

He hit it off with the family on his new ranch, and one person who did notice him was the thirteen-year-old son, Fred. Butch taught Fred to shoot cans off fenceposts while riding a horse. One day they were putting up hay. Fred was on top of the haystack when Butch tossed something at the kid's feet. It was a live rattlesnake. While Butch laughed, Fred jumped around until he finally killed the snake.

Not long after Belle Fourche, members of the Wild Bunch met up in the Little Snake River valley. During a three-day party, they started near Savery and moved like a drunken stampede toward Baggs.

They laughed about the many news reports surrounding the bad man, Cassidy, that proliferated with remarkable exaggerations. That he led a gang of five hundred, killed all who would cross him, and swore like a sailor in the desert.

> "He is the worst man in four states . . . the most notorious outlaw the West has ever had to cope with. The achievements of Jesse James and his followers place into tawdry insignificance before those of 'Butch' Cassidy and his five hundred. . . . As a killer he has earned a reputation during the last ten years probably equaled in the West only by that of 'Wild Bill' Hickok, peace to his ashes. . . . [Cassidy] is possessed of a fearful temper. . . . For picturesque profanity 'Butch' Cassidy hasn't his equal in the States."
>
> —*SAN FRANCISCO CALL*, APRIL 3, 1898

It was a hectic summer, and things continued like that into the fall. By the following spring of 1898, the governors of Utah, Colorado, and Wyoming met to discuss a plan for disposing of the Wild Bunch.

Only a month later, in May, the governors' prayers were answered. Word came that Butch Cassidy had finally been killed. Shot by a sheriff's posse on the Tavaputs Plateau. News articles ran features on the demise of the notorious outlaw.

Days earlier, the newly elected sheriff of Carbon County, Utah, had mounted a posse to search for stolen horses in an area north of the Book Cliffs. The posse had passed through Range Creek Canyon and crossed the Green River in Gray Canyon. They were pushing into the eastern Tavaputs when they stumbled across an outlaw camp. During a firefight, they killed two men still lying in their bedrolls while two others surrendered.

Explore the Outlaw Trail!

When it came to long rides across the West, these dudes did not mess around. In this story, the exploits ranged from **Adventure 86: Deadwood and Lead** to Baggs in **Adventure 63: Medicine Bow Mountains Museums** to Gray Canyon upstream of **Adventure 18: Green River, Utah**.

Back in town, the deceased were identified as Joe Walker and Butch Cassidy. The two outlaws were quickly buried. But when skepticism mounted, a small-town jailer who had briefly held Cassidy during the summer of 1892 was summoned. The bodies were exhumed and the jailer leaned in for a close look. It wasn't Cassidy.

By now the Wild Bunch rumor mill was in full swing, and soon the story was being told that Butch himself had attended his own funeral, riding through town in the back of a cart, hidden under a blanket.

In reality, the writing was on the wall. So were photos of Butch Cassidy, in the form of wanted posters using his mug shot from the territorial prison in Laramie. Sure, the thirty-two-year-old once named Bob had done plenty of illegal things. Cattle rustling. Horse theft. Robbed two banks and one mine to the tune of almost $40,000. But Butch Cassidy had supposedly done a whole lot more bad stuff than Bob ever had. So with that in Butch's mind, the three states of Wyoming, Utah, and Colorado were feeling a bit crowded. Later that year, he rode south through Arizona and onward into New Mexico Territory.

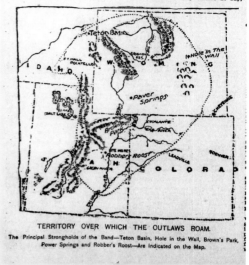

A map included in an article in the San Francisco Call *in 1898 (Library of Congress)*

WILD BUNCH STORIES

EPISODE 10

A Seemingly Normal Cowboy Named Jim Lowe, 1899

Long-lost brothers in the Mogollon Mountains • Wilcox, Wyoming • E. C. Woodcock • The Tall Texan and News Carver • The Pinkerton detectives • A friendly bartender named Jim Lowe

IN FEBRUARY 1899, a pair of cowboys named Jim Lowe and William McGinnis hired on with the foreman at the WS Ranch in New Mexico Territory. The ranch was on the San Francisco River in a high valley at the base of the Mogollon Mountains. William French, the owner of the spread, later said the two men were ranching naturals, with Lowe riding WS cattle across the range as trail boss and McGinnis breaking broncs in the corral.

The two men were perfect employees. The stocky blond one, Lowe, was so jovial he grinned every time he spoke. The taller dark-haired one, McGinnis, was quieter and more serious. They didn't get drunk, nor did they shoot up the nearby saloon in Alma after cattle drives. Issues with cattle theft became almost nonexistent. With the two men's help, the foreman was able to replace a number of slacking ranch hands with a seemingly endless supply of quality labor.

If French noticed anything odd, it was that when these new ranch hands showed up, Lowe and McGinnis met them as strangers, but the moment they thought no one was watching, they behaved like long-lost brothers. Friendly folks more comfortable when the boss wasn't looking, French supposed. The ranch was running so smoothly, he didn't have to keep close tabs on the men, who often spent weeks out at the horse camp 20 miles away.

. . . .

Meanwhile, 600 miles north in Wyoming, a few hours before sunrise on June 2, 1899, the Union Pacific Railroad's Overland Flyer No. 1 was traveling westbound at 50 miles an hour. It was a rainy night, and when the engineers saw a red-and-white warning light on the tracks ahead, they assumed the trestle bridge had washed out. The train screeched to a halt a mile past the town of Wilcox. When it stopped, several masked men jumped aboard. They ordered the employees and passengers to line up outside.

Going straight was apparently much easier for railroads than outlaws. This line eventually follows the Colorado River through Horsethief and Ruby Canyons (Adventure 15).

In the distance, one of the outlaws noticed the approaching headlight from a second train carrying overflow freight and passengers. Someone said it was carrying two cars of soldiers. The outlaws hustled their captives back aboard and ordered the last two cars uncoupled. The train was moved forward another mile past a small bridge. Then the outlaws dynamited the bridge and the train was moved another couple of miles down the track.

When the bandits proceeded to the express car, they found the agent, E. C. Woodcock, had locked himself inside and was yelling he'd shoot anyone who entered. The outlaws' reply was a stick of dynamite with a sizzling fuse. The door was blown off its hinges. Inside, the outlaws found Woodcock nearly unconscious. Unable to obtain the combination from Woodcock, the outlaws used dynamite to open the safe.

The explosion lit up the dark sky, with wreckage flying hundreds of feet. The express car's roof and walls were splintered, and the safe was blown open. The currency inside was damaged, with the right corners torn. The outlaws gathered the surviving cash and valuables and split into two groups.

One group went north into the Bighorn Mountains. The other group went south, including newer Wild Bunch members Ben "Tall Texan" Kilpatrick and William "News" Carver, who earned the nickname for his love of reading about the gang's exploits in the papers. He'd get his chance soon enough. The outlaws netted more than $40,000 in what would become one of the most infamous train robberies in American history.

Later that day, the Union Pacific dispatched a special train from Laramie carrying a mounted posse to the robbery site. These lawmen soon joined others already on the trail of the northern-bound trio. One posse confronted the outlaws at a ranch north of Casper, Wyoming. During a shootout, Harvey Logan shot and killed Sheriff Joe Hazen. This caused the posse to pull back and regroup, and Logan, Flat Nose Currie, and the Sundance Kid managed to escape to the north, crossing the Bighorn Mountains and disappearing in the Bighorn Basin.

A display at the John Jarvie Historic Ranch in Browns Park (Adventure 58)

News articles quickly credited the robbery to the Hole-in-the-Wall Gang, with Flat Nose Currie named as the leader and Cassidy identified as playing a key role. A few weeks later, the Pinkerton Detective Agency became involved. The first private detective agency in the US, Pinkerton had a seeing-eye logo and the slogan "We Never Sleep," which helped popularize the term *private eye*.

The Pinkertons sent Detective Charlie Siringo, who was particularly skilled at undercover work, to pursue a pair of Wilcox suspects spotted moving thirteen horses south from Wyoming toward Browns Park. Siringo picked up the southbound tracks of these mysterious men near Hanksville, Utah, and followed them down North Wash and Trachyte Canyon to Hite Ferry at Dandy Crossing.

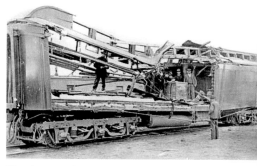

The destroyed train car from the Wilcox robbery (Creative Commons)

From there, Siringo followed White Canyon, coming at one point within a half mile of the suspects' camp but missed them. Next, he followed them east through Bluff, Utah, and into Arizona. By now, reports of the explosion-damaged currency had popped up along these suspects' route. But Siringo lost the trail in New Mexico and they got away.

Whether Butch and Elzy were involved in the Wilcox train robbery remained a mystery. They weren't with the gang at the holdup. But others claimed to have seen Butch in Wyoming during that time. Rumors suggested that the two men had come to assist with the planning and horse relay. Others said they were the mystery suspects heading south with the thirteen horses. Regardless, Jim Lowe and William McGinnis were back at the WS Ranch by sometime during June. A few days before July, McGinnis suddenly quit the ranch.

On the night of July 11, another train was robbed. This incident happened near Folsom, in far northeastern New Mexico. Gathering more than $50,000, three robbers fled north to a hideout on Turkey Creek. During the late afternoon on July 16, a five-man posse from Colorado confronted the men.

Elzy Lay was down by the creek filling his canteen when he was shot twice, in the shoulder and back. A horrific gunfight erupted, during which an injured Elzy, News Carver, and Sam Ketchum shot and killed the posse leader, Sheriff Farr. Before it was over, two more posse members were shot in their legs, and Ketchum took a bullet in the arm. The carnage ended with the posse abruptly retreating.

News Carver was the only one unharmed, and he helped his accomplices escape to a nearby cabin. Ketchum was too hurt to travel, so they left him in the cabin, and the following day he was arrested. The other two rode south. The injured Elzy rode hundreds of miles with two bullets inside him, all the way to a ranch near Carlsbad, New Mexico, before a posse nabbed him after a brief gun battle. Only News got away.

Elzy was taken to Santa Fe, where he gave the name William McGinnis and was charged with the murder of Sheriff Farr. In October, Elzy was convicted of second-degree murder and sentenced to life in prison. One of Butch's closest friends in the Wild Bunch was out of the game.

. . . .

Back at WS Ranch, Jim Lowe continued to work as trail boss while moonlighting as bartender and part-time owner of a saloon in the nearby town of Alma. Meanwhile, the WS Ranch owner, French, was starting to wonder who these ranch hands who worked for him really were.

Later that fall, a man showed up at the ranch to meet with French. He was a Pinkerton detective named Frank Murray, who wasn't investigating the Folsom robbery but another one, in Wilcox, Wyoming. Some of the currency with torn corners had shown up in New Mexico, traced to the store in Alma.

Murray showed French some photos of wanted men. French pointed at one of Jim Lowe, an outstanding fella. The best trail boss he'd ever had. "That's Butch Cassidy," explained Murray. Suddenly, the whole situation became clear. Whether French had realized it or not, the WS was a hideout on the outlaw trail.

Murray left the area a few days later to report his discovery. When French told Butch he'd been discovered, the outlaw only smiled. He'd already suspected Murray, who had been visiting the saloon under an alias. In fact, the night before Murray left, Butch had a drink with him, explaining how outlaws hiding at WS Ranch were planning on killing the detective.

Years later, Murray admitted what had happened. Butch had saved his life that night, arranging for him to leave unharmed. When Murray reached the agency offices in Denver, he filed his report. Yes, there were Wild Bunch members around Alma. Some had seen through Murray's cover, even threatened his life. Luckily, an unaffiliated citizen had tipped Murray off, and he managed to escape just in time. All thanks to a friendly bartender named Jim Lowe.

Explore the Outlaw Trail!

Outlaws and road-trippers seem to have something in common: visiting a bunch of places hundreds of miles apart over the span of a few weeks. In this story, the regular suspects were in and out of **Adventure 91: Wild Bunch Sites and Billy the Kid Scenic Byway, New Mexico**. Next up, how about the Bighorn Mountains, with one option being **Adventure 73: Cloud Peak Wilderness**. To follow part of Siringo's chase, consider this cluster: **Adventure 28: North Wash, Adventure 29: Hite Marina**, and then follow above White Canyon before venturing inside it with **Adventure 32: Natural Bridges National Monument**.

WILD BUNCH STORIES

EPISODE 11

The Trail Grows Hot, 1900–1901

Second thoughts on the outlaw trail • The Overland Limited • First National Bank of Winnemucca • The Fort Worth Five • Long arms of surrender • Alive or dead • Fleeing the West

BUTCH LEFT the WS Ranch during March 1900. On the way, he and a friend stole every riding horse from the neighboring Ashby ranch, whose employees had been stealing from the WS. The retaliation caused problems. Soon afterward, an Arizona sheriff became suspicious of the horses Butch was trailing and arrested him. A man named Jim Lowe appeared in court in late April and made bail, but was never seen again in those parts.

Meanwhile, up near Moab, Flat Nose Currie was killed by Grand County sheriff Jesse Tyler while stealing horses. A month later, Harvey Logan came looking for revenge, killing Sheriff Tyler and his deputy.

The ground underfoot was growing hot, and rumors began to circulate that Butch was having second thoughts about life on the outlaw trail. In Salt Lake City, attorney Orlando Powers, who had represented Matt Warner in 1896, claimed Butch came to see him.

"I'm getting sick of hiding out," said Butch. "There ain't a man left in the country who can go on the stand and identify me for any crime."

"You've robbed too many big corporations in your time," said Powers. "One of those companies would bring someone to the stand who would swear against you. No, you'll have to keep on the run, I'm afraid."

Matt Warner had been released from prison a few months before, and this time, he insisted on going straight. Matt said he put Butch in touch with the Utah governor, who considered amnesty until finding out Butch was suspected of the murder of Moab's Sheriff Tyler. Butch knew he hadn't been involved. He'd never killed anyone. Regardless, no offer was extended.

In late June, a story in the *Deseret Evening News* declared "Butch Cassidy to Surrender." The article claimed Cassidy was already in Salt Lake City, ready to turn himself in provided the governor didn't extradite him to Colorado. Along with an accurate physical description of Cassidy, likely obtained from the prison in Laramie, the article further mentioned that police were surveilling the house of his supposed wife.

All this came as news to Butch. After reading the article, he said he enjoyed it. In fact, he was willing to surrender if the terms were right. And why not go meet his wife, since he apparently had one now? Another proposed plan was to make Butch a train guard for the Union Pacific. But this discussion lurched to a halt on August 29, 1900, on the railroad tracks west of Tipton, Wyoming. All discussions were off. Butch had robbed another train.

Around 8:30 p.m., on the Overland Limited No. 3, a masked man climbed over the tinder and stuck a revolver in the engineer's back. With a procedure similar to what had been done in Wilcox, the cars were uncoupled and the train split. When the Wild Bunch surrounded the express car, they were surprised to discover that the agent was an old friend. Being blown up once was enough, and this time E. C. Woodcock quickly hid two packages of money before opening the door.

"Butch, you know that if it were my money, there is nobody that I would rather have steal it than you."

—E. C. Woodcock, a.k.a. George Furth in *Butch Cassidy and the Sundance Kid*, as written by William Goldman

The outlaws made off with $55,000 and went south along the Little Snake River through Baggs toward Browns Park, hitting horse relays along the way. A posse including Pinkerton Joe Lefors followed them as far as Powder Wash, where the outlaws herded a pack of range horses along with them and then let them scatter, which obscured their tracks. The outlaws, including Harvey Logan and Tall Texan Kilpatrick, escaped.

The press instantly blamed Butch Cassidy, declaring him ringleader of the robbery. And while Butch was involved with the planning, he wasn't present at Tipton. After all, he'd given his word long ago in exchange for a pardon from the governor of Wyoming. Instead, Butch and the Sundance Kid were 500 miles west, planning a different heist.

The First National Bank in Winnemucca, Nevada, was a large brick building that had been featured in an article earlier that year boasting it kept $82,000 on hand. Around noon on September 19, 1900, Butch, Sundance, and News Carver walked inside to investigate the claim.

"Gentlemen, throw up your hands," said Butch. "Be quick about it and don't make any noise."

Four bankers and one customer complied. The owner was taken to the vault, where he first tried to argue that the safe was on a timed lock and couldn't be opened. A knife blade to the throat helped him recall the combination, and soon the outlaws departed with $32,000 in mostly gold coins.

A few errant gunshots followed the robbers out of town. The deputy ran for the railroad station and pursued them by train. After a few miles, the lone steam engine overtook the outlaws and shots were exchanged at high speed. None landed.

The infamous Fort Worth Five photo. From left to right, back row: William "News" Carver, "Kid Curry" Harvey Logan; seated: "The Sundance Kid" Harry Longabaugh, "The Tall Texan" Ben Kilpatrick, and "Butch Cassidy" Robert LeRoy Parker (Creative Commons)

Their escape route turned north through the sagebrush of Basin and Range country toward the Jarbidge Mountains. They made the usual horse relays along the way. Yet again they escaped, working their roundabout way into Colorado before turning south for a prearranged rendezvous.

The outlaws arrived in Fort Worth, Texas, by train in October and November 1900, coming from the actual but fading Wild West around the same time that Buffalo Bill's Wild West Show was in town. They slipped through crowds who had watched a parade of authentically dressed Western performers on horseback, including Native Americans, cowboys, military riders, and lawmen. In the seedy brothel and bar district called Hell's Half Acre, five members of the Wild Bunch shared drinks at a saloon owned by "Mikey Mike" Cassidy, a man with a mysterious criminal past that few knew about. Butch even bought a bicycle during this trip, amusing himself with rides around town.

> "The Wild Bunch, as they have come to be called since their era has passed, numbered about twenty or, at most, twenty-five men. But there were never more than five or six on any one job, be it bank robbing or stealing a bunch of cattle. They were a loosely knit bunch, having no recognized leader but drifting around by twos or threes."
>
> —PEARL BAKER, *THE WILD BUNCH AT ROBBERS ROOST*

One evening on a whim, the outlaws bought new suits and bowler hats and went upstairs to a portrait studio. In good spirits, the men held back their laughter to pose for a photo. Seated in the front row were the Sundance Kid, the Tall Texan, and Butch Cassidy. Standing behind were News Carver and Harvey Logan. The outlaws loved the prints so much, they ordered fifty copies. The owner loved the shot too and later displayed a copy of his proud work in the waiting room.

For the outlaws, the photo was a mistake. A few months later, after the Wild Bunch had left town, a local police officer visited the gallery. The face of Harvey Logan caught his eye, so he took the photo back to the station. The Pinkertons called it their first real break in the case, and they used the images to make wanted posters for each man, which were sent out across the

West. The rewards totaled thousands of dollars and carried a new stipulation: wanted *dead* or alive. The railroads and banks had previously feared bad publicity for encouraging the killing of outlaws, but now they were getting their hands dirty. Bounty hunters and lawmen across the country joined in the hunt.

Less than six months later, in April 1901, News Carver and the Tall Texan were ambushed with other outlaws by lawmen in Sonora, Texas. When News went for his gun, he was shot six times.

"Die game, boys," were Carver's final words to his friends.

The Tall Texan lifted his long arms in surrender.

The last Wild Bunch robbery happened near Wagner, Montana, in July 1901. The Great Northern Railroad's Coastal Flyer No. 3 was westbound when all the classic signs of a Wild Bunch robbery occurred. A bandit came over the tender. The train was stopped and the cars separated. The express-car safe was dynamited. And the bandits rode south with three other outlaws and $40,000. This time the outlaws included Harvey Logan, the Tall Texan Kilpatrick, who had yet again gone free, and his girlfriend, Laura Bullion—the first time a woman had participated in a Wild Bunch robbery. After scattering north of the Missouri River Breaks, they reunited in the Little Rocky Mountains. It was almost too easy.

That fall, the Tall Texan and Laura Bullion were arrested in Saint Louis, Missouri, after using forged signatures on unsigned banknotes from the Great Northern robbery. Bullion was sentenced to five years in prison, and on her release, she went straight by opening a boardinghouse. Kilpatrick got ten to fifteen years. Nine months after his release in 1911, the Tall Texan robbed his final train, near Sanderson, Texas. He was beat to death with an ice hammer by the express-car agent.

In December 1901, a month after the Tall Texan was nabbed, it was Harvey Logan's turn after a saloon brawl near Knoxville, Tennessee. While Logan strangled a local tough, several officers beat Logan with billy clubs. The outlaw still got away into a creek channel, but not for long. He was captured within a few days. At trial, he received a sentence of twenty years. He escaped after less than two, during the summer of 1903. His final robbery came the following summer with a train on the Denver and Rio Grande Railroad outside Parachute, Colorado. A posse tracked him into a ravine

Explore the Outlaw Trail!

In these waning days of the Wild West, the outlaws ranged pretty far from their more familiar hideouts. Still, a few places relevant to the story include **Adventure 12: Moab** and the town of Baggs in **Adventure 63: Medicine Bow Mountains Museums.** Plus, learn about Buffalo Bill's Wild West Show in **Adventure 77: Cody.**

and injured him with gunfire. Harvey wouldn't let them have the satisfaction of taking him either way, so he put the final gun to his own head and pulled the trigger.

"Boy, I got vision and the rest of the world wears bifocals."

—Butch Cassidy, a.k.a. Paul Newman in *Butch Cassidy and the Sundance Kid*, as written by William Goldman

One by one, the Wild Bunch were taken just like the posters had suggested, alive or dead. Well, not all of them. In Fort Worth, a smirking Butch had proposed that all five of them follow his most outrageous plan yet: Leave it all behind. Give up the outlaw trail. Flee the West. Only the Sundance Kid, who was joined by Etta Place, heeded the advice. In February 1901, the three of them met in New York City.

The Many Battles of Browns Park, 1898

Constant turmoil • A lawless den of rustlers • Quite an active man for a dead man • Two Bar Ranch • A ruthless arrival

AS THE TWENTIETH century approached, life in Browns Park was in constant turmoil. The idyllic days when Native Americans, trappers, and homesteaders intermingled throughout a peaceful mountain valley were long gone. Now, many battle lines were being drawn. Not just between independent ranchers and the expanding cattle companies, but between husbands and wives, families and neighbors.

The valley had long been criticized from afar as a haven for outlaws. Some, like the Wild Bunch, behaved themselves while visiting, but others made Browns Park the locale of their trade. In February 1898, a pair of smalltime rustlers named P. L. Johnson and Jack Bennet were hanging around the John Jarvie store. A sixteen-year-old named Willie Strang had been left to visit with the ferry operator, Albert Speck Williams, one of two well-known African American residents in the valley. Johnson invited the boy Strang to join him and Bennet on a visit to Valentine Hoy's ranch on Red Creek.

While there, as a joke Strang spilled water on Johnson. Infuriated, Johnson shot at Strang as he ran away, hitting him in the back and killing him.

The two men fled to Powder Springs, the common hideout for area rustlers, where they joined forces with two dangerous escaped convicts, including the ruthless Harry Tracy. The four men decided to move their camp to Lodore Canyon, and they sent the only unwanted man, Bennet, into Browns Park for supplies.

Meanwhile, a posse trailed the other three toward the Gates of Lodore, coming across the embers of their dying fire one morning. When posse member Valentine Hoy approached between two rocks, Tracy shot him dead. The posse soon retreated.

Browns Park residents went into an uproar over the murder of two residents in short succession. The boy Willie Strang was a beloved face, and while Valentine Hoy was few residents' favorite, he was still one of their own. When Jack Bennet showed up at the Bassett Ranch store for supplies, the sheriff arrived to arrest him. Bennet was jailed in Herb Bassett's post office, where, the next day, a lynch mob came looking. Wearing masks, seven Browns Parkers dragged Bennet to a gatepost. A noose went around his neck, and they stood him on the Bassett buckboard. When they rolled the buckboard away, Bennet swung a full four minutes before dying.

Many residents were horrified by these bursts of violence and vigilantism. When P. L. Johnson was captured alive, calmer voices insisted he be taken to town to stand trial. Claiming the death was an accident and that he only meant to scare the boy, Johnson was acquitted. The residents' worst fears came to pass, and the killer of Willie Strang went free. This once again confirmed the limited reach of law and order in Browns Park.

The lynching of Jack Bennet had sent a message. Other small-time outlaws left the valley, looking for new opportunities. Regardless of any departures, the many newspapers covering these dramatic events reinforced an outside perception that Browns Park was a lawless den of rustlers. It was a view the larger cattle companies were eager to indulge.

Around this time, Ann Bassett returned to Browns Park after attending several prestigious academies across the country. Each one had found her too wild a pupil, prone to bursts of rebelliousness and angry tantrums. Ann had set her sights on returning to life as a free-spirited cowgirl on the open range.

Complicating her return was the presence of Tom Hicks, a new ranch hand and cook hired by Bassett manager Matt Rash. Both Ann and Josie despised Hicks, who was prone to bragging about his many kills in the Indian Wars. He would often stare at the beautiful Josie and repeatedly ask her age.

Hicks was the least of Josie's worries at the time. She and her husband of six years, the hard-drinking Jim McKnight, were having problems. In

Graveyard at the John Jarvie Historic Ranch in Browns Park (Adventure 58)

March 1900, after escalating arguments and physical altercations, Herb took his twenty-six-year-old daughter to Steamboat Springs, Colorado, to file a restraining order. Local headlines reported the scandal of the young century: divorce.

To lure Jim McKnight back to serve the papers, Josie pretended to be ill at a friend's house. Meanwhile, the deputy sheriff waited inside. When Jim discovered the ruse, he flew into a rage and was shot by the deputy sheriff. Tom Hicks rode to Vernal for a doctor, and Jim survived. The actual events seemed too plain for the local rumor mill, and soon the story evolved to Josie having shot her ex-husband.

"No, I did not shoot him," Josie would explain. "If I had, I wouldn't have missed."

"The stories I've read, why, the most ridiculous fool things I ever read. . . . That Charles Kelly said that I shot [Jim]. Well, he was quite an active man for a dead man."

—Josie Bassett, as quoted by Grace McClure in
The Bassett Women

Once Jim had moved to Vernal to open a saloon, Josie followed her father's suggestion and sold the ranch. With her young sons, she moved to Rock Springs—a choice she'd later come to regret. As Josie's days with her first husband on a Browns Park ranch came to an end, her younger sister Ann was hoping for better luck on both accounts.

Not long after Ann's return home, the twenty-two-year-old became romantically involved with Matt Rash. The thirty-five-year-old manager of the Bassett Ranch had recently been made president of the Browns Park Cattle Association. In this official capacity, Matt represented the interests of the independent Browns Park ranchers against the larger cattle companies.

These days, the biggest threat came from Ora Haley's Two Bar Ranch, which had moved its headquarters to the nearby Little Snake River. With

A portrait of Ann Bassett taken in 1904

eyes on the park's fertile grazing lands, Haley sent his devoted manager, Hi Bernard, into the valley with two objectives. One goal was to stop the spread of valley sheepherders. The other goal was to convince the independent ranchers to allow Two Bar cattle to mix with smaller herds. Come market time, all would be swept up in company roundups, with the independent livestock being returned afterward. On behalf of the valley ranchers, Matt declined both offers.

Instead, Matt proposed a boundary line. The "divide" was a natural limestone ridge located halfway between Browns Park and the Little Snake River. Soon, Browns Park ranchers were taking turns patrolling the divide, pushing back any cattle that tried to cross. The solution worked exactly as Browns Park ranchers hoped, which was a problem for Two Bar's planned encroachment. Only the occasional strays from their herds crossed the divide, which were typically turned back by valley residents or occasionally appropriated by small-time rustlers.

Ann Bassett, whose own ranch had discreetly taken a few head of cattle from the company herds over the years, sent a defiant letter to Hi Bernard. "When you visit," wrote Ann, "stick to the road. The hoofprints of your cattle and horses are an eyesore in the park."

On behalf of Ora Haley, Hi Bernard responded in a few ways. He'd grown up poor and had little compassion for the little guys who fought a losing battle. Better to join the winning side and accept the corporate realities of the future. Bernard continued buying up smaller area ranches, while also swearing out complaints against alleged rustlers in the park. Next, Two Bar Ranch joined forces with several other larger cattle operations east of Browns Park to form the Snake River Stock Growers Association.

If Two Bar was going to invade Browns Park, the first thing that had to be done was clear out the rustlers. And Haley and Bernard conveniently saw anyone who opposed them, including family ranchers, as rustlers. After all, everyone knew the valley was a lawless place that harbored bank robbers and murderers. In secret, these cattle barons pooled their money and hired a stock detective with an infamous reputation as a ruthless killer for hire. Then they set him loose on Browns Park with the goal of making the residents comply.

Explore the Outlaw Trail!

With the story in Browns Park deepening, here are a few places to bring the tales to life: **Adventure 58: John Jarvie Historic Ranch**; the Gates of Lodore are part of **Adventure 59: Eastern Browns Park**; stop by the nearest towns, including **Adventure 43: Vernal** and **Adventure 53: Green River and Rock Springs (Wyoming)**.

. . . .

Stories from the outlaw trail resume in Part 4, The Ends of the Outlaw Trail—Stories Conclude, with Wild Bunch Stories: Episode 13, From Manhattan to Patagonia, 1901–1903.

The Sierra Madre is located near the Snowy Range in Southwestern Wyoming (chapter 8).

PART III

TRAVELING THE
OUTLAW TRAIL

Action Loot Giddyup

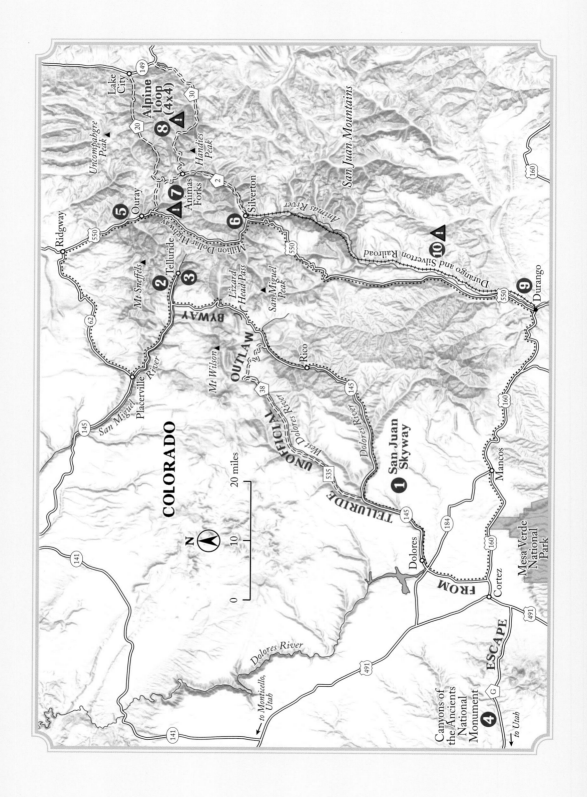

COLORADO

San Juan Mountains

Lake City

Alpine Loop (4x4) **8** **1**

Uncompahgre Peak

Handies Peak

20

Animas Forks **7**

Ouray **5**

Ridgway

Silverton **6**

550

Mt Sneffels

Telluride **2** **3**

62

Lizard Head Pass

San Miguel Peak

550

Durango and Silverton Railroad **10** **9** Durango

Million Dollar Highway

Animas River

BYWAY

OUTLAW

San Miguel River

Placerville

Mt Wilson

Rico

145

145

160

Mancos

160

Durango

145

UNOFFICIAL

West Dolores River

38

Dolores River

535

San Juan Skyway **1**

TELLURIDE

145

Dolores

184

160

Mesa Verde National Park

N

20 miles

10

0

141

Dolores River

to Monticello, Utah

FROM

Cortez

ESCAPE

Canyons of the Ancients National Monument

491

G

to Utah **4**

491

141

CHAPTER 1

San Juan Mountains

SOUTHWESTERN COLORADO

THE WHOLE KIT AND CABOODLE: In the early 1890s, the San Juan Mountains were booming with mining activity, which served as the backdrop for the earliest exploits of Butch Cassidy and a nascent Wild Bunch. Today, this rugged subrange of the Rocky Mountains, located in southwestern Colorado, is an excellent travel destination with fascinating history, plenty of outlaw connections, and many awesome adventures. To the west of the mountains, Mesa Verde National Park and Canyon of the Ancients National Monument have trails to fascinating ruins.

X MARKS THE SPOT: The entire region is covered in Latitude 40° Recreation Topo Map: Southwest Colorado Trails.

THE TICKING CLOCK: Visitors flock to the San Juan Mountains year-round. Winter is popular for skiing at area resorts such as Telluride and Wolf Creek. Spring comes late, and summer is peak season for adventure travel such as hikes out of Telluride and Ouray. Fall, when the aspens change to golden yellow, is a favorite time for many visitors.

THE YARNS: The San Juan Mountains appear in two Wild Bunch Stories: Butch Cassidy's dramatic first robbery, at the San Miguel Valley Bank in Telluride, is described in Episode 1, Escape from Telluride, 1889. How Butch came to Telluride and got involved with Matt Warner and Tom McCarty is found in Episode 2, The Beginnings of Bob Parker, 1866–1889.

1

San Juan Skyway

THE LOWDOWN: This 235-mile loop on scenic highways links up mountain towns and historic sites in the San Juan Mountains, including many of the places listed in this chapter. How convenient! Along the way you'll be surrounded by jagged peaks with many stunning roadside viewpoints. Estimated total driving time is six hours. While the byway is entirely paved and suitable for all two-wheel-drive vehicles, this route is not for the faint of heart . . .

THE HARDSHIPS: The loop has many sheer precipices and cliffs lacking guardrails, plus

Fall colors on display along the San Juan Skyway

several passes at 10,000 to 11,000 feet. Drivers should have mountain-driving experience, follow speed limits, and proceed cautiously.

THE GIDDYUP: You can hop on the horse—er, byway, anywhere on the loop, described here clockwise from the southwest. From Cortez, at the junction of US 491 and US 160, head east a short way and turn left (north) to follow CO 145 northeast for 76 miles through Dolores, Stoner, Rico, and over Lizard Head Pass (with beautiful alpine views, including Mount Wilson) to reach Telluride. Next, the highway turns northwest and after 16 miles reaches Placerville. Turn right (northeast) on CO 62 and continue about 23 miles to Ridgway. Turn

right (south) on US 550 and proceed about 11 miles to quaint Ouray (with views of Mount Sneffels). Next comes a famous 23-mile stretch called the **Million Dollar Highway**, known for hairpin switchbacks and cliff-side views, on the way to Silverton. Continue by descending through two passes at the western edge of the San Juans to reach Durango in 48 miles. Turn right (west) on US 160 and continue through Mancos, past Mesa Verde National Park, to reach Cortez in 46 miles.

THE SUSPECTS: The Colorado Department of Transportation offers byway information (see Resources).

X MARKS THE SPOT: The most detailed online map is available from the Durango Area Tourism Office's website (see Resources).

THE SNORT: Breweries, distilleries, saloons, and more abound on the byway. See the adventures below for some options but know there's more to be found.

RIDE ONWARD: If you want to drive the approximate route of Butch Cassidy, Matt Warner, and Tom McCarty during their flight from the San Miguel Valley Bank robbery, check out Adventure 4.

THE YARNS: Long before there was a new-fangled skyway, part of this loop was used regularly by a young Butch and accomplices, described in Wild Bunch Stories, Episodes 1, Escape from Telluride, 1889; and 2, The Beginnings of Bob Parker, 1866–1889.

2

Telluride Historic District

THE LOWDOWN: The Telluride of today is a mountain ski town with a national historic landmark district, but in 1899 it was the site of Butch Cassidy's first major robbery. The downtown historic district includes about three hundred buildings from the late 1800s and early 1900s, located on and around Colorado Avenue. Highlights include the Telluride Historical Museum and a walking tour.

THE ACTION: A walking tour of the town feels a bit like stepping back in time to the Old West—with some modern posh. Today, the historic buildings mostly house pricey shops that would make a nineteenth-century outlaw's mouth water. The walking tour highlights more than fourteen sites, include the restored **Sheridan Opera House**, built in 1913, which

hosts an annual Wild West Fest each June. THE SCENE OF THE CRIME: 110 N. Oak Street, Telluride, CO 81435. THE SUSPECTS: 970-728-6363; sheridanoperahouse.com. X MARKS THE SPOT: The city of Telluride offers an online guide and map (see Resources).

THE LOOT: Outlaw enthusiasts should stop by the **Mahr Building**, which has a commemorative plaque marking the site of Butch's 1889 robbery. THE SCENE OF THE CRIME: 129–131 W. Colorado Avenue, Telluride, CO 81320; GPS 37.9376, −107.8114.

MORE LOOT: The **Telluride Historical Museum** was built in 1896 as a hospital. Today the museum has exhibits about the area's history, including geology, Native inhabitants, mining booms, Butch Cassidy's robbery, and more. THE TICKING CLOCK: Open Monday–Saturday early June to mid-October; Thursday–Saturday early December to early April. THE TAKE: Modest admission fees for adults and students, children free. THE SCENE OF THE CRIME: 201 W. Gregory Avenue, Telluride, CO 81435. THE SUSPECTS: 970-728-3344; telluridemuseum.org.

THE DIGS: The 1895 **New Sheridan Hotel** is a historic, restored brick hotel and restaurant with walls lined by hundreds of historic photos from the Old West. THE SCENE OF THE CRIME: 231 W. Colorado Avenue, Telluride, CO 81435. THE SUSPECTS: 970-728-4351; newsheridan.com.

THE SNORT: Telluride has two breweries, Smuggler-Union Brewery downtown and Telluride Brewing Company on the western outskirts.

THE YARNS: The Telluride bank robbery was Robert Leroy Parker's first heist, described in Wild Bunch Stories, Episodes 1, Escape from Telluride, 1889; and 2, The Beginnings of Bob Parker, 1866–1889.

Idarado Legacy Trail and Bridal Veil Falls

THE LOWDOWN: A pair of linked trails allow visitors to walk upcanyon from downtown Telluride to the base of a plummeting waterfall.

THE ACTION: Idarado Legacy Trail is an easy dirt path, 2 miles one-way, running along the San Miguel River from Telluride Town Park to the Bridal Veil Falls trailhead near the Pandora Mill site. Stop here or continue steeply uphill to the falls (see below). **THE SCENE OF THE CRIME:** Start hiking the Idarado Legacy Trail from the Telluride Town Park and Campground, 500 E. Colorado Avenue, Telluride, CO 81435; GPS 37.936, –107.8068.

MORE ACTION: From the trailhead near the Pandora Mill site, the rugged, steep **Bridal Veil Falls Trail** ascends about 850 feet for 1.2 miles one-way to the base of the 365-foot falls. Nearby, a rough four-wheel-drive road switchbacks more gradually up to the top of the falls and beyond—an option used by hikers and high-clearance four-wheel-drive vehicles. **THE SCENE OF THE CRIME:** Pandora Mill site trailhead's small parking lot; GPS 37.9287, –107.7765.

THE DIGS: The **Telluride Town Park and Campground** operated by the city is in a pleasant riverside setting a few blocks east of downtown. **THE SCENE OF THE CRIME:** 500 E. Colorado Avenue, Telluride, CO 81435; telluride.com.

Opposite: The Idarado Legacy Trail just outside downtown Telluride

RIDE ONWARD: Near Bridal Veil Falls is the eastern trailhead for the Telluride Via Ferrata, a 2-mile technical climbing route that traverses the cliffs on the north side of town. Guided trips are available from outfitters in town (see Resources).

Escape from Telluride Unofficial Outlaw Byway

THE LOWDOWN: This unofficial byway follows the outlaws' escape route from Telluride after their 1899 bank robbery. Along the way, it leads to some of the most impressive Ancestral Puebloan ruins in the region. While many of the roads are unpaved, under normal weather and road conditions the route should be passable for two-wheel-drive vehicles with good clearance. The route starts in Telluride and ends in Utah north of Moab at I-70. Following the outlaws' escape route any farther becomes increasingly nonsensical, with plenty of roundabout routing and backtracking. I mean, these dudes were bank robbers, not travel agents.

THE GIDDYUP: From Telluride, follow CO 145, part of the **San Juan Skyway** (Adventure 1) south over scenic Lizard Head Pass for 21 miles. Turn right (west) onto unpaved Dunton Road (FR 535/CR 38) and continue over a pass and along the West Dolores River. After 10.5 miles, you'll pass the **Dunton Hot Springs**, a ghost town turned guest ranch resort (duntondestinations.com/hot-springs). About 2.25 miles farther, on the left (east) is the trailhead for the **Geyser Spring Trail**, a 1.5-mile one-way hike up to a sulfurous blue mineral pool that's supposedly

Colorado's only true geyser. Continuing south on Dunton Road (FR 535/CR 38), eventually pass two Forest Service campgrounds (West Dolores and Mavreeso) and in 19 miles rejoin CO 145.

Head south for 23 miles to the town of Cortez and turn right onto US 160, heading west through town for about 2.5 miles. Turn left (south) onto US 491 and go 2.5 miles. Turn right onto CR G and head west along the southern edge of **Canyons of the Ancients National Monument**. After about 13 miles, consider a stop at **Sand Canyon and Rock Creek trailhead** to hike to the monument's Ancestral Puebloan ruins (see BLM brochure in Resources).

Continue driving west on CR G, which becomes Ismay Trading Post Road (CR N5068) in Utah, for about 17.25 miles. Turn right (north) onto Cajon Mesa Road (CR N5067) and follow it 4.5 miles. For a side trip to the incredible ruins at **Hovenweep National Monument**, turn right onto Hovenweep/Reservation Road (CR N413) and proceed about 6 miles into the monument. To continue on the unofficial byway, return to or stay on Cajon Mesa Road/Reservation Road (CR N5067) heading west. In about 9.25 miles you'll reach a T junction; turn right onto Montezuma Canyon Road and follow it up **Montezuma Canyon**. After 9 miles, turn right to stay on Montezuma Canyon Road and continue following upcanyon. In about 7.25 miles, the impressive **Three Kiva Pueblo** is on the left.

Continue following Montezuma Canyon Road for another 27 miles (during the final 5 miles, the road switchbacks out of Montezuma Canyon and follows tributary Verdure Creek roughly west) to US 191. Turn right (north) and proceed to Monticello, with side trips possible into the **Blue (Abajo) Mountains**

(Adventure 17) and the **Needles District** of Canyonlands National Park (Adventure 16). Continue north into **Moab** (Adventure 12), with a possible side trip to **Arches National Park** (Adventure 13), then continue north to I-70 near Thompson Springs.

THE HARDSHIPS: Between Cortez and US 191, the route described above is unpaved, rugged, and remote—with little to no cell reception. Along the way, a maze of side roads intersect the suggested route, and there aren't always signs. Only drivers confident with backcountry navigation should attempt this adventure. Study the route beforehand, using either a satellite view like Google Maps or the BLM's map website (see Montezuma Canyon in Resources). If you're uncertain, alternate routes exist on paved highways. The shorter route is US 491 north from Cortez to Monticello. The longer and more scenic route is US 491 south, US 160 west, CO 41 north, UT 162 west through the historic town of Bluff (check out the Bluff Fort museum), and north on US 191.

THE SNORT: Breweries along the way can be found in Telluride, Dolores, Cortez, and Moab.

THE YARNS: This escape route is described in two Wild Bunch Stories, Episodes 1, Escape from Telluride, 1889; and 3, On the Outlaw Trail, 1889.

5

Ouray and Perimeter Trail

THE LOWDOWN: This mountain town is nestled in a stunning valley on the US 550 portion of the San Juan Skyway. Like many such towns, its economy has shifted from mining to tourism. Possibly due to the absence of a ski resort, Ouray offers a more casual and relaxed vibe compared to some Colorado mountain towns. (This is where outlaws might go to celebrate after robbing Telluride.)

THE ACTION: Circling the cliffs above town, the **Ouray Perimeter Trail** is a scenic and challenging 6.5-mile loop that links up several valley highlights, including four waterfalls and five bridges. Over the course of the entire loop, the trail gains 1,600 feet of elevation. Along the way, there are around a half dozen trailheads and access routes leading back to town, meaning you can shorten this hike as desired. Box Cañon Falls Park and Ouray Hot Springs (see below) can both be reached via the Perimeter Trail. **THE SCENE OF THE CRIME:** The trail begins across from the Ouray Visitors Center, 1230 Main Street, Ouray, CO 81427. **X MARKS THE SPOT:** The Ouray Trail Group has an online hiking map for the Ouray Perimeter Trail (see Resources). **THE HARDSHIPS:** With the trail oscillating above and below 8,000 feet, make sure you're acclimated to the elevation before attempting this hike.

MORE ACTION: **Box Cañon Falls Park** is a private park on the southwest edge of town, with short trails and stairways leading inside a dramatic bedrock grotto with a view of a plummeting waterfall. **THE TICKING CLOCK:** Open daily. **THE TAKE:** Modest fee for adults and kids

The Perimeter Trail above Ouray

4–17, younger children free. THE SUSPECTS: 970-325-7080 (for URL, see Resources).

THE LOOT: Near the town's visitor center, **Ouray Hot Springs** is a popular attraction among families and visitors, with several large pools of different temperatures. THE TAKE: Moderate admission fee for adults and kids 4–17, younger children free. THE SCENE OF THE CRIME: 1220 Main Street, Ouray, CO 81427. THE SUSPECTS: 970-325-7073; ouray hotsprings.com.

THE SNORT: For its tiny size—fewer than one thousand residents—Ouray has a big collection of saloons and breweries, including Ouray Brewery, Red Mountain Brewing, Colorado Boy Brewery, KJ Wood Distillers, and more. Enjoy!

RIDE ONWARD: The Ouray Via Ferrata opened during spring 2020, a technical climbing route through the Uncompahgre River Gorge above town; for guides and other information, see ourayviaferrata.org. Also nearby is Mount Sneffels, but you'll need to do your own research for the challenging hike up this 14er.

6
Silverton Historic District

THE LOWDOWN: Silverton is a mountain town that makes for a good stop during a driving tour along the San Juan Skyway (Adventure 1). The quaint town is a common starting point for trips to the Animas Forks Ghost Town (Adventure 7) and the Alpine Loop 4x4 Trail (Adventure 8). The northern terminus for the Durango and Silverton Railroad (Adventure 10) is located here. Basically, you'll be going out of your way not to stop here.

THE ACTION: The pleasant downtown historic district makes for a good walking tour, with plenty of buildings from the late 1800s and turn of the twentieth century. THE SUSPECTS: Silverton Chamber of Commerce, silvertoncolorado.com.

THE HARDSHIPS: Silverton rests at an elevation of 9,318 feet, so bring your own oxygen with you.

THE LOOT: The San Juan County Historical Society operates the **Mining Heritage Center**, a museum with a restored 1902 county jail and exhibits of realistic underground tunnels and machinery. THE TAKE: Modest fee. THE SCENE OF THE CRIME: 1557 Greene Street, Silverton, CO 81433. THE SUSPECTS: 970-387-5838.

THE SNORT: Two breweries in a town of six hundred? I'll take those odds. Avalanche Brewing Company and Golden Block Brewery are both downtown.

7

Animas Forks Ghost Town

THE LOWDOWN: A picturesque ghost town at over 11,000 feet, Animas Forks was once one of the highest mining towns in the US. During its heyday, it was home to the *Animas Forks Pioneer*, a newspaper operating the highest-elevation printing press ever located in the US.

THE LOOT: About ten structures, many of them restored and stabilized, can be explored throughout the preserved townsite. Some of the structures can be entered, while others have collapsed or only the foundations remain.

THE GIDDYUP: Animas Forks is located on a spur road that connects Silverton with the

Alpine Loop 4x4 Trail (Adventure 8). From Silverton, take CR 2 north along the upper Animas River for about 13 mostly unpaved miles, with the final 4 miles after Eureka Gulch recommended for high-clearance and/or four-wheel-drive vehicles.

THE SCENE OF THE CRIME: GPS 37.9314, −107.5707.

THE SUSPECTS: Bureau of Land Management, blm.gov/visit/animas-forks.

RIDE ONWARD: Four miles south of Animas Forks, where CR 2 crosses the Animas River, a popular and challenging side scramble (west) up Eureka Gulch leads to several stunning bedrock waterfalls. **THE SCENE OF THE CRIME:** GPS 37.8799, −107.5679.

THE HARDSHIPS: Given the elevation of about 11,200 feet, pace yourself here.

8

Alpine Loop 4x4 Trail

THE LOWDOWN: This famously rugged, 65-mile national backcountry byway with incomparable views links two high mountain passes: Engineer Pass at 12,800 feet and Cinnamon Pass at 12,640 feet. The small ghost town of Animas Forks (Adventure 7) is located below the challenging switchbacks leading up to Engineer Pass. The Capitol City ghost town is located on the northern side of the loop. The roads on the Alpine Loop were originally used by miners with mule-drawn carts during the 1800s.

A structure at the Animas Forks Ghost Town, with a section of the Alpine Loop in the background

THE GIDDYUP: Most drivers begin the Alpine Loop from the town of Ouray (Adventure 5) or Silverton (Adventure 6), though you can also join the loop near Lake City and several other spots. The description below begins from Silverton—but note this listing is provided for orientation purposes only. Given that the Alpine Loop is considered a challenging and potentially dangerous route, you must do supplementary research to decide if this adventure is right for you.

THE ACTION: From Silverton head northeast on CR 2 through Eureka and Animas Forks. Most drivers follow the clockwise route, which is considered safer because you climb the challenging switchbacks to Engineer Pass at 12,800 feet. Next, head east on CR 20 through the Capitol City ghost town to Lake City. Turn south on CO 149 for about 2 miles. Turn west on CR 30 and follow past Lake San Cristobal, over Cinnamon Pass at 12,640 feet, and return to near Animas Forks.

THE SUSPECTS: Colorado Department of Transportation (for info, see Resources).

THE LAW: Law?! There ain't no law up there—er, speed limit is 15 miles per hour. Passenger cars, recreational vehicles, and travel trailers are not recommended. Semi-trucks are prohibited. Uphill traffic has the right of way on all roads.

THE TICKING CLOCK: Typically open from late May or early June through late October; closed in winter.

X MARKS THE SPOT: The Forest Service offers a decent online brochure and map, and Colorado Tourism has information on its website (see Resources).

THE HARDSHIPS: Road conditions can change, including presence of snow, mud, fallen rocks, and more. Drive carefully and bring a full tank of gas, spare tire, patch kit, and extra food and water.

9

Durango

THE LOWDOWN: There's so much to do in and around Durango, I can't cover it all—from hiking the many trails in the mountains surrounding the town to whitewater kayaking or rafting the Animas River. This adventure focuses on a downtown walking tour with Old West vibes and stops. Founded in 1880 by the Denver and Rio Grande Railroad, Durango's downtown is a nationally registered historic district with many buildings from the late nineteenth and early twentieth centuries that now often house modern restaurants and shops.

THE LOOT: Most of the historic district's notable buildings are located along ten blocks of Main Avenue, including the Strater Hotel (see below) and the Durango and Silverton Railroad Depot and Museum (Adventure 10). Both the Durango Business Improvement District and the Durango Area Tourism Office have free online guides for self-guided walking tours (see Resources).

MORE LOOT: The **Strater Hotel** is a historic Victorian brick building dating to 1887. Its interior features mahogany woodwork, period wallpaper, decorative antiques, a restored saloon, and exhibits about the Old West. Walk-in visitors are welcome. THE SCENE OF THE CRIME: 699 Main Avenue, Durango, CO 81301. THE DIGS: Luckily, you can stay the night without robbing a bank. THE SUSPECTS: 800-247-4431; strater.com.

EVEN MORE LOOT: The **Animas Museum** includes a Law and Disorder exhibit about the Wild West era in La Plata County, plus a Native American gallery about the

Basketmaker peoples, and more. THE SCENE OF THE CRIME: 3065 W. Second Avenue, Durango, CO 81301. THE SUSPECTS: animas museum.org.

RIDE ONWARD: Keep your legs moving by continuing onto the **Animas River Trail**, a 7-mile paved walking and cycling path alongside the Animas River (switching sides in a few spots). THE SCENE OF THE CRIME: From downtown, follow Ninth Street west to the riverside path.

THE SNORT: I don't even know where to begin. How much time does your liver have? On or near Main Avenue there are roughly a hundred—give or take eighty-five—microbreweries, taverns, wine bars, "spiritoriums," et cetera. Steamworks Brewing, Carver Brewing, and Animas Brewing are some popular options; Ska Brewing is south of downtown.

10

Durango and Silverton Railroad

THE LOWDOWN: This family-friendly historic tourist train has run continuously since 1881 through deep canyons along the Animas River. The train robbery scenes in the film *Butch Cassidy and the Sundance Kid* were filmed on this railroad. But don't go getting any crazy ideas.

THE LOOT: Most guests start from Durango on a roundtrip ride to Silverton, though alternative itineraries are possible. THE TICKING CLOCK: From roughly May to October, trains depart daily, with the most common route being the 45 miles between Durango and Silverton, which takes 3.5 hours each way. During winter, and at other select times of

year, the train runs a shorter, 26-mile route from Durango called Cascade Canyon. THE TAKE: Unless you jump from a horse onto the train, you'll have to pony up for this one. Some tickets are under a hundred but most are well over it. THE SCENE OF THE CRIME: Durango Depot, 479 Main Avenue, Durango, CO 81301. THE SUSPECTS: 970-247-2733; durangotrain.com.

MORE LOOT: Even if you're not riding the train, make sure to stop by the Durango Depot for the free **D&SNG Museum**, with 12,000 square feet of exhibits related to railroading, transportation, and mining history. THE TICKING CLOCK: Open daily during summer.

11

Upper Arkansas River Valley

THE LOWDOWN: If you're looking for an outlaw-themed side trip to south-central Colorado, consider the beautiful Upper Arkansas River Valley, which has tons of worthwhile sites and activities. To the west loom the Collegiate Peaks. To the east, the tumbling river runs along the flanks of high-desert granite hills and peaks. The mountain towns of Leadville, Buena Vista, and Salida are each worth a stop. This adventure provides just a basic overview, organized north to south, for an area that could very well offer a rewarding weeklong destination.

THE LOOT: **Leadville** is a former silver-mining and gambling town at the headwaters of the Arkansas River with several museums and a small historic district. The town offers a free online walking-tour guide (see Resources). Doc Holliday was briefly a resident after his

Whitewater rafting on the Arkansas River through Browns Canyon

heyday at the OK Corral in Tombstone, Arizona, allegedly becoming a regular at the **Silver Dollar Saloon**, established in 1879 and still open today. **THE SCENE OF THE CRIME:** 315 Harrison Avenue, Leadville, CO 80461. **THE GIDDYUP:** From I-70, head south either on US 24 for 32 miles if coming from the west or on CO 91 for 22 miles if coming from the east. **THE SUSPECTS:** For more information about visiting Leadville, 710-486-9914; leadville.com.

THE SNORT: Breweries abound throughout the valley, and some folks come just for that reason: Two Mile Brewing Company (Leadville), Eddyline Brewery (two locations in Buena Vista), Browns Canyon Brewing Company (near Nathrop), Elevation Beer Company (Poncha Springs), and Tres Litros Beer Company and Soulcraft Brewing (Salida)—plus distilleries, saloons, and more.

THE ACTION: The adventure town of **Buena Vista** is a popular hub for whitewater rafting and kayaking. There are many possible runs, ranging from class II to V, throughout the valley. One of the top rafting experiences in the country runs through **Browns Canyon National Monument** as either a half-day or full-day class III–IV trip. **THE DIGS:** Many rafting outfitters' outposts between Buena Vista and Salida offer cabins or camping. **THE SUSPECTS:** For information about trip options and outfitters, see buenavistacolorado.org/rafting.

MORE ACTION: Hundreds of miles of hiking and mountain-biking trails can be found throughout the valley and surrounding mountains. The options around Buena Vista include some easier hikes and a short mountain-bike ride. In addition to strolling through the historic downtown, for an easy walk check out the 0.5-mile **Riverside Trail** on the Arkansas River's western bank. For a moderate hiking or mountain biking option, cross the bridge and continue on the **Barbara Whipple Trail**, a 3.3-mile loop with about 500 feet of elevation gain. Many spur trails allow you to extend the hike or ride. THE SCENE OF THE CRIME: The typical starting point for the town trails is the Buena Vista River and Whitewater Park at the eastern end of Main Street. The trailhead is on the western side of the pedestrian bridge, near where kayakers play on the constructed river features. X MARKS THE SPOT: The Buena Vista Recreation Department has a solid map for all trails in town at buenavistarec.com/trails. There's also the Latitude 40° Recreation Topo Map: Salida Buena Vista (see Resources).

MORE LOOT: The **St. Elmo Ghost Town**, at 10,000 feet in the Collegiate Peaks west of Buena Vista, is a family favorite with about forty historic buildings to explore. Along the way, consider a stop at **Mount Princeton Hot Springs Resort**. THE GIDDYUP: From Leadville, head south on US 24 for 33 miles to Buena Vista, then continue south 8 miles to CR 162 and turn right (west) to follow it 8 miles to the hot springs. To reach St. Elmo, continue west on CR 162 for 11.5 miles. THE SUSPECTS: mtprinceton.com; uncover colorado.com/ghost-towns/saint-elmo.

EVEN MORE LOOT: **Salida** is the valley's biggest city, with five thousand residents. The pleasant downtown has been designated a national historic district, with 136 preserved buildings from its Old West past, and guided walking tours are available. The **Salida Museum** has exhibits about local history, mining, and railroads. THE GIDDYUP: From Buena Vista, head south on US 285 for 24 miles and turn left (east) onto US 50 for 5 miles. THE SCENE OF THE CRIME: The museum is at 406½ W. Rainbow Boulevard, Salida, CO 81201. THE SUSPECTS: For the town, salidachamber.org/first-timers-guide. For the museum, salidamuseum.org.

RIDE ONWARD: At the southern end of the valley, the Royal Gorge is an impressive canyon rising over the Arkansas River. The three main ways to see it are during a class IV whitewater raft trip (see THE ACTION, above), on the historic Royal Gorge Route train ride (see YET MORE LOOT, below), or at the **Royal Gorge Bridge and Park**. This private park offers various methods to explore the gorge, including driving across a famous suspension bridge, ziplining across the gorge, climbing on a guided via ferrata course, and more. The park also has trails and camping. THE GIDDYUP: From US 50 either 49 miles east of Salida or about 7.5 west of Cañon City, turn south onto CR 3A and proceed about 4 miles. THE SCENE OF THE CRIME: 4218 CR 3A, Cañon City, CO 81212. THE TAKE: Moderate to high, depending on which option(s) you choose. THE SUSPECTS: 719-275-7507; royalgorgebridge.com.

YET MORE LOOT: The **Royal Gorge Route Railroad** is a historic tourist train following the Arkansas River through the deep chasm of the Royal Gorge, site of the Colorado Railroad War during the 1870s (see Old West Stories below). THE GIDDYUP: From Salida, take US 50 east for 56 miles to Cañon City. THE SCENE OF THE CRIME: 330 Royal Gorge Boulevard, Cañon City, CO 81212. THE TAKE: Well, it's not an arm and a leg—it costs just one or the other. Coach tickets are less than a Ben Franklin, but most other options are more. THE SUSPECTS: royalgorgeroute.com.

OLD WEST STORIES: THE ROYAL GORGE WAR

It was the late 1870s when silver was found in the high mountain town of Leadville, Colorado, near the headwaters of the Arkansas River. And two powerful railroad companies both wanted to lay tracks and reap the rewards. Except for each other, the most formidable obstacle lying in either railroad's way was the Royal Gorge: an imposing canyon with sheer 1,000-foot-high cliffs of granite that were only 30 feet apart at the canyon's narrowest.

On one side of the war was the Atchison, Topeka, and Santa Fe Railroad, with a terminal in Pueblo, east of Cañon City, the gateway to what was called the Grand Canyon of the Rockies. The other combatant was the Denver and Rio Grande Railroad, which had already laid tracks in the Arkansas River Valley to within a mile of Cañon City.

In the spring of 1878, the Santa Fe Railroad sent a crew to the mouth of the Royal Gorge with orders to begin grading for a track. The Santa Fe Railroad had blocked the Rio Grande Railroad, and the war was on. Over the following two years, the battle was fought mostly in the courts, with the case eventually reaching the US Supreme Court.

Meanwhile, on the ground the two railroads dug in for a standoff. While the Santa Fe was building through the narrowest parts of the gorge, allies of the Rio Grande were rolling boulders from above or throwing tools into the river. Both railroads hired armed guards, with the Santa Fe employing Bat Masterson and Doc Holliday to raise a posse of sixty hired guns.

After the Supreme Court ruled in favor of the Denver and Rio Grande Railroad and its victory seemed at hand, the posse led by Masterson seized Rio Grande train stations from Cañon City to Denver. When the Rio Grande raised a larger force of a hundred, Masterson told his posse to stand down, and the so-called war was over.

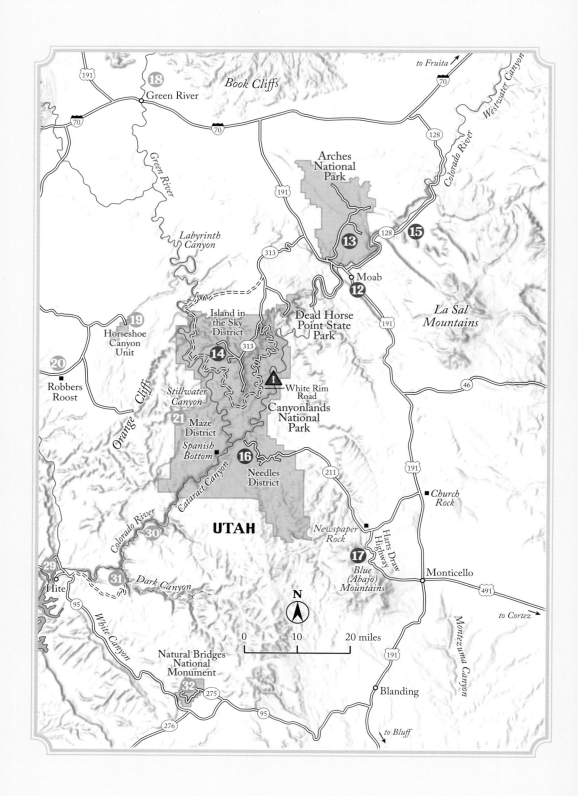

to Fruita

Book Cliffs

Green River

(18) Green River

Labyrinth Canyon

Arches National Park

(13)

(15)

Moab

(12)

La Sal Mountains

Horseshoe Canyon Unit

(19)

Island in the Sky District

(14)

Dead Horse Point State Park

Robbers Roost

(20)

Orange Cliffs

Stillwater Canyon

White Rim Road

Canyonlands National Park

(21) Maze District

Spanish Bottom

(16)

Needles District

UTAH

Cataract Canyon

Church Rock

Newspaper Rock

Colorado River

(30)

Harts Draw Highway

(17)

Monticello

Blue (Abajo) Mountains

to Cortez

(29)

Hite

(31) Dark Canyon

N

0   10   20 miles

White Canyon

Natural Bridges National Monument

(32)

Blanding

Montezuma Canyon

to Bluff

CHAPTER 2

Canyonlands and Moab

SOUTHEASTERN UTAH

THE WHOLE KIT AND CABOODLE: For hundreds of years, southeastern Utah has been a desert adventurer's paradise for everyone from ancestral Native Americans to fur trappers, from outlaws to modern adventurers. During the days of the Wild West, this area served as the ridiculously scenic backdrop for countless exploits by livestock rustlers and fleeing robbers. Today, modern bandits mostly steal experiences while wearing hiking boots or riding atop mountain bikes.

THE LOOT: The area is home to two of Utah's world-famous Mighty Five national parks. **Canyonlands** has three far-flung districts: Island in the Sky and the Needles are covered in this chapter; the Maze District and the Horseshoe Canyon Unit are covered in the next chapter. **Arches** is much smaller and more accessible, very close to the town of Moab.

THE TICKING CLOCK: Due to a somewhat lower elevation—around 4,000 feet at Moab and about 1,000–2,000 feet higher on the surrounding mesas—Moab and the Canyonlands region have a relatively wide season, with visitation ramping up through March and staying busy into November. Winters in Moab are relatively mild, with daily highs in the mid-40s to low 50s. Spring and fall are pleasant to warm, with many days in the 60s and 70s. Summers come out blazing like a bandit fleeing a bank robbery—expect days in the high 80s into the 90s and low 100s.

12

Moab

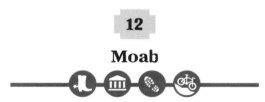

THE LOWDOWN: In the old days, Moab was a sleepy crossing of the Grand River (later renamed the Colorado River) for travelers and outlaws on the lam. Today, it's a major outdoor adventure destination and gateway to the Canyonlands region. The town offers access to national and state parks, several mountain ranges, four-wheel-drive routes, mountain biking, hiking, and coffee shops with prices that could turn any dirtbag into a bandit. There's way too much to include it all here, so below are a few highlights that have relevant outlaw connections—plus several spots that feel too Wild West-y not to mention.

THE HARDSHIPS: Welcome to Moab! The biggest little city in southeastern Utah has about five thousand residents—plus approximately 1.3 million tourists, give or take, during high season, April through October. Just saying: get your brake pads checked—cuz, pardner, you're gonna need them on the main drag.

THE LOOT: For outlaw enthusiasts, the **Moab Museum** features stories and several objects related to Wild West history in the area. There's a set of leg irons reportedly used to detain Wild Bunch gang members captured near Robbers Roost—possibly a reference to the arrest of Silver Tip, told in Wild Bunch Stories, Episode 15, The Battle at Roost Canyon, 1899. Additionally, there is a letter handwritten in 1890 by Grand County Sheriff Westwood requesting the funds to purchase the irons. A revolver from the 1920s and oral histories from the Old West round out the collection. THE TAKE: Modest fee. THE SCENE OF THE CRIME: 118 E. Center Street, Moab, UT 84532. THE SUSPECTS: 435-259-7985; moabmuseum.org.

MORE LOOT: Enjoy walking around downtown to explore the many shops, including the excellent **Back of Beyond Books** (83 N. Main Street). You can extend your walk on the **Mill Creek Parkway**, a 2-mile paved walking and cycling path that starts near South Main Street between E. 100 Street and E. 200 Street and ends at Rotary Park. For visitor information, stop by the **Moab Information Center**, at the corner of Main and Center Streets, and bask with fellow dirtbags in the warm glow of free Wi-Fi. THE SUSPECTS: discovermoab.com. More information about Moab's world-famous mountain biking can be found in local bike shops, where you can also arrange a rental and/or shuttle.

THE ACTION: Just above town, the famous **Slickrock Trail** is a challenging, 10.5-mile mountain biking and hiking route over petrified dunes of bare Navajo sandstone. THE GIDDYUP: To reach the trailhead, from US 191 head east on East Center Street. After four blocks, turn right onto Fourth East Street and proceed about 0.5 mile. Turn left onto South Mill Creek Road, which becomes Sand Flat Road. After 3 miles, you'll reach the Slickrock trailhead. X MARKS THE SPOT: Local bike shops carry the Latitude 40° Recreation Topo Map: Moab Singletrack Utah (see Resources). THE TAKE: Modest entry fee per vehicle. THE SUSPECTS: grandcountyutah.net/654/Slickrock-Bike-Trail.

RIDE ONWARD: The La Sal Mountains rise dramatically to the east above Spanish Valley, offering a variety of adventures, driving tours, hikes, and a famous mountain-bike trail called the **Whole Enchilada**, with 7,000 feet of descent during a 34-mile (shuttle-assisted) ride.

THE SNORT: And the answer to the final question posed in Becoming an Outlaw Adventurer is, drum roll please, the **Moab Brewery**. It's an excellent spot for post-adventure beers and burgers. Everyone and their best friends know this, so expect a wait—but still worth it.

THE JIG: Finding parking. Pro tip: remember to breathe.

THE YARNS: Moab is a setting for two Wild Bunch Stories featured in this book: Episodes 3, On the Outlaw Trail, 1889; and 15, The Battle at Roost Canyon, 1899.

Opposite: Prickly pear cactuses bloom during spring in the high desert landscape near Moab.

13

Arches National Park

THE LOWDOWN: In recent years, the entry road to the fantastic Arches National Park saw a line of vehicles backing up from the fee station toward town. Increasingly, the alternative became waiting for the geologic formation of new sandstone arches in other less-visited places. To reduce overcrowding, in 2022, the park service introduced a timed-entry reservation system from early April to early October. Despite the crowds, the incredible landscape of Arches is definitely worth a visit. For a more Wild West-y feel, consider visiting during the low season from late fall to early spring—or go in the middle of a moonless night like an outlaw.

THE JIG: It's possible the new timed-entry system will evolve during the first few years of implementation, so check the park website for updates. At time of research, timed-entry tickets were released on recreation.gov in monthly blocks, three months in advance, following a release schedule posted on the park website.

THE ACTION: It's all good stuff here, which is why it's so busy. The park road leads to many scenic viewpoints and trailheads. A popular highlight along this road is the moderate, 3-mile roundtrip hike with 480 feet of elevation gain to **Delicate Arch**, which slightly resembles a pair of legs wearing cowboy chaps. THE SCENE OF THE CRIME: At 11.7 miles on the park road, turn right (east) and drive 1.2 miles to the trailhead. THE LOOT: At the trailhead, Old West enthusiasts should make sure to check out the early 1900s Wolfe Ranch.

MORE ACTION: Another solid destination (apologies, as always, for the rock pun) is

from the trailhead at the end of the park road. Hike a moderately easy gravel trail 1.6 miles roundtrip to **Landscape Arch**, famous for the 1991 video of its partial collapse (easily found online). And of course there's plenty more to check out, so set aside a day or two if you can.

THE DIGS: The park road ends 17.7 miles from the park entrance at the very popular **Devils Garden Campground**.

THE HARDSHIPS: Heat and sun exposure can be an issue here. During summer and hot days, hike early in the morning or evening. Hat, sunscreen, even long sleeves can be helpful.

THE GIDDYUP: The park entry station is on the northeast side of US 191 about 4 miles north of downtown Moab.

THE SUSPECTS: 801-259-8161; nps.gov/arch.

THE TAKE: Park entry and camping fees.

X MARKS THE SPOT: The park service has good maps on their website. For more detail, check out the National Geographic Trails Illustrated Topo Map #211, Arches National Park.

THE YARNS: For one of the best Wild West chases in national park history, please see Wild Bunch Stories, Episode 3, On the Outlaw Trail, 1889. Episode 15, The Battle at Roost Canyon, 1899, also involves the park area.

14

Island in the Sky District

THE LOWDOWN: Island in the Sky is an isolated mesa about 2,000 feet above the Green River that's connected to the adjacent landscape by a narrow isthmus of rock only a hundred feet wide called the Neck. Because it's so close to Moab, this is the most accessible and popular of the three districts in Canyonlands

Mountains bikers finish the White Rim Loop by ascending Mineral Bottom Road.

National Park. In addition to several unique hikes, stunning viewpoints, and a famous four-wheel-drive road, there are a few outlaw connections for enthusiasts.

THE LOOT: For outlaw enthusiasts, the views to the west along the main road—particularly at **Green River Overlook** (near Willow Flat Campground) but also those around **Grand View Point** at the end of the main road—are the best drive-up spots for seeing the distant Orange Cliffs, which border the infamous Robbers Roost region and which Butch Cassidy once used as a hideout (see THE YARNS below).

THE ACTION: Hikers and photographers will want to walk the 0.25-mile (one-way) path to the famous **Mesa Arch**, known for its iconic archway view east toward the La Sal Mountains that appears on inspirational

posters in countless physical therapy offices across the country (the trailhead is 6 miles southwest of the visitor center on Grand View Point Road). Two other unique hikes include the 2-mile roundtrip **Aztec Butte Trail** to several Ancestral Puebloan granaries and the roughly 1-mile roundtrip **Upheaval Dome** hike (both trails are located on Upheaval Dome Road, at its beginning and end, respectively).

THE GIDDYUP: From US 191 about 8 miles north of Moab, turn left (south) onto UT 313. At a junction in about 15 miles (to the left is Dead Horse Point State Park), continue straight onto Island in the Sky Road and follow it to the entry station. This visitor center is about a 40-minute drive from Moab—but traffic can get bad during high season, especially in midmorning. The one-way park road continues another 20 or so miles to a fork near the campground; to the right is Upheaval Dome, continuing straight leads to Grand View Point.

THE SUSPECTS: National Park Service, 435-719-2313; nps.gov/cany/planyourvisit/island inthesky.htm.

X MARKS THE SPOT: The NPS map and guide are available on entry. The National Geographic Trails Illustrated Topo Maps include #310, Island in the Sky, for just that district or #210, Canyonlands National Park, for all three districts.

THE DIGS: Willow Flat Campground has about a dozen sites—first come, first served.

MORE ACTION: The **White Rim Road** is a famous, 71-mile, four-wheel-drive road that today is popular for 4x4 driving and mountain biking. When combined with other unpaved and paved roads—like the twisty Shafer Trail and Mineral Bottom Road, which switchbacks dramatically down to the Green River (and was once called Horsethief Trail)—the result is a roughly 100-mile loop. THE LAW: Prior to embarking on the White Rim Road, all users must obtain a day-use or overnight permit online or at the park's visitor center, where you can also obtain maps and route guides. THE SUSPECTS: nps.gov/cany/plan yourvisit/whiterimroad.htm. THE HARDSHIPS: The White Rim Road loop is tough driving and takes time. If you attempt a day drive, know you're getting into more than ten hours of bouncing behind the wheel.

RIDE ONWARD: Nearby there's the **Horsethief Trail System**, with just a few of the many mountain bike trails in the area. The trails start from **Horsethief Campground**

An abandoned uranium-mining cabin on the Green River near Canyonlands National Park

(BLM) just off UT 313 about 3 miles north of the turnoff to Dead Horse Point State Park.

THE YARNS: Butch Cassidy and accomplices made a camp in the shade of the **Orange Cliffs** during spring 1897, shortly after the Castle Gate robbery. The hideout camp appears in Wild Bunch Stories, Episode 8, Into the Roost, 1897.

15

Colorado River Trips

THE LOWDOWN: Moab is a hub for several awesome desert paddling trips in the Canyonlands region, mostly on the Colorado River. Plus there are several trips on the nearby Green River that are discussed in Adventure 18. The trips below are described from upstream to downstream.

THE ACTION: **Ruby-Horsethief** is a 25-mile class I–II trip on the Colorado River, starting from Loma boat launch in Fruita, Colorado, and ending at Westwater boat ramp in Utah. This trip is a popular friends and family float, with groups typically taking two to four days using rafts, kayaks, paddleboards, and other watercraft. River runners frequently wave to passing trains, and there's a dugout cabin a few miles into the run. **THE LAW:** The Bureau of Land Management requires advance camping permits for multiday trips (see Resources).

EVEN BIGGER ACTION: **Westwater Canyon** is a classic, 17-mile, class III–IV whitewater trip on the Colorado starting from the Westwater boat ramp and typically ending at Cisco Landing on UT 128 between I-70 and Moab, though lower takeouts are possible. There's an outlaw cave on this run, which passes through a gorge of Vishnu schist similar to the inner

gorge of Grand Canyon. Most boaters opt for an overnight trip, though long day trips are also common. **THE LAW:** BLM requires advance permits for both types of launches (see Resources).

SOME TOWN ACTION: The **Moab Daily** is a class II–III trip on the Colorado just northeast of town, paralleling UT 128 for about 13 miles between Hittle Bottom Recreation Area and Take Out boat ramp. This is a great show-yourself-down option, though guided trips are also available. **THE SUSPECTS:** Check the BLM website for information and a map (see Resources).

RIDE ONWARD: **Meander Canyon** of the Colorado River is a classic class I float trip for about 51 miles through Canyonlands National Park. Put-in is at Potash boat ramp on Potash Road (UT 279), and most trips end at Spanish Bottom, just below the confluence with the Green River. Because there's no takeout—it's in the middle of the most beautiful nowhere you'll ever see—this run requires prearranging a jet-boat pickup (for small boats only) from Tex's Riverways of Moab, or boaters must continue downstream through class III–V Cataract Canyon (Adventure 30: Cataract Canyon River Trip). **THE LAW:** You'll need a permit and specialty equipment to follow park-service regulations (see Resources). **THE SUSPECTS:** For more information about jet-boat pickup, see texsriverways.com/meander -canyon.

THE HARDSHIPS: Self-guided river trips in canyon country—even easier class I–II sections—are often best left to river runners experienced with upcanyon wind bursts, sudden thunderstorms, blistering heat, possible high water (typical in late spring through early summer), and being self-sufficient for long days on the water. Bring plenty of drinking water, food, and common sense.

THE YARNS: The minor outlaw Blue John Griffith was a boatman who spent time in the Westwater area. He is featured in several Wild Bunch Stories, including Episode 15, The Battle at Roost Canyon, 1899.

16

Needles District

THE LOWDOWN: Compared with Island in the Sky, the Needles District of Canyonlands National Park is farther from Moab, with more-rugged adventures. But it's a must-visit spot for slot-canyon hiking enthusiasts and anyone who likes ridiculously impressive rock spires jutting into the air. Bring a whiplash brace.

THE ACTION: Old West enthusiasts should check out the preserved Cowboy Camp near the start of the short **Cave Spring Loop**. Continuing on this fun 0.6-mile loop trail involves ducking inside the cave and climbing two ladders. THE GIDDYUP: From the visitor center, head west on UT 211 and follow signs for Cave Spring.

MORE ACTION: Several long out-and-back and loop hikes are possible in the Needles District. One of the best is the 11-mile **Chesler Park–Joint Trail Loop**, which feels like exploring an outlaw hideout if there ever was one. Start from the Elephant Hill trailhead

THE HARDSHIPS: This is rugged country. Be in shape and bring lots of water, food, and your A-game.

THE GIDDYUP: From US 191 south of its junction with UT 46, take UT 211 west for about 35 miles to the park entrance. After a quarter mile, the visitor center is on the right.

The park road continues past scenic viewpoints and well-signed turnoffs to district attractions. From the visitor center, the turnoff to Cave Spring is less than a mile, and the campground road is 2 miles farther. To reach the Elephant Hill trailhead, from the north spur of the campground road head west on an unpaved road for 3 miles.

THE SUSPECTS: National Park Service, 435-719-2313; nps.gov/cany/planyourvisit/needles.htm.

X MARKS THE SPOT: In addition to park service maps, there's the National Geographic Trails Illustrated Topo Map #311, The Needles.

THE DIGS: The popular Needles Campground has about thirty sites, half of which can be reserved.

RIDE ONWARD: On the road to the Needles, stop by **Newspaper Rock State Historic Monument** to view an impressive petroglyph panel, with carvings spanning two thousand years of Native American cultures.

17

Blue Mountains

THE LOWDOWN: Typically called the Blue Mountains in outlaw lore and the Abajo Mountains by Spanish explorers, this small range rises to the west of Monticello, Utah, and to the south of the Needles District. The Blues were once home to the Carlisle Ranch, an outlaw-friendly stopping point.

THE LOOT: Most travelers can get a good feel for this range by driving the 19-mile paved **Harts Draw Highway**, especially scenic during midfall when the aspen groves turn

The Peekaboo Trail in the Needles District of Canyonlands National Park

bright yellow and orange. There are several viewpoints along the way.

THE ACTION: The range's high point is Abajo Peak at 11,360 feet, with the mountainous areas to the west being most popular among ATVers and dirt bikers following the many off-highway vehicle (OHV) trails and dirt roads. Most OHV trails are multiuse, also allowing hiking, mountain biking, and horseback riding, while a few trails are nonmotorized. In winter, the Blues are popular for skiing, snowshoeing, and snowmobiling.

THE GIDDYUP: From US 191 in Monticello, head west on W. 200 S. Street, which becomes Abajo Drive, then North Creek Road, then FR 101, and then FR 136 (a lot of names, but stick to the main road and you'll be fine). After about 9.5 miles, the Harts Draw Canyonlands overlook is on the right. The road ends at UT 211. Turn left for Newspaper Rock and the Needles (Adventure 16) or turn right to return to US 191.

THE DIGS: Two small campgrounds, Dalton Springs and Buckboard Flat, are off FR 101, with plenty more dispersed sites throughout the range.

THE SUSPECTS: US Forest Service, which publishes an "Abajo Mountains Guide" (see Resources).

X MARKS THE SPOT: National Geographic Trails Illustrated Topo Map #703, Manti–La Sal National Forest.

RIDE ONWARD: A more-rugged road trip is the unpaved **Abajo Loop State Scenic Backway**, which connects Monticello and Blanding, Utah, covering about 37 miles on

Forest Roads 105, 101, 079, and 095. THE SUSPECTS: US Forest Service, which offers a route guide (see Resources).

THE YARNS: The Blue Mountains and the Carlisle Ranch regularly appear in outlaw lore, including several Wild Bunch Stories in this book. See Episode 3, On the Outlaw Trail, 1889.

MODERN EXPLORATIONS: PHOTOGRAPHY ON THE OUTLAW TRAIL

The sun will come out tomorrow? • Hideouts and bandit routes • Is that a hat or a satellite dish? • Hey, stranger • Favorite places

Imagine fifty people lined up near the edge of a cliff in the twilight of dawn. Clutching cameras, tripods, phones, and backpacks, we looked like we were waiting to be robbed.

Welcome to Mesa Arch, one of the most popular spots in the West for sunrise photography. It was a cool morning in late September atop the Island in the Sky District of Canyonlands National Park. Many of us had been waiting more than thirty minutes, and the mood was a mixture of giddiness and impatience.

"Maybe it doesn't come up this morning?" joked someone.

"It's not daylight savings today, is it?" added someone else, maybe me, checking their imaginary watch. "We could be here for hours."

One of the most iconic vistas in the West, Mesa Arch is located atop Island in the Sky.

Meanwhile another wise guy—okay, also me—took things way too far: "The Aztecs sacrificed people to keep the sun moving."

The photographer to my left laughed. The person to my right rolled their eyes and started cautiously backing away.

· · · · · ·

When I began photographing the outlaw trail for this book, I wanted to shoot a mix of lesser-known spots—like remote hideouts and forgotten bandit routes—plus well-known spots that most people didn't realize had outlaw connections. The emphasis was always on finding the best photos to showcase each region—with bonus points when something looked particularly Wild West-y.

That's how I found myself huddled in a small cave during a hailstorm at Vedauwoo Recreation Area in the Laramie Mountains. I'd hiked into the granite formations during a break in a thunderstorm, figuring I'd find shelter in an area known for hiding outlaws.

Once the storm broke, I carefully scrambled upward, searching for my shot. I felt quite proud to be the only person in sight braving the wet rock. I was going to earn that dramatic cloudy background or eat granite trying.

Luckily, I slipped only a few times—minor losses of traction, let's call them. Around the thirteenth time, I was rolling around on the ground, happy no one was around to see me, when I looked up. A young fella wearing a floppy straw hat was sprinting across the summit, jumping over crevices.

As a rule of thumb for this book, anytime I saw someone wearing a head covering that even marginally resembled a cowboy hat—wide-brim sun hat, birthday sombrero from a Mexican restaurant, college graduation mortarboard, aluminum foil–covered dish from Halloween satellite costume (could happen)—I maybe kind of stalked them around the desert. Breathy pretentious voice: "for the art."

Other times, I was hiking leg-burning mountains for vantage points. Squeezing through slot canyons for dizzying visuals. Approaching friends and strangers with odd questions like, "Hey, can you glance longingly into the horizon while standing next to that bicycle?"

I guess what I'm getting at is the outlaw trail can take you to some of the most stunning photography spots in the West (see Suggested Trips in Part 1). Keep an eye on the photo captions throughout this book for more information.

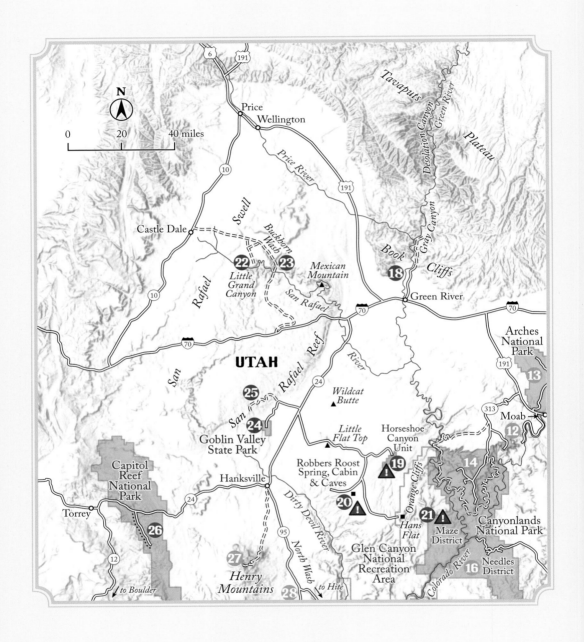

CHAPTER 3
Robbers Roost and San Rafael Swell
SOUTH-CENTRAL UTAH

THE WHOLE KIT AND CABOODLE: Robbers Roost is simultaneously one of the most famous and least understood of the hideouts along the outlaw trail. When people unfamiliar with the history hear the word *hideout*, they may picture a specific point on a map, like a cave or cabin. There were certainly plenty of such pinpoint hideouts along the outlaw trail, but just as often there was another type: an inaccessible region where many individual hiding spots and grazing areas could be used. Robbers Roost fits this latter category. (See the San Rafael Swell introduction later in this chapter.)

Even today, many writers and websites mistakenly describe Robbers Roost like it's a single X on the map—a destination that can be checked off the list with the right GPS coordinates. They might say, "Robbers Roost is *east* of North Wash. *Near* the Maze. A great side trip *from* Horseshoe Canyon."

Bzzzt! (Game show wrong-answer buzzer.) That's like being atop Island in the Sky and asking, "Where's Canyonlands?" All three of those places mentioned above are *part of*

Robbers Roost—they fall within its historical borders.

THE SCENE OF THE CRIME: Robbers Roost is essentially a 2,000-square-mile parallelogram. The northernmost corner is the town of Green River, Utah (a great starting point for the adventures in this chapter). The northeastern border follows the sinuous Green River to the confluence—now located in Canyonlands National Park—with the Grand River, today called the Colorado River. The southeastern border runs down the Colorado River through Cataract and Narrow Canyons to a southernmost corner at Hite Crossing. From there, the southwestern border follows Trachyte Canyon and North Wash to the town of Hanksville. Closing this parallelogram, the northwestern border follows the San Rafael Reef back to the town of Green River.

Within these borders is a desolate region of high mesas, drifting sand dunes, and deeply eroded canyons that are challenging, but not impossible, to navigate through. There are several historical trails, many caves, and very few water sources. Add all this together, and it was the perfect area for outlaws to evade capture.

Overlanders travel through Robbers Roost.

This chapter covers the northern bulk of the Roost and the Swell. The next chapter covers the Roost's southern periphery.

Which Planet?

Well, since you ask, the Robbers Roost area, as seen in satellite images from outer space, has been compared to Mars.

THE SUSPECTS: The area inside Canyonlands National Park is managed by the National Park Service and the area outside the park is managed by the Bureau of Land Management, but don't expect many rangers to be patrolling the area.

X MARKS THE SPOT: BLM produces a high-resolution Robbers Roost Map as a PDF for download (see Resources).

THE TICKING CLOCK: Adventurers can visit the Robbers Roost and San Rafael Swell area year-round. Winters are typically mild, with highs in the 40s and lows in the teens, though colder temps are possible. Summers are blistering, with highs in the 90s, lows in the 50s and 60s. Thus, spring and fall are the preferred seasons. To approximate local weather, check forecasts for Green River, Utah, and Hanksville, Utah.

THE HARDSHIPS: Today, Robbers Roost is one of the most remote and logistically challenging areas to visit in this book. There are no services inside the Roost, with the nearest gas stations, stores, and restaurants in Hanksville or Green River. Don't expect to have cell service in most parts. Visitors need a solid vehicle, typically a high-clearance four-wheel- or all-wheel-drive vehicle, or they should possess solid two-wheel-driving skills and outlaw-level guts. Bring all water, supplies, and food. Take enough fuel. Check your spare tire and tools. If you get into trouble, you'll probably be on your own.

THE GIDDYUP (TO THE Y JUNCTION): Since three Robbers Roost adventures below (19, Horseshoe Canyon; 20, Robbers Roost Spring, Cabin, and Caves; and 21, The Maze District) all require first navigating to the oft-referenced Y junction (with a sign that usually has more bullet holes than information), those directions are located here.

From Green River head west on I-70 for about 10 miles. Exit onto UT 24, turn left, and head south for about 25 miles. Just past Temple Mountain Road (the road to Goblin Valley State Park), turn left (east) onto unpaved Lower San Rafael Road/Hans Flat Road (toward Hans Flat Ranger Station in Canyonlands National Park) and follow it for about 24 miles to the Y junction. From here, follow the driving directions in each adventure.

THE YARNS: Robbers Roost is the setting for several dramatic Wild Bunch Stories featured in this book, including Episodes 3, On the Outlaw Trail, 1889; 7, Desperadoes at Castle Gate, 1896–1897; and 8, Into the Roost, 1897.

18

Green River, Utah

THE LOWDOWN: Located just south of the impressive Book Cliffs, the town of Green River and the river it's named after offer several under-the-radar adventures and a great museum. Plus it's a central starting point for this chapter's adventures.

THE LOOT: History buffs will want to check out the **John Wesley Powell River History Museum** on Main Street by the river—you'll spot it. Exhibits about the 1869 expedition mix with exhibits about river history and ecology. THE TAKE: Modest fee. THE SUSPECTS: johnwesleypowell.com.

THE ACTION: There are several high-quality paddling trips on the Green River, which are harder to access than those near Moab but well worth the effort. Due to their remote nature, and the possibility of stiff upcanyon winds, these runs are best for experienced river runners. The more user-friendly option is the **Green River Daily** through scenic Gray Canyon. This fun, 8-mile, class II day trip sees occasional kayakers and rafters and far less overall usage than popular runs on the Colorado River upstream from Moab. Put-in is at Nefertiti Access and takeout is at Swaseys Beach boat ramp (see THE GIDDYUP below). THE SUSPECTS: Bureau of Land Management (see Resources).

MORE ACTION: For those who want to explore Gray Canyon on their feet, a rough riverside trail with excellent scenery starts from road's end near Nefertiti. About 2 miles upstream you'll reach Rattlesnake Canyon, a sinuous side canyon that can be explored for several miles. (Make sure to review "slot canyons" and "flash floods" in the Ask an Outlaw FAQ in Part 1.)

THE GIDDYUP: To reach Gray Canyon from the town of Green River, head east on Main Street a half mile past the river and turn left (north) onto Hastings Road. Continue about 9.5 miles to Swaseys Beach. To reach Nefertiti, continue on Hastings Road for about 8.5 miles (after 2.5 miles, check out the old cabin on the left). Note that beyond Swaseys Beach, the road is unpaved and becomes increasingly rougher as you progress upcanyon. Most two-wheel-drive vehicles with good clearance should be fine under normal conditions.

RIDE ONWARD: For an even more remote and challenging paddling adventure, check out two multiday trips downstream (see chapter 2 map): **Labyrinth Canyon** is 45 miles through BLM land, and **Stillwater Canyon** is 55 miles through Canyonlands National Park, with a complicated egress.

Plan Your Own Trip!

For more information about paddling trips (including access points, shuttle directions, permits, and regulations) on the Green River through Desolation, Gray, Labyrinth, and Stillwater Canyons, plus Cataract Canyon on the Colorado—and the story of the 1869 first expedition through Grand Canyon—please check out my book *Paddling the John Wesley Powell Route*.

THE YARNS: Green River, Utah, makes many appearances in outlaw lore, including several mentions in this book. See Wild Bunch Stories, Episode 3, On the Outlaw Trail, 1889.

19

Horseshoe Canyon

THE LOWDOWN: Located on the eastern side of Robbers Roost, Horseshoe Canyon is a satellite unit of Canyonlands National Park that's known for several remarkable Barrier Canyon–style rock art panels, including the famous Great Gallery. Of Wild West significance, Butch Cassidy and other outlaws used

Horseshoe Canyon and the surrounding area as a hideout during the 1890s.

THE ACTION: The typical way to access the rock art in Horseshoe Canyon is by hiking a 3.5-mile (one-way) trail, with around 1,000 feet of elevation loss from the west-side rim-top trailhead to the canyon floor. THE HARDSHIPS: The descent into Horseshoe Canyon is steep. Don't go down if you can't go back up.

THE GIDDYUP: The area's roads are typically passable by most high-clearance two-wheel-drive vehicles during normal conditions but usually impassable when wet, and four-wheel drive is recommended (and sometimes necessary) due to deep sand drifts from changing winds. To reach the Horseshoe Canyon trailhead parking area, first navigate to the Y junction using the driving directions in the chapter introduction. At the Y junction stay left (east) and continue about 5 miles. Turn right at the National Park Service sign, and continue around 2 miles to the trailhead. THE SCENE OF THE CRIME: GPS 38.4738, –110.2002.

THE SUSPECTS: National Park Service, 435-719-2313 (for URL, see Resources).

THE LAW: No camping or backpacking is allowed inside Horseshoe Canyon within the national park boundary. Visitors may camp at the west rim trailhead on public land managed by the Bureau of Land Management. There is a vault toilet but no water.

THE TAKE: Unlike Canyonlands's three main districts, there is no entrance fee to visit Horseshoe Canyon.

X MARKS THE SPOT: National Geographic Trails Illustrated Topo Map #210, Canyonlands National Park.

THE YARNS: See Wild Bunch Stories, Episodes 7, Desperadoes at Castle Gate, 1896–1897; and 8, Into the Roost, 1897.

20

Robbers Roost Spring, Cabin, and Caves

THE LOWDOWN: This cluster of historic sites found deep within Robbers Roost is popular with outlaw enthusiasts. Reaching these sites is half the fun, requiring driving many miles on unpaved roads, which are typically passable by most high-clearance two-wheel-drive vehicles during normal conditions, but four-wheel drive is recommended (and sometimes necessary) given that roads can be covered by deep sand drifts from changing winds. These roads are usually impassable when wet.

THE LOOT: Robbers Roost Spring was used by rustlers and outlaws, and it remains in use by ranchers today. Located just above the start of the South Fork of Robbers Roost Canyon, the spring is not much of a site itself but worth a look when combined with the other two sites below.

THE ACTION: The so-called **Butch Cassidy Cabin** is just an impressive brick fireplace, all that remains of a cabin that was certainly used by some outlaws, though not necessarily by Butch himself. To reach the cabin, from the dirt parking area walk upstream (west) along the stream bed for less than a half mile, then search to the north.

Silvertip Spring Caves are famous for a shootout between a posse led by Sheriff Tyler of Moab against the outlaws Blue John

Looking into lower Robbers Roost Canyon with the Henry Mountains rising in the distance

Griffith, Silver Tip, and Indian Ed Newcomb. To find the caves, from the cabin area return to the main wash and walk about 500 feet upstream. Then turn north and follow a tributary drainage into a small, narrowing canyon below the grotto of Silvertip Spring. The two caves are in the western cliffs.

THE GIDDYUP: To reach all three sites, start by following the driving directions to the Y junction in the chapter introduction. Turn right and head south for about 7 miles. At the three-way signed intersection, take the 90-degree right turn (west) onto an unnamed road leading toward Robbers Roost Spring and follow it for 6 miles. Turn left onto a rough dirt road and follow this 1,000 feet into a dirt parking area above the spring called "Butch Cassidy Cabin Parking."

RIDE ONWARD: Instead of turning toward Robbers Roost Spring, continue driving the unnamed road for under 4 miles (definitely less than 4 miles or you'll go off a cliff) for an increasingly dramatic drive across a narrow mesa running above the Middle and North Forks of Robbers Roost Canyon. This canyon has access to a variety of challenging routes for hiking and nontechnical or technical slot canyoneering.

THE YARNS: Bring this visit to life by reading Wild Bunch Stories, Episodes 8, Into the Roost, 1897; and 15, The Battle at Roost Canyon, 1899.

21

The Maze District

THE LOWDOWN: Occupying the southeast corner of Robbers Roost, the Maze is the most isolated and rugged of Canyonlands National Park's three districts. Visits to the Maze require a four-wheel-drive or all-wheel-drive vehicle (or guided tour) and plenty of time. Highlights include 4x4ing, camping, hiking, mountain biking, and visiting stunning viewpoints. The gateway to the Maze is Hans Flat Ranger Station, located about two hours from Green River, Utah. Because of the slow driving speeds and distances involved, day trips are mostly unfeasible and the vast majority of visits last three days or more.

THE LAW: Permits are required for all overnight trips in the Maze.

THE GIDDYUP: To reach the Maze, start by following the directions to the Y junction in the chapter introduction. Turn right (south) and drive for about 21 miles to the Hans Flat Ranger Station. Note the ranger station is at the boundary of the co-managed Orange Cliffs unit of Glen Canyon National Recreation Area, and it takes another three to six hours on rough 4x4 roads to reach the canyons of the Maze. THE SCENE OF THE CRIME: GPS 38.2552, −110.1798.

THE SUSPECTS: National Park Service, 435-719-2313 (for URL, see Resources).

THE LOOT: Inside the Maze District, one popular destination is the **Doll House**, with towering rock spires to explore that are similar to those at the Needles. The Doll House is reached by a series of rough 4x4 roads in about six or seven hours from Hans Flat. (Note: you can also reach the Doll House via a steep hiking trail from Spanish Bottom during Colorado River trips.) Another popular stop is the **Maze Overlook**, offering views into the heart of the district.

THE HARDSHIPS: Because of the challenges associated with this remote adventure, make sure to conduct your own research before attempting it (for starters, check out the National Park Service information; see

Resources). There are no services available in the Maze, so bring all the water, food, fuel, supplies, and equipment you need to stay safe. And, I'm sorry, did you ask about shade? Bring about fifty hats.

The San Rafael Swell

THE LOWDOWN: The San Rafael Swell is a roughly 3,000-square-mile region of entrenched canyons and uplifted rock formations located northwest of Robbers Roost. Geologically speaking, the Swell is an anticlinal dome. Its jagged eastern edge, colloquially called the San Rafael Reef, is visually comparable to the Water Pocket Fold (geologically, a monoclinal fold) in Capitol Reef National Park to the south. But unlike that relatively smaller and narrower national park, the Swell is about ten times larger. There's only one paved road passing through: I-70, which splits the Swell in half. With mostly dirt roads and rough 4x4 tracks, the Swell remains one of the most remote parts of the Colorado Plateau, and the challenges and precautions related to visitation are the same as for the three adventures above in Robbers Roost.

THE LOOT: During the Wild West era, the Swell was home to several camps regularly used by outlaws. Meanwhile, a few routes through it were part of the outlaw trail, with some leading onward to Robbers Roost.

THE ACTION: Today, there are a variety of hiking and biking trails, mostly unmaintained and without much if any signage, plus a few surprising paddling trips and some great camping opportunities, mostly primitive and dispersed.

THE HARDSHIPS: This place is riddled with the words *no* and *little*. As in, no water, no

services, no food, no fuel, little shade, and little to no cell coverage. Plan ahead and be prepared!

THE SUSPECTS: In 2019 the new San Rafael Swell Recreation Area was created, along with fourteen interwoven wilderness areas. The area continues to be managed by the Bureau of Land Management (see Resources).

X MARKS THE SPOT: National Geographic Trails Illustrated Topo Map #712, San Rafael Swell.

THE YARNS: The San Rafael Swell makes an appearance in two Wild Bunch Stories in this book: Episodes 3, On the Outlaw Trail, 1889; and 8, Into the Roost, 1897.

22

Little Grand Canyon

THE LOWDOWN: The most dramatic part of the northern San Rafael Swell is a 1,200-foot-deep gorge of colorful horizontal rock units. Coincidentally, its bottommost layer (Moenkopi Formation) is the same rock as the top layer of the real-deal Grand Canyon.

THE LOOT: Both the **Little Grand Canyon Overlook** and the **Wedge Overlook** have stunning views of the river winding through canyons surrounded by multilayered sandstone cliffs, buttes, domes, and spires. Adventures 22 and 23 can be combined for an excellent long day or a multiday camping trip.

THE ACTION: The mostly flat **Good Water Rim Trail** is popular among hikers and mountain bikers. It starts near the Wedge Overlook and heads 16 miles one-way along the rocky and sandy rim of Good Water Canyon, with amazing views into the Little Grand Canyon in many spots.

A pair of mountain bikers take a break on the Good Water Rim Trail.

THE GIDDYUP: There are several routes to the Little Grand Canyon, but the most common starts from I-70, about 28 miles west of Green River, Utah. Take exit 131, turn right onto unpaved Buckhorn Draw Road, and follow as it winds about 20 miles to Swinging Bridge over the San Rafael River. Continue through Buckhorn Wash (pictographs and hikes discussed in Adventure 23) for about 9.5 miles and turn left onto Green River Cutoff Road. After only a few hundred feet, take the next left onto the Wedge Cutoff Road and continue 1.5 miles. Take a left onto South Wedge Road and proceed about 4.5 miles to the clifftop Little Grand Canyon Overlook. **THE SCENE OF THE CRIME:** GPS 39.0930, −110.7588. To reach the Wedge Overlook, follow a dirt road that parallels the rim for about a half mile.

X MARKS THE SPOT: Maps for the Good Water Rim Trail can be found online (see Resources), but note that, at the time of this writing, the trail is not included in the National Geographic Trails Illustrated Topo Map #712 recommended in the San Rafael Swell intro above.

THE DIGS: A small campground is located near the Wedge, plus many primitive dispersed camping areas throughout the Swell. And did you say reservations? Ahem, sorry, pardner.

THE HARDSHIPS: When you're out here, you're really out there. Be fully self-sufficient when exploring the Swell.

RIDE ONWARD: Why just walk or bike the Little Grand Canyon when you can paddle it with a kayak, canoe, paddleboard, or small raft? The run is 17 miles of mellow class II with anything but mellow scenery. THE SCENE OF THE CRIME: Put-in is at Fullers Bottom (GPS 39.1174, –110.8539) and takeout is at Swinging Bridge (GPS 39.0809, –110.6671). THE SUSPECTS Bureau of Land Management (see Resources for a map and information about the Fullers Bottom put-in).

THE YARNS: The Little Grand Canyon appears in two Wild Bunch Stories, Episodes 3, On the Outlaw Trail, 1889; and 8, Into the Roost, 1897.

23

Buckhorn Wash

THE LOWDOWN: The dirt road through Buckhorn Wash (a.k.a. Buckhorn Draw) is one of the scenic highlights in the northern San Rafael Swell, with plenty of attractions along the way. Trails and routes go up pretty much every side canyon, while named and unnamed arches can be found lurking in unexpected places. Go looking, and you'll find more than enough to keep you occupied. In the Swell, all roads are unpaved and only periodically maintained, though they should be passable for most vehicles during normal conditions and weather. When wet, the clay-dirt roads quickly become impassable for most vehicles.

THE LOOT: A major highlight of this canyon is the **Buckhorn Wash Pictograph Panel**, about 4 miles north of Swinging Bridge. This impressive collection of Barrier Canyon Style and Fremont Culture pictographs was created an estimated 1,000 years ago.

THE ACTION: About 2 miles north of Swinging Bridge, on the east side of Buckhorn Wash, a popular trio of short hikes (about 1 to

3 miles one-way) can be found at **Calf, Cow, and Pine Canyons**. X MARKS THE SPOT: These trails and others are best found using the National Geographic Illustrated Topo Map #712, San Rafael Swell—but note the area has many trails not listed on maps.

THE DIGS: A small campground is at Swinging Bridge (small fee).

THE GIDDYUP: From Green River, Utah, take I-70 west for about 28 miles to exit 131. Turn right onto unpaved Buckhorn Draw Road and follow as it winds about 20 miles to Swinging Bridge over the San Rafael River. Continue 2 miles to the three canyons and short hikes mentioned above. Note, there is no trailhead, this is the Swell, just park somewhere and start wandering around until you get the hang of the place. Continue driving another 2 miles to the Buckhorn Wash Pictograph Panel.

THE HARDSHIPS: Prepare to be fully self-sufficient when exploring the Swell.

THE YARNS: Buckhorn Wash is the site of a haphazard shootout in Wild Bunch Stories, Episode 8, Into the Roost, 1897.

24

Goblin Valley State Park

THE LOWDOWN: Named by cowboys who stumbled across the thousands of squat, mushroom-shaped hoodoos eroded from Entrada Sandstone, Goblin Valley is located near the San Rafael Reef on the northwestern edge of Robbers Roost.

THE ACTION: One highlight is that visitors are allowed to scramble on top of the rock formations. For this reason, most visitors wander off-trail through the hoodoos from the main parking area at Goblin Overlook. It's a fun activity for kids and, no judgment, child-like adults. (Though, one time, an impulsive dad carrying his child up the hoodoos got cliffed-out and had to hand the kid down to me for safety—so maybe a little bit of judgment?)

Additionally, there are several short, marked hiking trails. One favorite near the park's eastern boundary is the **Goblin's Lair Trail**, a strenuous 1.5-mile one-way hike into a slot canyon that requires scrambling over boulders. The hike begins from the Goblin Overlook parking lot, starting with 0.5 mile on the **Carmel Canyon Loop**, a moderate and scenic alternative hike that passes through the heart of the hoodoos in 1.5 miles.

MORE ACTION: The park's **Wild Horse Mountain Biking Trail System** includes five short, intersecting loops that total 7 miles, starting from a trailhead near the campground.

THE GIDDYUP: From I-70, 10 miles west of Green River, take UT 24 south for about 24 miles. Turn right (west) onto Temple Mountain Road. In about 5 miles, turn left (south) onto the park road and reach Goblin Valley State Park in just under 7 miles.

THE SUSPECTS: Utah State Parks (see Resources).

THE TAKE: Day-use and camping fees.

THE DIGS: The park campground has tent and RV sites, a disc golf course, and hot showers, making it an excellent base for exploring the San Rafael Reef (Adventure 25). Available for reservation are two tent yurts, modeled after Mongolian *gers*, that have become semi-famous on Instagram—because, you know, the internet.

Opposite: Crack Canyon in the San Rafael Reef

25

San Rafael Reef

THE LOWDOWN: The highlight of the southeastern edge of the Swell, the San Rafael Reef is a 75-mile fold of sharply tilted Navajo and Wingate Sandstones. Visible for miles, this defining feature creates startling fins, peaks, domes, and deeply entrenched slot canyons perfect for exploring on foot. The hikes below range in difficulty and length, and can be made shorter and often easier by simply turning around early.

THE TICKING CLOCK: If you plan to get out of the car, maybe don't go in summer. Spring and fall are your best bet for hiking. Winter is cold but may work for those people who wear shorts during snow flurries. To approximate local weather, look up forecasts for Green River and Hanksville.

THE ACTION: Starting from spots along the unpaved Behind-the-Reef Road, a series of hiking routes plunge through the slot canyons that cut through the reef. Note these are not maintained trails like those found in a national park but hiking routes that became established over the years. Easier routes include **Wild Horse Creek**, about 4 miles one-way, and the stunning sandy-bottomed **Chute Canyon**, also about 4 miles one-way. The very impressive and more challenging **Crack Canyon**, up to 6 miles one-way, is like a nontechnical canyoneering route involving scrambling over rock jumbles and using short ropes (often left by past visitors, but no promises) to navigate past several short dry falls. THE SCENE OF THE CRIME: These hikes are found not far from the junction of Temple Mountain Road along Behind-the-Reef Road, which offers

a good point for orientation: GPS 38.6675, –110.6876.

THE HARDSHIPS: During normal weather conditions, most two-wheel-drive vehicles with normal to high clearance can navigate the challenging Behind-the-Reef Road, though some drivers may prefer having four-wheel drive. It's rough—drive slowly! ALSO: Don't expect much in the way of trailheads. With the new rec area designation, the situation is evolving, but part of the Swell's appeal is that it remains undeveloped. There may be a sign here or there, but it's just as likely there won't be one. Instead, study a topo map and monitor the reef topography for the head of each canyon. Then watch for signs of other visitors, like tire tracks leading down short spur roads to the most basic of parking areas.

THE GIDDYUP: From UT 24, about 24 miles south of I-70, turn west onto Temple Mountain Road. Continue 7 miles (past the turnoff south to Goblin Valley State Park) to the junction with Behind-the-Reef Road. From the junction, Wild Horse Canyon is around mile 1.5, Crack Canyon is around mile 4, and Chute Canyon is around mile 6.25. Beyond that, the Behind-the-Reef Road becomes more of a double-track trail, best suited for ATVs.

MORE ACTION: On the south side of the reef, a longer loop hike of around 10 miles combines **Little Wild Horse Canyon** and **Bell Canyon Trails**. **THE GIDDYUP:** Follow the directions above to Temple Mountain Road, but after 5 miles turn left onto the road to Goblin Valley State Park. After about 6 miles, but before entering the park, turn right (west) onto unpaved Wild Horse Road and continue about 5.5 miles to the trailhead for the Little Wild Horse–Bell Loop. **THE SCENE OF THE CRIME:** GPS 38.5834, –110.8028.

X MARKS THE SPOT: Don't expect a lot of city luxuries like trail signs, so bring a map! A topo map like the National Geographic Trails Illustrated Topo Map #712, San Rafael Swell is strongly recommended. The Bureau of Land Management has a good PDF map to download of the Temple Mountain Recreation Area, which includes the reef (see Resources). Or you can try the guidebook *Hiking and Exploring Utah's San Rafael Swell* by Michael Kelsey.

THE DIGS: A primitive campground is near the Temple Mountain junction, and many primitive camping areas can be found throughout the Swell.

RIDE ONWARD: Mountain biking and bike-packing are increasingly popular throughout the San Rafael Swell. But given the risks from sun exposure, dehydration, and remoteness, you'll need to do your own research about the trails, roads, and routes. However, if you feel comfortable with riding in the desert, definitely check it out.

THE YARNS: The San Rafael Reef appears in Wild Bunch Stories, Episode 8, Into the Roost, 1897.

26

Capitol Reef National Park

THE LOWDOWN: Capitol Reef National Park protects the startling Waterpocket Fold, a geologic monocline, or fold of sedimentary rocks, that extends roughly north-to-south for 100 miles. The park is located south of the San Rafael Reef, which offers similar landscapes but is geologically different, being the jagged edge of an anticline, or dome, of warped rocks.

While there isn't evidence of much outlaw activity in the park, local lore suggests that outlaws did pass through. The main activities are driving tours on paved and unpaved park roads and hiking the many trails.

THE LOOT: Old West enthusiasts will want to check out the **Fruita Historic District**, which preserves several sites, including a frontier homestead, a schoolhouse, Fremont Culture petroglyphs, and more. Heading south from the visitor center, the park's **Scenic Drive** is a 7.9-mile paved road winding behind the Waterpocket Fold. Along the way, two dirt spur roads lead to the Grand Wash and Capitol Gorge trailheads. The park service recommends spending about 1.5 hours to drive this route (for a guide to Scenic Drive, see Resources).

THE ACTION: Though Butch Cassidy has no direct connection to the rock feature bearing his name, **Cassidy Arch** is still an impressive site. Several routes of varying length and difficulty lead to the arch, so review the park website's hiking guide and map to decide which is right for you. A shorter and easier option is the 1.7-mile one-way cliff-top **Cassidy Arch Trail**, making for a 3.5-mile round-trip.

An excellent but longer option combines the **Grand Wash Trail** with the **Cassidy Arch Trail** for an 8-mile out-and-back. From the Grand Wash trailhead, hike about 2 miles west through Grand Wash's impressive narrows, then look for the Cassidy Trail junction on the right and follow it about 1.7 miles (with 670 feet of elevation gain) to the arch.

THE GIDDYUP: From Hanksville, take UT 24 west for about 37 miles to the visitor center at Fruita. For the Cassidy Arch trailhead, from the visitor center head south on the park's Scenic Drive for about 3.5 miles, then turn left onto unpaved but graded Grand Wash Road and reach the trailhead in less than 1.5 miles. For the Grand Wash trailhead, from the visitor center head east on UT 24 for 4.5 miles.

THE SUSPECTS: National Park Service, nps .gov/care.

X MARKS THE SPOT: National Geographic Trails Illustrated Topo Map #267, Capitol Reef.

THE DIGS: The large Fruita Campground has more than seventy sites, which are fully reservable from roughly spring through fall.

RIDE ONWARD: A number of unpaved driving tours are possible inside the park (see Resources). Adventurous explorers may want to visit the **South (Waterpocket) District** using the Notom-Bullfrog and Burr Trail Roads. Both of these roads are typically suitable for two-wheel-drive vehicles during normal conditions. Visiting the North District and **Cathedral Valley** requires a four-wheel-drive vehicle for the rough Hartnet Road.

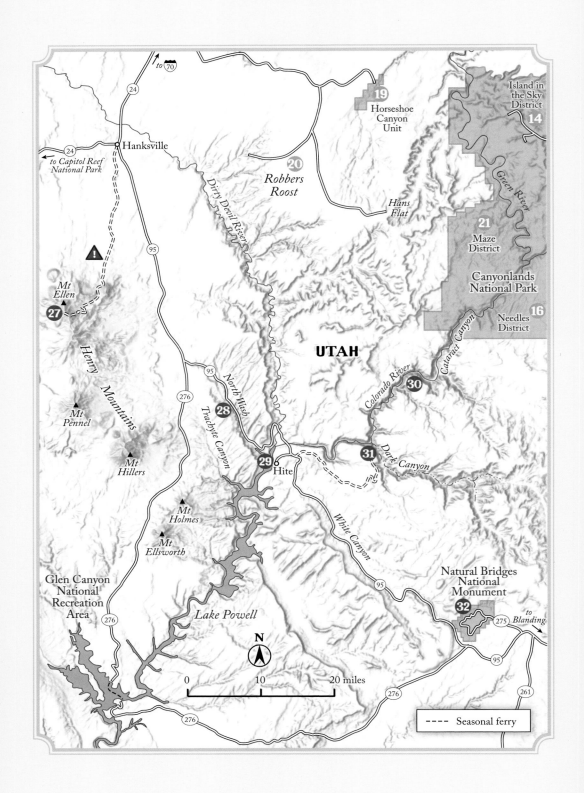

to 70

24

19 Horseshoe Canyon Unit

Island in the Sky District

14

Hanksville

24

to Capitol Reef National Park

20 Robbers Roost

Hans Flat

Green River

95

Dirty Devil River

UTAH

21 Maze District

Canyonlands National Park

27

Mt Ellen

Herry Mountains

95

North Wash

28

Trachyte Canyon

Colorado River

30

Cataract Canyon

Needles District

16

Mt Pennel

Mt Hillers

29 Hite

31 Dark Canyon

276

Mt Holmes

Mt Ellsworth

White Canyon

95

Natural Bridges National Monument

Glen Canyon National Recreation Area

Lake Powell

32

275

to Blanding

276

N

95

0   10   20 miles

276

261

- - - - Seasonal ferry

CHAPTER 4

Henry Mountains and North Lake Powell

SOUTHERN UTAH

THE WHOLE KIT AND CABOODLE: Like an afterthought to the better-known La Sal Mountains and southern Lake Powell, the Henry Mountains and northern Lake Powell are a nearly forgotten corner of southern Utah. Glen Canyon National Recreation Area extends from the western edge of Canyonlands National Park to just beyond the Arizona state line, and the NRA borders the southern tip of Capitol Reef National Park.

Here you won't find a lot of highfalutin things like services, visitor centers, or smooth roadways. What you will find is a rugged, less-visited region perfect for making your own discoveries. A place where outlaws once hid now hides endless adventure potential. Mount up your posse and bring plenty of water.

THE SNORT: Which way to the saloon? More like, which way to a supermarket? There's a small grocery in Hanksville, along with some restaurants, motels, gas stations, and convenience stores—one of which is built into a cliff. Note that in 2022, the store, gas station,

and facilities at Hite Marina were closed after the concessionaire stopped operating (though they may reopen with a new concessionaire in the future).

THE YARNS: The Henry Mountains appear in several Wild Bunch Stories in this book, including Episode 8, Into the Roost, 1897.

27

Mount Ellen Summit Hike

THE LOWDOWN: The last mountain range to be mapped and named by white Americans in the United States, the Henry Mountains rise just across the Dirty Devil River from Robbers Roost. From Mount Ellen southwest of Hanksville to Mount Holmes and Mount Ellsworth near Glen Canyon, this remote area offers some excellent 4x4 exploration, a few stunning viewpoints, several worthy hikes, frequent mentions in outlaw lore—and it's visited by about thirty-eight people a year, feels like.

THE ACTION: A popular hike is the gradual, 2-mile one-way, 1,000-foot ascent to the summit of **Mount Ellen** at 11,522 feet. From the top, you'll have a remarkable view down on Robbers Roost, the San Rafael Swell, and the Capitol Reef region. While the hike is basically a walk up to the summit, this is high-altitude adventuring, and you'll want to be in good physical condition and, ideally, acclimated to higher elevations.

THE HARDSHIPS: Winds can be wild atop Mount Ellen. If you find yourself leaning at an angle into the gusts at the trailhead, it may not be the day for summiting. If weather—particularly rain, hail, or snow develops—bail out to lower elevations. Don't push this one. Flee like an outlaw and return another day.

THE GIDDYUP: The road to the trailhead is 98 percent unpaved, quite rough, and steep in places, requiring a high-clearance vehicle during normal weather conditions, with four-wheel drive or all-wheel drive recommended. From UT 24 in Hanksville, start from the west side of town. Head south on East 100 North Street/Sawmill Basin Road for about 23 miles—into the mountains, across an unbridged creek bed, and through Lonesome Beaver Campground. At Wickiup Pass—there should be a sign, but why promise such things?—turn right (south) onto BLM-14635 and follow this road for about 2.75 miles. At Bull Creek Pass, there's a small parking area

The trailhead for the summit hike up Mount Ellen

next to the Mount Ellen trailhead, with the summit rising to the north. **THE SCENE OF THE CRIME**: GPS 38.0858, −110.8024.

THE SUSPECTS: Bureau of Land Management, blm.gov/visit/henry-mountains.

X MARKS THE SPOT: There's no National Geographic map, but BLM produces a topo map PDF that can be downloaded from the website above.

THE DIGS: The small Lonesome Beaver Campground has some sites, with plenty more dispersed camping options available throughout the Henrys.

RIDE ONWARD: There's more to explore in the Henrys, including Mounts Pennel and Hillers, which are also called the Little Rocky Mountains.

THE YARNS: About 15 miles south of Hanksville on Sawmill Basin Road is the turnoff (to the east) for Granite Road, so named for the infamous Granite Ranch, known for harboring plenty of outlaws. The ranch is also the location of *Blue John in Relief*, a temporary statue briefly installed by Deputy Marshal Bush; see Wild Bunch Stories, Episodes 8, Into the Roost, 1897; and 15, The Battle at Roost Canyon, 1899.

28

North Wash

🚗 👣 🚲

THE LOWDOWN: A highlight of driving the 48 paved miles of UT 95 between Hanksville and Hite Crossing is the scenery surrounding North Wash. The Henry Mountains loom to the west. To the east are a series of lesser-known slot canyons marking the edge of Robbers Roost. Though some of these side canyons are easy to walk up, exploring the

tighter and more remote slot canyons should be done only by those folks with solid back-country navigation skills.

THE ACTION: At **Hog Springs Recreation Area,** an easy 1-mile one-way trail passes through a brushy narrows to a small waterfall and pool. This is probably North Wash's only "official" trail, but there's much more to discover. **THE GIDDYUP**: Drive UT 95 south of Hanksville for 34 miles to the small picnic area and the trailhead. **THE SCENE OF THE CRIME**: GPS 37.9628, −110.4913.

X MARKS THE SPOT: Other than standard USGS topo maps, your best bet for exploring North Wash is the 2009 guidebook *Hiking and Exploring Utah's Henry Mountains and Robbers Roost* by Michael Kelsey.

THE TICKING CLOCK: Hiking in North Wash is a spring or fall kind of thing, with summer months being way too hot. Winters are mild.

THE HARDSHIPS: Everyone—road trippers, hikers, and cyclists—needs to carry ample water during a trip into North Wash. The closest resupplies (other than treating spring or creek water) are located in Hanksville or Blanding. For warnings and tips related to slot-canyon hiking, check out Ask an Outlaw (FAQ) in the How to Use This Book chapter in Part 1.

MORE ACTION: While most travelers drive through North Wash, UT 95 is also popular with **road cyclists** for out-and-back day trips or self-supported or van-supported multi-day tours, sometimes starting and ending in Moab.

RIDE ONWARD: Running nearly parallel to the south of lower North Wash is another side canyon of the Colorado River, called Trachyte Canyon. Today, it is occasionally hiked or backpacked, though there is no "official" trail, meaning backcountry navigation skills are essential. **THE GIDDYUP**: Trachyte

Canyon—including the main wash and side canyons—can be accessed via UT 276, but you'll need to do your own research to plan your entry, route, and exit.

THE YARNS: North Wash was a common route for travelers and outlaws heading to and from Hite Ferry at Dandy Crossing near the old town of White Canyon on the Colorado River. As in, they'd take the route just north of Trachyte Canyon—a.k.a. North Wash. (These days, Hite marks the northern extent of Lake Powell, though with the droughts in recent years, there's often current moving through here.) See Wild Bunch Stories, Episode 10, A Seemingly Normal Cowboy Named Jim Lowe, 1899.

29

Hite Marina

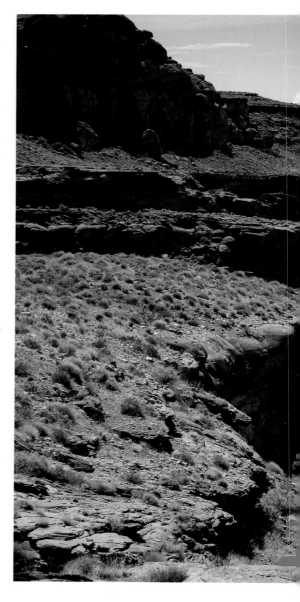

THE LOWDOWN: This remote ranger station and former marina rests at the northern end of Lake Powell in the Glen Canyon National Recreation Area. The area has excellent adventure potential, but very few visitors actually stop, with most passing through on driving tours between other points of interest, like Capitol Reef National Park (Adventure 26) and Natural Bridges National Monument (Adventure 32). Unfortunately, in 2022 the Hite store, campground, and adventure outpost shut down, and the park service is currently seeking a new concessionaire. I've left this adventure in this book in hopes that by publication time, the situation will have improved. Check with the park service for updates.

THE ACTION: The original Hite Marina, built in anticipation of a full reservoir, sits high and dry a quarter mile up from the currently less-than-half-full "Lake" Powell—in recent years, the reservoir has once again resumed flowing, albeit slowly through silty lake sediments, as the Colorado River. There had been discussions about extending a boat ramp for paddlers that reaches the lower water level

A cyclist rides UT 95 through North Wash

of recent years, at one time scheduled to be completed in 2021; in reality, a new ramp may not happen. Instead, it's mostly rafters who come through, taking out from Cataract Canyon whitewater trips (Adventure 30) at the dirt North Wash boat ramp across the river from Hite.

THE GIDDYUP: Hite Marina is just off UT 95 near the Hite Crossing Bridge, about 49 miles south of Hanksville and 73 miles west of US 191.

THE SUSPECTS: National Park Service, nps.gov/glca.

THE DIGS: Given the major overhaul at **Hite Marina Campground** in recent years, it seems likely that it will eventually reopen. It has bathrooms with flush toilets and showers—amenities otherwise unseen for miles in all directions. The campsites have fire rings and picnic tables, but campers must provide their own shade.

THE SNORT: They never sold beer or whiskey at the Hite store, but gather 'round, young-uns, and hear how they once sold snacks, maps, books, sunscreen, and even gas.

THE YARNS: See Wild Bunch Stories, Episodes 10, A Seemingly Normal Cowboy Named Jim Lowe, 1899; and 15, The Battle at Roost Canyon, 1899.

30

Cataract Canyon River Trip

THE LOWDOWN: Cataract Canyon on the Colorado River is one of the most remote rafting adventures in the Lower 48. This trip involves a mix of mellow floating, memorable side hikes, and some exhilarating whitewater. Most trips start near Moab, pass through Canyonlands National Park, and end at northern Lake Powell (Adventures 12, 14, 16, and 29, respectively).

THE ACTION: From Potash boat ramp to Spanish Bottom, the trip begins as an idyllic class I–II float for 50 miles, with the lower 31 miles passing through Canyonlands National Park. Next comes 15 miles of intense whitewater, including several of the biggest rapids in the US—Big Drops I, II, and III, with the last also called Satan's Gut—regularly run by commercial groups. The final 30 miles involve a very slow float, or rowing, or motoring out between crumbly banks of reservoir-deposited sediments through Narrow Canyon, with the trip ending at the North Wash boat ramp. Along the way, side canyon explorations lead to hidden waterfalls and dramatic rock formations, including the Doll House in the Maze District of Canyonlands.

Commercial guests typically fly from take-out to put-in, while most private groups drive a vehicle shuttle (five and a half to seven hours roundtrip, depending on the route). For more information about running your own DIY private trip (experienced whitewater boaters only) in Cataract Canyon, please check out my book *Paddling the John Wesley Powell Route*.

THE HARDSHIPS: I don't even know where to start for this one. Does it help to know that the confluence was one of the last spots to be properly mapped in the United States? Bring two of everything, including raft guides.

THE SUSPECTS: Canyonlands National Park manages the Colorado River for the majority of this trip: nps.gov/cany.

THE LAW: A permit (and fee) is required for all private boating groups. For information on permits and regulations and a list of commercial outfitters, see Resources.

THE SCENE OF THE CRIME: Most trips begin at Potash boat ramp (Adventure 14) and end at the North Wash boat ramp off UT 95; GPS 37.8883, −110.4007.

X MARKS THE SPOT: A good topo map is National Geographic Trails Illustrated Topo Map #210, Canyonlands National Park. There are also two waterproof river maps: Belknap's Waterproof Canyonlands River Guide All New Edition by Buzz Belknap and RiverMaps Colorado and Green Rivers in the Canyonlands by Tom Martin.

As viewed from "Poop Rock," which means exactly what you think it might, a raft group navigates the intimidating Big Drop rapids in Cataract Canyon on the Colorado River.

THE YARNS: Cataract Canyon makes quite an appearance in chapter 10 of Pearl Baker's book *The Wild Bunch at Robbers Roost*. In this book, see Wild Bunch Stories, Episode 15, The Battle at Roost Canyon, 1899, in which Blue John Griffith hikes to Spanish Bottom at the head of Cataract Canyon.

31

Sundance Trail, Dark Canyon

THE LOWDOWN: Dark Canyon is a deep and rugged tributary drainage of the Colorado River through Narrow Canyon. Part of Dark Canyon is a Bureau of Land Management primitive area and part of the canyon is a Manti–La Sal Forest Service wilderness area. There are only a few trails into Dark Canyon, with the Sundance Trail (4.5 miles, one-way) considered one of the "easier" access routes. That said, calling the Sundance Trail easy is wildly inaccurate . . .

THE ACTION: The crux of this hike comes midway, where the **Sundance Trail** descends 1,000 feet in 0.3 mile down a 30- to 45-degree landslide to reach the canyon floor. On the landslide descent, be careful careful careful. Go slow and pick your steps and handholds like you're a hard-to-please wine connoisseur in Napa. While you could hike in and out of Dark Canyon in a long day, a better choice is to backpack down and stay for at least three days and two nights, which allows a full day to explore the bottom of lower Dark Canyon, where the creek tumbles over many instream waterfalls. Once on the canyon floor, you can hike downstream to the Colorado River in about 3.5 miles one-way, while other hikes go upcanyon and into side canyons.

THE HARDSHIPS: How long do you have? This is desert wilderness adventure at its best. Make sure to carry enough water for the descent and ascent. Given the daily shade at the canyon bottom, there is typically flowing water in the Dark Canyon creek.

THE SUSPECTS: Dark Canyon is jointly managed by the Forest Service and BLM. For a downloadable USFS trail guide, see Resources. Current conditions for the Sundance Trail can be obtained from the BLM field office in Monticello, Utah, 435-587-1500. For more information, see Resources for the website.

THE GIDDYUP: From UT 95 at Hite Marina, head south on the highway and in 0.25 mile veer left (east) onto a dirt county road. Head roughly southeast for around 7.5 miles (on Google Maps the road numbers are 2081 and 256) before turning northeast, always keeping an eye out for occasional trailhead signs, until a final left (northeast) turn onto the trailhead road. These roads are minimally maintained and conditions may change due to weather, but the route is normally passable for confident drivers in two-wheel-drive vehicles with normal to high clearance, though some drivers will prefer having four-wheel drive. Look, it's basically an adventure just getting there, but study maps and a satellite view beforehand and you'll find it. THE SCENE OF THE CRIME: The trailhead has a luxurious sand and rock parking lot at GPS 37.8477, −110.1911.

X MARKS THE SPOT: National Geographic Trails Illustrated Topo Map #703, Manti–La Sal National Forest.

RIDE ONWARD: Another option is to thru-hike the Dark Canyon Wilderness, with most backpackers starting at one of several trailheads to the east inside Manti–La Sal National Forest, heading downcanyon, and exiting via the Sundance Trail. Or if you enjoy prolonged foot pain, why not tackle the 800-mile Hayduke Trail from Arches to Zion? (Find info—a.k.a. survivor tales—online.)

THE YARNS: Though the Sundance Trail shares a name with the Wild Bunch's beloved Kid, there is no evidence confirming such an outlaw connection. That said, legends do suggest that the remote canyon was used to hide stolen livestock.

The steep landslide descent into Dark Canyon on the Sundance Trail

32

Natural Bridges National Monument

THE LOWDOWN: In 1883 ferry operator Cass Hite searched White Canyon for gold and instead found three stunning natural bridges carved by White Canyon Creek, which became Utah's first national monument, in 1908. Today, the bridges are known by Hopi names Sipapu, Kachina, and Owachomo. This small national monument, which also protects ancestral rock art and ruins, could be fully explored in one long day.

THE ACTION: Each natural bridge can be viewed from above with easy walks to lookouts off the monument's loop road or visited at ground level with short but steep hikes. Another option is to hike the 10-mile full loop trail, which traverses the mesa top and White Canyon while visiting all three natural bridges.

THE GIDDYUP: From UT 95, about 44 miles east of Hite Crossing and 30 miles west of US 191, turn north onto UT 275 and continue about 4 miles into the monument.

THE SUSPECTS: National Park Service, nps.gov/nabr.

X MARKS THE SPOT: At the visitor center pick up the park brochure (with a map) and hiking guide (also downloadable from the park service website above).

THE DIGS: The monument has a small campground with about a dozen sites, all first come, first served.

RIDE ONWARD: Heading west from the monument, the 30 miles along UT 95 makes for an excellent road trip across Cedar Mesa and through Bear Ears National Monument. Bears Ears offers some of the best Ancestral Puebloan ruins in the region. But that's a whole 'nother place to explore, requiring your own research.

THE YARNS: White Canyon was a major east-west route for prospectors, cowboys, and outlaws traveling between southeastern Utah and southwestern Colorado. Sometimes these travelers followed White Canyon from above, and other times they descended into it. Pinkerton detective Charlie Siringo tracks a pair of suspected outlaws down North Wash and along White Canyon in Wild Bunch Stories, Episode 10, A Seemingly Normal Cowboy Named Jim Lowe, 1899.

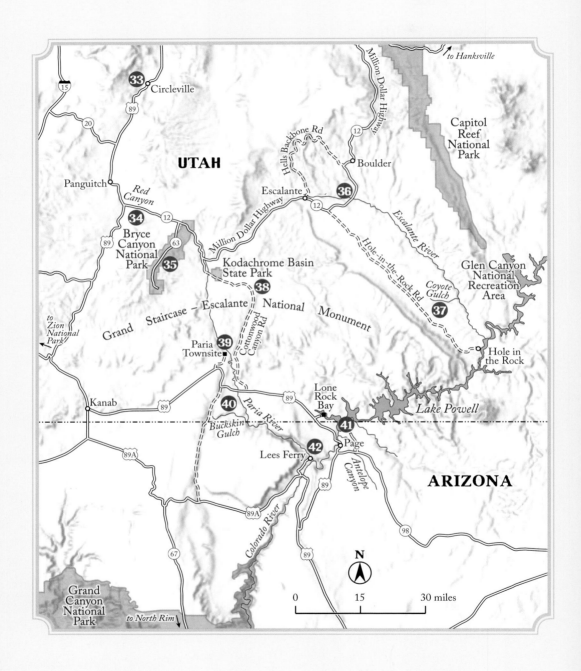

to Hanksville

15

③③ Circleville

89

20

Capitol
Reef
National
Park

Million Dollar Highway

12

UTAH

Hells Backbone Rd

Boulder

Panguitch

Red
Canyon

Escalante

③⑥

12

Million Dollar Highway

Escalante River

③④

12

Hole-in-the-Rock Rd

89

63

Bryce
Canyon
National
Park

③⑤

Kodachrome Basin
State Park

Coyote
Gulch

Glen Canyon
National
Recreation
Area

③⑧

to
Zion
National
Park!

Grand Staircase – Escalante National Monument

③⑦

Cottonwood Canyon Rd

Paria ③⑨
Townsite

Hole in
the Rock

Kanab

89

③⑨ 40

Paria River

89

Lone
Rock
Bay

Lake Powell

Buckskin
Gulch

④①

89A

Lees Ferry ④②

Page

Antelope Canyon

ARIZONA

89A

Colorado River

89

67

98

N

Grand
Canyon
National
Park

to North Rim

0   15   30 miles

CHAPTER 5
Grand Staircase and South Lake Powell
SOUTHWESTERN UTAH– NORTHERN ARIZONA

THE WHOLE KIT AND CABOODLE: A massive series of sedimentary rock layers, the Grand Staircase stretches across 100 miles of dramatic landscapes in southwestern Utah. From top to bottom, the staircase starts with plateaus like the Paunsaugunt and Aquarius, where you'll find Butch Cassidy's boyhood home. Next, the staircase descends through the hoodoos of Bryce Canyon National Park, the dizzying canyons of Grand Staircase–Escalante National Monument, the sunken slots around the Paria River Canyon, and the sheer cliffs of Lake Powell in Glen Canyon National Recreation Area. The final hurrah is a precipitous drop into Arizona's Grand Canyon southwest of Lees Ferry. Today the Grand Staircase remains a remote area with few paved roads but plenty of trails to explore.

33
Butch Cassidy's Boyhood Home

THE LOWDOWN: A highlight for outlaw enthusiasts, the childhood home of Robert Leroy Parker is now a historic homestead near the little town of Circleville in southwest Utah.

THE LOOT: Information stations throughout the site describe the remaining historic structures. Visitors can enter the cabin where Butch Cassidy grew up. There's also a small shed, where Cassidy presumably did chores. A newfangled vault toilet replaces the long-gone outhouse, where Cassidy presumably—OK, moving on.

THE TAKE: Maybe pay your respects by guarding your valuables? Otherwise, this site is free.

THE SCENE OF THE CRIME: The site is on the north side of US 89, about 3 miles southwest of Circleville. You can't miss it.

THE TICKING CLOCK: Open daily during daylight hours.

THE SUSPECTS: Website? Outlaws don't have websites.

THE YARNS: The family spread makes an appearance in two Wild Bunch Stories in this book: Episodes 2, The Beginnings of Bob Parker, 1886–1889; and 17, Phantoms of the Outlaw Trail, 1922 . . . .

34

Red Canyon and Thunder Mountain Trail

THE LOWDOWN: Red Canyon is a national forest recreation area west of Bryce Canyon, offering similar hoodoo scenery and outdoor activities but seeing fewer visitors. The many trails passing through dramatic rock formations and rolling canyon terrain are open to hiking, mountain biking, and horseback riding. Several off-highway vehicle (OHV) trails see mostly ATVs and some mountain bikes. Add it all together, and there are plenty of adventures to find here.

THE LOOT: Starting from US 89, 7 miles south of Panguitch, **Scenic Byway 12** runs east through Red Canyon for about 14 miles to UT 63, the turnoff for Bryce Canyon National Park (Adventure 35), then continues another 111 miles along the northern edge of Grand Staircase–Escalante National Monument (providing access to, from west to east,

Adventures 38, 36, and 37) and ends at Torrey, near Capitol Reef National Park (Adventure 26). The Red Canyon Visitor Center, on UT 12 at 3.5 miles east of US 89, offers drinking water, information, and a trail map.

THE ACTION: The many trails through Red Canyon hoodoos on the north side of UT 12 are remarkably scenic and perfect for a full day of hiking or mountain biking. The **Cassidy Trail**, named for Butch, starts from the Red Canyon trailhead and extends 9 miles one-way. Along the way, it intersects several other worthy trails that can be used to make loops of various lengths. For a shorter 5-mile option, after about 2.5 miles on the Cassidy Trail, turn left (west) onto the **Rich Trail** to return via a figure-eight loop.

For strong hikers or mountain bikers, a longer 12-mile loop can be made by following the Cassidy Trail for about 4.5 miles and turning left (west) onto the impressive **Losee Canyon Trail**. After about 3 miles, turn left (south) onto the Casto–Losee Canyon Road and follow it for 2 miles to UT 12. Turn left (east) onto one of the social trails that have been trodden on either side of the highway for about 0.75 mile, past the lower Thunder Mountain trailhead, and onto the paved Red Canyon Bicycle Trail (see below). In about 1.75 miles you'll return to the starting trailhead. Of course, you could make an epic MTB loop by tacking on the Thunder Mountain trail . . .

MORE ACTION: The 7-mile **Thunder Mountain Trail** on the south side of UT 12 is considered by some to be one of the most scenic mountain bike rides in all of Utah, winding beneath stacks of hoodoos, through canyons, and across ridges. The suggested downhill direction is from southeast to northwest, with a final mile on the Grandview Trail. Thunder Mountain can be ridden as a 15-mile

Mountain biking the mixed-use trails through Red Canyon

loop by adding the paved shared-use 18-mile Red Canyon Bicycle Trail and Coyote Hollow Road (FR 113).

EVEN MORE ACTION (YOU'RE INSATIABLE!): The dedicated and paved **Red Canyon Bicycle Trail**—popular for road cycling, running, and walking—mostly parallels UT 12 and UT 63 from the lower Thunder Mountain trailhead near the Red Canyon Visitor Center to Inspiration Point inside Bryce Canyon National Park (see Resources).

MORE LOOT: To this day, locals claim there are ruins of an outlaw cabin where Butch hid at the top of Casto Canyon (see **THE YARNS**), near where the Cassidy Trail joins the **Casto Canyon Trail**. Sure enough, ruins of a cabin can be found there. This would make for an almost 10-mile hike one-way, so it may be more realistic to mountain-bike there.

THE HARDSHIPS: These fun trails are at high elevation, with lots of sun, so it's easy to overdo it—especially when mountain biking. Make sure you're in good shape, acclimated, and realistic about how many miles you can go in a day.

THE GIDDYUP: On UT 12, with approximate distances from US 89, the lower Thunder Mountain trailhead is on the right at mile 2.75 and the Red Canyon trailhead is on the left at mile 4.5. To reach the upper Thunder Mountain trailhead, at mile 7.5 turn right (south) onto Coyote Hollow Road (FR 113) and follow it for about 2 miles.

THE SUSPECTS: Powell Ranger District of Dixie National Forest, fs.usda.gov/main/dixie/home.

X MARKS THE SPOT: Besides the visitor center trail map, check out National Geographic

Trails Illustrated Topo Map #705, Mount Dutton, Aquarius Plateau.

THE DIGS: The **Red Canyon Campground** is a popular spot just off UT 12, with almost forty first-come, first-serve sites, flush toilets, and showers.

THE SNORT: Restaurants, motels, supplies, and even a few bars can be found along UT 12 between Panguitch and Bryce.

THE YARNS: Local lore claims that in his teenage years, before leaving Circleville and assuming the name Butch Cassidy, Robert Leroy Parker got into a fistfight over a girl in nearby Panguitch. Thinking he had killed the unconscious young rival, Parker fled to Red Canyon and hid out. Meanwhile, the bruised but breathing suitor awoke and raised a posse to chase Parker through the canyons. This all makes for great material, but the story is likely apocryphal, given that it doesn't appear in any of the detailed biographies about Butch's life. It also seems unlikely that, in the era of countless robberies and murders, a posse would be raised over a fistfight. Still, it's entirely possible that some outlaws, maybe Mike Cassidy and possibly Butch, did use the confusing paths through remote Red Canyon to discreetly travel west across the Paunsaugunt Plateau when moving stolen livestock. Learn about these early days in Wild Bunch Stories, Episode 2, The Beginnings of Bob Parker, 1866–1889.

35

Bryce Canyon National Park

THE LOWDOWN: Bryce Canyon is a relatively small national park that contains the world's highest density of hoodoos, a.k.a. rock towers. Given the park's unique offerings, its 56 square miles regularly make many visitors' list of favorite national parks.

THE ACTION: Hiking through hoodoos is what it's all about here, with most foot traffic occurring between viewpoints along the scenic **Rim Trail**, which extends 5.5 miles above Bryce Amphitheater. Most people access the Rim Trail from parking lots near the Bryce Canyon Lodge or at Sunset Point.

Other visitors enjoy hiking the short, steep trails that lead down inside the stunning Bryce Amphitheater. One excellent choice is the 1.5-mile **Navajo Loop,** with 500 feet of elevation change, which starts from Sunset Point and leads through famous Wall Street.

A longer 3-mile loop into Bryce Amphitheater starts from Sunrise Point on the **Queens Garden Trail**, which takes 1.8 miles one-way to connect to the bottom of the Navajo Loop. To see Wall Street, take the southern (climber's left) side of the loop up to Sunset Point and turn right on the Rim Trail to return to Sunrise Point.

MORE ACTION: The park's longer hikes are less crowded, offering a more outlaw-country feel. One option (day-hiking only) is the **Fairyland Loop**, a strenuous 8-mile trail with 2,300 feet of elevation gain that starts from Fairyland Point and passes through a fascinating landscape. Elsewhere in the park, you'll find the 8.8-mile **Riggs Spring Loop** and the 23-mile **Under-the-Rim Trail**—both open for backpacking trips. THE LAW: Permit required for backcountry camping.

THE JIG: With the rim ranging in elevation from 7,500 to 9,100 feet, the temps are typically milder here than at other Utah national parks. A good place to cool off when the lower-elevation destinations over-heat.

THE HARDSHIPS: Despite this park's milder temps due to higher elevation, the sun can be intense here during summer. Hikers should take sun protection and plenty of water. Oh, and watch out for tour buses.

THE LOOT: Most visitors take the shuttle bus or drive the 18 miles on scenic UT 63 south through the park to **Rainbow Point**. Along the way are many pullouts with vistas down into the stone amphitheaters.

THE TICKING CLOCK: Bryce can be extremely busy from roughly March through October. Visitation peaks during the summer months when every hoodoo seems to be surrounded by five gawkers. For a calmer experience, aim to visit from November to February when there's a chance of beautiful snowy landscapes after storms.

THE SUSPECTS: National Park Service, 801-834-5322; nps.gov/brca.

THE GIDDYUP: From US 89 south of Panguitch, turn east onto UT 12 and drive 17 miles. At the junction with UT 63, turn right (south) into the park entrance.

X MARKS THE SPOT: National Geographic Trails Illustrated Topo Maps #219, Bryce Canyon National Park, or #714, Grand Staircase, Paunsaugunt Plateau.

THE DIGS: The park offers several popular campgrounds for tents and RVs. Just outside the park entrance, there are hotels, restaurants, and stores.

RIDE ONWARD: Road cycling is popular on the 15 miles of UT 63 from Inspiration Point to Rainbow Point, which makes for an excellent 30-mile out-and-back road ride with 1,600 feet of climbing. For a longer distance, some continue onto the 18-mile (one-way) Red Canyon Bicycle Trail (Adventure 34).

THE YARNS: Bryce Canyon, in a way, is where the whole Wild Bunch saga began. Butch's mentor Mike Cassidy hid stolen livestock in the breaks, or hoodoos, around the Bryce Amphitheater. The park of today doesn't offer much interpretation about the Wild West, but scant mentions in my research point to the area being an occasional setting for outlaw exploits. Bryce Canyon makes an appearance in Wild Bunch Stories, Episode 2, The Beginnings of Bob Parker, 1866–1889.

Grand Staircase–Escalante National Monument

THE WHOLE KIT AND CABOODLE: Grand Staircase–Escalante National Monument (GSENM) is such a massive piece of protected public land that it would be impossible to include more than a few brief highlights here. At the time of this writing, it was 1,568 square miles—after a controversial 47 percent reduction by the Trump administration in 2017. So what's an outlaw adventurer to do?

During the Old West, the area was so remote and rugged, with such a small population and little cash to grab, that it doesn't seem to have had much historical outlaw activity. For the most part, wanderers came here on their way to other places. When they did pass through, most history books point to it being mostly along the western side of the monument around Kanab, Cottonwood Canyon, and the Paria River. That said, if you're interested in exploring GSENM on the way to or from other outlaw-relevant sites, there are several scenic driving routes to consider, with many hiking side trips possible along the way.

THE HARDSHIPS: These adventures and roads—even the paved ones—are really out there. Self-sufficiency fully applies. Bring extra everything: water, food, maybe even two maps.

THE SUSPECTS: It's the Bureau of Land Management, and they're up to their usual tricks (see Resources)

THE YARNS: In Wild Bunch Stories, Episode 15, The Battle at Roost Canyon, 1899, the outlaw Silver Tip travels through the Grand Staircase.

36

Million Dollar Highway and Calf Creek

THE LOWDOWN: West of Red and Bryce Canyons, the stunning canyons of the Escalante River area have a pair of routes worth exploring. One is the paved Million Dollar Highway—part of scenic UT 12— suitable for all vehicles but not for the faint of heart (the other is described in Adventure 37).

THE GIDDYUP: Scenic Byway 12 runs for 124 miles from just west of Red Canyon (Adventure 34), past Bryce Canyon (Adventure 35), and along the northern edge of GSENM to Torrey, near Capitol Reef National Park (Adventure 26). Driving the byway takes about two and a half hours— slightly longer than two routes to the north but definitely worth it. From Escalante, at roughly the midpoint on UT 12, drive east 15 miles to reach Calf Creek.

THE LOOT: The section of UT 12 between Escalante and Boulder, Utah, is known as the **Million Dollar Highway**, passing through tributary canyons of the Escalante River in eastern GSENM. Completed by the Civilian Conservation Corps (CCC) in 1940 after five years of intense dynamiting and backbreaking construction, this highway offered the first

A vehicle passes out of sight at the Cockscomb on Cottonwood Canyon Road (Adventure 38).

paved all-weather route between Escalante and Boulder. Up until its completion, Boulder still received mail by mule train during part of the year.

THE ACTION: A popular highlight along the Million Dollar Highway, **Calf Creek Recreation Area** offers a 3-mile (one-way) hiking trail to 126-foot-tall **Lower Calf Creek Falls**. THE SUSPECTS: Bureau of Land Management, blm.gov/visit/calf-creek-recreation-area-day-use-site. X MARKS THE SPOT: National Geographic Trails Illustrated Topo Map #710, Canyons of the Escalante. THE DIGS: Calf Creek has thirteen first-come, first-serve campsites.

RIDE ONWARD: **Hells Backbone Road** is a 38-mile unpaved alternate route between Boulder and Escalante, typically suitable for high-clearance two-wheel-drive vehicles during normal weather conditions. Completed by the CCC in the early 1930s, the road passes above the **Box–Death Hollow Wilderness**, which contains a number of challenging hiking and backpacking trails and routes. THE SUSPECTS: Escalante Ranger District, Dixie National Forest (see Resources).

37

Hole-in-the-Rock Road and Coyote Gulch

THE LOWDOWN: Hole-in-the-Rock Road is an unpaved road heading southeast from Escalante, leading to some of the best slot canyons in the region through GSENM and finishing in Glen Canyon National Recreation Area, dead-ending above Lake Powell.

THE GIDDYUP: Hole-in-the-Rock Road departs UT 12 near Escalante and continues

for 62 miles, becoming increasingly rough the farther southeast you drive. That said, confident drivers with normal-clearance two-wheel-drive vehicles often make it quite far on the road (and even up some of the side roads). However, the final 5 miles require four-wheel drive.

THE LOOT: Along the **Hole-in-the-Rock Road**, side roads provide access to trails and unmarked routes leading to remote highlights like arches and slot canyons, with many of the latter being tributaries to the Escalante River. These side roads are often even sandier and rougher than the main road, typically requiring four-wheel drive.

Hole-in-the-Rock Road ends at the **Hole-in-the-Rock historic site**. In 1879–80, 150 Mormon pioneers spent six months traveling overland for 250 miles by wagon train, hoping to find a shortcut in their attempts to settle near present-day Bluff, Utah. For two months they wintered at Forty-Mile Spring, using mostly hand tools and some blasting powder to widen a crack of Navajo sandstone into a "hole" wide enough for lowering wagons down to the Colorado River, where they built a ferry, then continued through even rougher terrain east of Glen Canyon and eventually established the town of Bluff.

THE ACTION: Coyote Gulch, with access to famous **Jacob Hamblin Arch**, is the most popular side canyon off Hole-in-the-Rock Road. There are two routes into Coyote Gulch, neither of which is maintained. The longer and easier hiking route that's popular among backpackers starts on Hole-in-the-Rock Road roughly 33 miles from UT 12 and follows Hurricane Wash east for about 7 miles one-way to the arch in Coyote Gulch.

A shorter but more challenging way into Coyote Gulch is the **Sneaker Route**, which starts from a water tank on Fortymile Ridge

The iconic Jacob Hamblin Arch in Coyote Gulch

Road and requires using a grab rope (sometimes one has been left by other hikers, but if not you will need your own 150-foot rope) to descend a 45-degree slickrock segment of Navajo sandstone.

RIDE ONWARD: You can follow Coyote Creek downstream about 5.5 miles to its confluence with the Escalante River, then head upstream a short way to **Stevens Arch**. Or you can follow the Escalante downstream for many twisty miles, though lake sediments can make it challenging to reach Lake Powell.

THE HARDSHIPS: Hole-in-the-Rock Road is unpaved, rough, and remote. Expect shifting sand drifts, exposed sections of bedrock, and no services. Whichever of these hikes to Jacob Hamblin Arch you choose, you'll need to conduct your own research, but for strong adventurers, it is an experience well worth the effort. Understand that neither route involves trails: while there may be rock cairns, these are unmaintained routes along wash bottoms—with sand, cobbles, and likely shallow water crossings—and over slickrock. Plan accordingly and be prepared.

THE SUSPECTS: GSENM is managed by the Bureau of Land Management; Glen Canyon NRA is managed by the National Park Service (see Resources).

X MARKS THE SPOT: National Geographic Trails Illustrated Topo Map #710, Canyons of the Escalante.

38

Cottonwood Canyon Road

THE LOWDOWN: On the west side of GSENM, the 46-mile Cottonwood Canyon Road—also called Cottonwood Canyon's Scenic Backway by the Bureau of Land Management—starts not far from Bryce Canyon and heads south along the Cockscomb, past the Paria River, and ends near the southern Lake Powell area (Adventure 41). Along the way you'll find a state park, a pair of arches, hiking trails, and some of the most jagged scenery this side of a rooster convention.

THE GIDDYUP: On UT 12 about 13 miles east of Bryce Canyon, in the small town of Cannonville, turn south on Kodachrome Road (a.k.a. Main Street), which is paved for 9 miles to Kodachrome Basin State Park. Continue south on unpaved Cottonwood Canyon Road (Road 400) for up to 37 miles.

THE SUSPECTS: BLM, blm.gov/visit/cottonwood-canyons-scenic-backway.

X MARKS THE SPOT: Download BLM's free online map (see Resources); also National Geographic Trails Illustrated Topo Map #714, Grand Staircase, Paunsaugunt Plateau.

THE ACTION: **Kodachrome Basin State Park**, with its colorful rock formations, is named after the famous Kodak 35mm film. One unique feature is the sixty-seven stone spires called sand pipes, towering above the landscape. A number of hiking trails, from short to moderate length, wind through the park's rock formations. THE SUSPECTS: Utah State Parks, stateparks.utah.gov/parks/kodachrome-basin. THE DIGS: Kodachrome Basin State Park has three campgrounds.

THE LOOT: South of Kodachrome, the next highlight on the road is **Grosvenor Arch**, a pair of sandstone arches located in the cliffs high above the roadway. Continuing south, the road follows the base of the **Cockscomb**, a roughly 15-mile ridge with jagged triangular segments of uplifted Navajo and Entrada bedrock. As you continue south on Cottonwood Canyon Road toward US 89, you enter the Paria River valley (Adventure 39).

MORE ACTION: Along Cottonwood Canyon Road, there are several side-canyon hikes to explore. About 5 miles south of Grosvenor Arch, the **Cottonwood Narrows Trail** is an easy 1.75 miles one-way through a slot canyon of varying width. A northern and southern trailhead are both located on the road about 1 mile apart. Walk the road back to your starting trailhead for a 2.75-mile loop.

Lower Hackberry Canyon Trail is a bit more challenging, given there's usually water in the stream bed of the 1.5-mile narrows that starts not far from the road. The trailhead is about 10 miles south of the southern end of Cottonwood Narrows. Hackberry Canyon continues for many miles beyond the narrows, and some people backpack this canyon as an out-and-back.

THE HARDSHIPS: Cottonwood Canyon Road can be rough and sandy, impassable during wet weather, and it's generally preferred to have a high-clearance and/or four-wheel-drive vehicle—or just a lot of outlaw-style guts and, I don't know, a hatchback or something.

39

Paria Townsite and Paria Box

THE LOWDOWN: The Paria River and surroundings are the site of several tales and haphazard chases from outlaw lore, with bandits fleeing through the canyon to escape pursuing lawmen. A few highlights have Wild West connections, including the ruins at Paria Townsite.

THE LOOT: The **Paria Townsite** (a.k.a. Pahreah or Old Paria) is a small ghost town, with a few stone structures remaining from the late nineteenth century, that feels straight out of a Wild West movie. There's a reason for that. The valley around the Paria Townsite was used as a movie set during the mid-twentieth century, most famously in 1976's *The Outlaw Josie Wales* starring Clint Eastwood. Sadly, the re-created buildings from the old set burned down during the early twenty-first century, but the stunning valley itself is well worth a visit. The remaining structures are located on the northeast side of the riverbed against the hillside below the cliffs. There are several unofficial trails in the area, but in general find the stream bed, look for footprints, and you'll find the ruins.

THE GIDDYUP: There are two ways to access Paria Townsite. The easier option is to drive there. From Lower Hackberry Canyon trailhead (Adventure 38), continue south on Cottonwood Canyon Road for 14.5 miles. Turn right (west) onto US 89 and continue for 13 miles. At the sign for Paria Townsite, turn right (northeast) onto an unpaved road and follow it for 5.5 miles to some sandy parking areas.

The adventurous option is a slot-canyon hike from Cottonwood Canyon Road 2.5 miles south of Lower Hackberry Canyon trailhead through the Paria Box.

THE ACTION: The **Paria Box** is a hiking route along the Paria River stream bed into the narrows. The typical start is from the Paria Box trailhead on Cottonwood Canyon Road, about 12 miles north of US 89. The hiking route from the road, through the Box, to Paria townsite is about 2.25 miles one-way and may require walking in shallow water. Another way to access the Box is from the Paria Townsite to the west.

MORE ACTION: The **Toadstools Trail** can be reached from US 89, 1.5 miles west of the southern end of Cottonwood Canyon Road.

This 1-mile trail leads to hoodoos shaped like—you guessed it.

THE SUSPECTS: Bureau of Land Management, Paria Contact Station, a field office just off US 89 about 43 miles east of Kanab, 435-644-1217; blm.gov/visit/paria-hwy-89-wayside.

EVEN MORE ACTION: Today, lower Paria Canyon is a wilderness area with a challenging but nontechnical out-and-back day hike, most commonly accessed from White House trailhead south of US 89. Others undertake a multiday backpacking thru-trip to Lees Ferry (advanced permits required); much of this route is through the cold, ankle-deep water of the Paria River, and experienced desert explorers should conduct their own research into this excellent adventure.

MORE LOOT!: In the nearby town of Kanab on US 89, check out the **Little Hollywood movie museum**, which documents the use of the region as a movie set for countless Western films over the years. THE SCENE OF THE CRIME: 297 W. Center Street, Kanab, UT 84741. THE SUSPECTS: 435-644-5337; littlehollywood museum.org.

RIDE ONWARD: About 30 miles west of Kanab is **Zion National Park**, a favorite of many travelers that's better known for exceptional canyon scenery than Wild West history. Not only is Zion the most visited of Utah's Mighty Five, but it's one of the most popular national parks in the US, averaging around 4.5 million annual visitors in recent years. Numbers like that are enough to keep most outlaws at bay—though they might attract pickpockets who prefer the crowds. But despite the chaos, Zion is definitely worth a visit. For a quieter time, consider late fall to early spring.

THE YARNS: The outlaw Silver Tip was arrested at an abandoned cabin on the upper Paria River; see Wild Bunch Stories, Episode

15, The Battle at Roost Canyon, 1899. It's unlikely, though, that the location was at Paria Townsite, which was still occupied as late as the 1920s.

40

Wire Pass to Buckskin Gulch

THE LOWDOWN: The hiking highlight in the Paria Canyon area is the day hike from Wire Pass to Buckskin Gulch, which takes people inside a series of narrows and slots. At 13 miles long, Buckskin Gulch is the longest slot canyon in the Southwest—and possibly the world. **THE ACTION:** Most day hikers start on the **Wire Pass Trail**, which reaches Buckskin Gulch in 1.7 miles. From there, most hikers head southeast (to the right) into the deeper parts of **Buckskin Gulch**. Continue as far as you have time and return the way you came. **THE GIDDYUP:** From US 89 about 38 miles east of Kanab, turn south onto unpaved House Rock Valley Road, best suited to high-clearance vehicles, with two-wheel drive sufficient during normal weather conditions. Continue about 8.3 miles to the Wire Pass trailhead. **THE SCENE OF THE CRIME:** GPS 37.0191, −112.025. **THE SUSPECTS:** Bureau of Land Management, blm.gov/visit/wire-pass. **THE LAW:** Day hiking does not require a permit, but permits must be obtained in advance for all overnight trips in Buckskin Gulch and Paria Canyon; recreation.gov/permits/74984. **THE TAKE:** Modest per-person fee for day use. **X MARKS THE SPOT:** National Geographic Trails Illustrated Topo Map #859, Paria Canyon, Kanab.

THE HARDSHIPS: Due to the dangers of flash floods, it's critically important to *never* enter a slot canyon like Wire Pass or Buckskin Gulch when there's a threat of thunderstorms. If you see rain clouds building near or far, immediately exit the slot canyon and return another day.

41

Southern Lake Powell

THE LOWDOWN: The southern end of Lake Powell, near Page, Arizona, is the hub for the entire reservoir. There are several marinas, and while motorboat traffic may get hectic, paddlers can still explore some quieter spots. Two accessible options include what's called lower lower Antelope Canyon (to distinguish it from the famous slot-canyon tours called Upper and Lower Antelope Canyon) and Lone Rock Bay, which requires beach driving. The whole lakeshore is in Glen Canyon National Recreation Area. On the south side, the lake and a shoreline buffer zone are currently in the park service's jurisdiction, while inland is the Navajo Indian Reservation. **THE ACTION:** In particular, a paddling trip into lower lower **Antelope Canyon** is a real highlight, requiring about 4 miles of paddling roundtrip. From the Antelope Point Marina boat ramp, paddle southwest along the southern shore of Lake Powell for 1 mile. Turn left (southeast) into Antelope Canyon. You can paddle up into the narrowing slot canyon for about 1 mile. Return as you came. **THE GIDDYUP:** To reach Antelope Point Marina, from US 89 south of Page, take AZ 98 east a few miles, then turn left (north) onto Navajo Route 222 and go about 6.5 miles (stay

straight, don't turn off to the marina) to reach the boat ramp.

MORE ACTION: An excellent half-day trip into **Lone Rock Canyon** launches from the beach at Lone Rock Bay, centered on a bay with, yes, a giant lone rock. Launch from anywhere on the beach at the park service primitive camping area. Paddle north about a half mile, staying west of the Lone Rock, to enter Lone Rock Canyon. From there you can explore several arms of the canyon, with one winding north for almost 1 mile. (Note that during 2022, drought caused the reservoir level to drop so much that Lone Rock Bay completely dried up—do make sure there's water before trying to paddle!) **THE DIGS:** Lone Rock Bay has a huge park service primitive camping area along the beach. **THE GIDDYUP:** To reach Lone Rock Bay, from US 89 about 9 miles northwest of Page, turn right (east) onto paved Lone Rock Road. After 2 miles, beyond the bathroom facilities, the paved road ends and vehicles (four-wheel drive recommended) must drive on unmaintained and often loose sand trails to reach the beach.

THE SUSPECTS: National Park Service, nps.gov/glca.

THE TAKE: Both Antelope Point Marina and Lone Rock Bay are park-service fee areas.

THE HARDSHIPS: During high season, roughly May through September, launch in the early morning to avoid the increasing motorboat traffic. Stay close to shore when paddling in the reservoir's main channel. Keep a watch out for wakes—if things get rowdy, turn your boat and paddle head-on over the approaching waves. If the wind rises or weather forms, don't go out; return to the marina or seek shelter as needed.

Opposite: Hikers pass through the depths of Buckskin Gulch.

THE JIG: In Page, you can arrange boat rentals and guided paddling tours, including some that use motorboats to access farther-away side canyons (see Resources).

42

Lees Ferry and Glen Canyon

THE LOWDOWN: Lees Ferry is a National Park Service unit that is often overlooked by travelers, but those who do visit are often pleasantly surprised. Located at the beginning of Marble Canyon, Lees Ferry is near the northern edge of Grand Canyon National Park, though it is actually just inside Glen Canyon National Recreation Area. Here you can find several worthy hikes and a remarkable paddling trip.

THE LOOT: Originally called Pahreah Crossing, **Lees Ferry** was once the main crossing on the Colorado River for many miles due to the inaccessibility of the Grand Canyon downstream and, with a few exceptions, Glen Canyon upstream. Many outlaws no doubt passed through, aided from 1872 to 1877 by ferry operator and fugitive John D. Lee, one of the participants in the Mountain Meadows Massacre. In 1857 Mormon militiamen—allegedly fearing incursions by non-Mormons into the region—disguised themselves as Native Americans and murdered 120 members of an emigrant wagon train on the Old Spanish Trail in southern Utah. Federal investigation was delayed by the Civil War, and it wasn't until twenty years later that Lee was convicted and executed for his role. Controversially, he was the only participant ever brought to justice.

Today, visitors can explore several historic buildings at Lees Ferry. The **Lees Ferry Fort** is a series of stone structures located at the site of the old ferry, near the trailhead for the River Trail, discussed below. Nearby, the **Lonely Dell Ranch Historic Site** is a preserved pioneer homestead that was occupied by John D. Lee and several subsequent Mormon families during the nineteenth century. Today, a 1-mile walking tour loops through the ranch and orchard.

THE **ACTION:** Several excellent hikes of varying difficulty can be found at Lees Ferry. Starting from the trailhead near the boat launch, the **River Trail** is an easy 1-mile one-way hike along the banks of the Colorado River. The more challenging highlight from this trailhead is to the **Spencer Trail**, which veers uphill from the River Trail about 0.3

mile from the parking lot. The Spencer Trail is about 2.25 miles one-way with 1,700 feet of elevation gain to the top of the Echo Cliffs, where you are rewarded with a dramatic view into upper Marble Canyon as the Colorado drops away into the start of the Grand Canyon. Another nearby hike is the **Cathedral Wash Trail**, which descends a side canyon to the Colorado in 1 mile one-way.

THE **GIDDYUP:** From US 89 at Bitter Springs, about 23 miles south of Page, Arizona, head north on US 89 Alt for about 14 miles. Just past Navajo Bridge (a popular stop to walk across the bridge and visit the NPS interpretive center), turn right (north) onto Lees Ferry Road. Reach the Cathedral Wash trailhead on Lees Ferry Road in 1.5 miles from US 89 Alt. To reach the Lonely Dell historic site, continue on Lees Ferry Road another 4 miles,

Hiking the Spencer Trail above the Colorado River at Lees Ferry

turn north onto River Drive, and proceed less than a half mile. To reach the boat launch and main trailhead, continue on Lees Ferry Road another 0.5 mile (6 miles from US 89 Alt).

THE SUSPECTS: National Park Service, nps.gov/glca/planyourvisit/lees-ferry.htm.

THE DIGS: Lees Ferry Campground, with more than fifty campsites, often has space; all are first come, first served.

MORE ACTION: The **Glen Canyon Backhaul** section of the Colorado River is a remarkable class I–II paddling trip. Because there is no vehicle access near Glen Canyon Dam, this adventure requires arranging a backhaul ride on a motorboat up from Lees Ferry. Then you can paddle the 15 river miles back down to Lees Ferry. THE SUSPECTS: Current operations are offered by Wilderness River Adventures (see Resources).

RIDE ONWARD: Oh, and since you're already here, why not consider the river-trip-of-a-lifetime down the Grand Canyon?

THE HARDSHIPS: Stopping yourself from stowing away on a raft that's heading downstream.

THE YARNS: Lees Ferry was a common river crossing for outlaws, including a tense episode for outlaw Tom McCarty sometime before teaming up with Butch Cassidy in 1889. As described by Charles Kelly in *The Outlaw Trail*, McCarty and accomplices were being chased by the US Border Patrol after a cattle raid into Old Mexico. After making it across the river ahead of the lawmen, the outlaws supposedly hid in the canyons and country along the Paria River (Adventure 39).

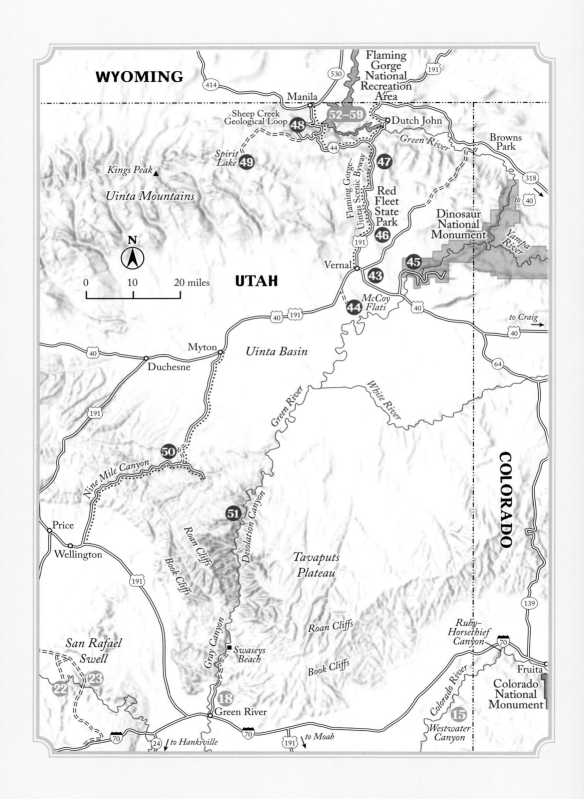

CHAPTER 6
Uinta Basin and Eastern Uinta Mountains
NORTH-CENTRAL UTAH

THE WHOLE KIT AND CABOODLE: A subrange of the Rockies in far northeastern Utah, the Uinta Mountains run parallel to the Wyoming border for about 130 miles. With elevations rising to 13,534 feet at Kings Peak, the highest point in Utah, the Uintas are the tallest east-west-trending mountain range in the United States.

The Uinta Basin and Uinta Mountains were the setting for many Wild West stories and Wild Bunch exploits. And like many such stories, some were probably true and others myth. Speaking of myths, one common whopper told about the Uinta Mountains themselves is that they are the *only* east-west-trending mountain range in the US. Certain qualifications bring this claim a little more in line with reality. The Uintas are one of only two major mountain ranges in the US to trend east-west, with the other being the Transverse Range in Southern California.

Most visitation to the Uinta Mountains happens on the western side, closer to Salt Lake City in the Uinta-Wasatch-Cache National Forest, including spots around the Mirror Lake Highway (UT 150). This chapter offers a few lesser-visited spots in the Eastern Uintas and Ashley National Forest, between Flaming Gorge and Browns Park in the north and Vernal and the Uinta Basin to the south, including the Tavaputs Plateau south of the Uinta Basin (see Tavaputs Plateau introduction below).

X MARKS THE SPOT: National Geographic Trails Illustrated Topo Map #711, High Uintas Wilderness.

THE YARNS: Given their ruggedness and high elevation, the Uintas seem to have presented an obstacle to outlaws and rustlers, who mostly traveled around them. There are, however, several prospecting tales, including one about Matt Warner, who was allegedly transported (with his ankles tied) along the Old Carter Military Road to Ogden, Utah, for his murder trial. See Wild Bunch Stories, Episode 6, A Most Desperate Plot, 1896.

43

Vernal

THE LOWDOWN: An up-and-coming town—which has been up-and-coming since the days of the Wild West—Vernal makes a good base for exploring the Uinta Basin and eastern Uinta Mountains (Adventures 44 and 47–49), Red Fleet State Park (Adventure 46), and Dinosaur National Monument (Adventure 45). You can even access Flaming Gorge National Recreation Area and the Browns Park area if you don't mind some day-trip driving. Also, a giant pink dinosaur welcomes visitors to town, so there's that.

THE GIDDYUP: Vernal is on US 191 at its junction with US 40.

THE LOOT: The **Utah Field House of Natural History State Park Museum** is an impressive modern facility with an appropriately long name, given the exhibits span the entire 4.6 billion years of Earth history, with an emphasis on local dinosaurs. The visitor center in the lobby offers a brochure and map for an Outlaw Country driving tour. **THE SCENE OF THE CRIME:** 496 E. Main Street, Vernal, UT 84078. **THE SUSPECTS:** Utah State Parks, state parks.utah.gov/parks/utah-field-house.

Nearby, the **Uintah County Heritage Museum** covers local history, including the Ute tribes, white settlers, and outlaws like Matt Warner of the nascent Wild Bunch. **THE SCENE OF THE CRIME:** 155 E. Main Street, Vernal, UT 84078. **THE SUSPECTS:** uintah museum.org.

Opposite: The Hog Canyon Trail near the Josie Bassett Morris Cabin is a perfect example of this area's hidden gems.

MORE LOOT: A Wild West–themed self-guided driving tour (Day Trip 6, Outlaw Country) explores the region surrounding Vernal, along the way passing through Crouse Canyon, a likely route for outlaws traveling into Browns Park. Other stops on the 84-mile loop include the majority of Browns Park highlights (Adventures 58 and 59), and it passes scenic Flaming Gorge Reservoir (Adventures 52, 55, 56, and 57). **THE SUSPECTS:** Download a brochure and map at dinoland.com/play.

THE SNORT: Vernal Brewing Company has good food and makes some pretty mean session beers.

THE YARNS: Located at the crossroads of several outlaw trails, the town of Vernal and its frontier saloons are all over Wild West lore. See Wild Bunch Stories, Episodes 6, A Most Desperate Plot, 1896; and 17, Phantoms of the Outlaw Trail, 1922 . . . , and Browns Park Stories, Episode 12, The Many Battles of Browns Park, 1898.

44

McCoy Flats Trail System

THE LOWDOWN: Built for mountain biking but also popular among hikers and trail runners, the McCoy Flats Trail System winds through tablelands and small canyons just south of Vernal.

THE GIDDYUP: From downtown Vernal, drive south on US 191/US 40 for 6 miles and turn left (south) onto McCoy Flat Road. Head southeast for 3 miles to McCoy Flat Corral, a shelter, and the trailhead. **THE SCENE OF THE CRIME:** GPS 40.3505, −109.5819.

THE SUSPECTS: Bureau of Land Management, blm.gov/visit/mccoy-flats-trailhead.

Mountain biking at McCoy Flats, a pleasantly surprising trail system just south of Vernal

X MARKS THE SPOT: A system map is available at the trailhead. Trail maps are available at Altitude Cycle (580 E. Main Street, Vernal, UT 84078).

THE ACTION: This fun cross-country trail system offers about 40 miles of intersecting loop trails with a mix of surfaces, from packed-dirt flow trails to bedrock ledges and other rocky, technical sections. The trails are mostly singletrack, with some double mixed in, offering a range of difficulty from beginner to advanced.

45

Dinosaur National Monument (Utah Side)

THE LOWDOWN: There are plenty of highlights on the Utah side of Dinosaur National Monument, from a few short hiking trails with nice scenery that link up around the Split Mountain area to many excellent petroglyph sites throughout the park, including the famous Fremont Culture lizards. There are also two outlaw highlights in the park, one you can drive to and the other requiring a boat.

THE JIG: Note that it takes two and a half hours to travel between the monument's Utah side and the northern end of the Colorado side in Browns Park (Adventure 59).

THE LOOT: The most popular attraction on the monument's Utah side is the **Quarry Exhibit Hall**. Visitors can view thousands of fossilized dinosaur bones left embedded in the original rock face. Access is only by shuttle from the Quarry Visitor Center. **THE SCENE OF THE CRIME:** GPS 40.4382, −109.3078.

MORE LOOT: The **Josie Bassett Morris Cabin** is a well-preserved structure located on Cub Creek that was built by the famous Josie Bassett of Browns Park. She homesteaded and lived here for the final fifty years of her life before her death in 1963.

THE ACTION: Two short trails depart from the Josie Bassett Morris Cabin. One leads 0.25 mile one-way into **Box Canyon**, Josie's natural corral. Another trail takes 0.75 mile one-way to penetrate the dramatic Weber Sandstone cliffs of **Hog Canyon**. THE GIDDYUP: From Vernal, head east on US 40 for about 13 miles to Jensen, turn left (north) onto UT 149, and proceed 6 miles to the monument visitor center. Continue east on the park road to a fork and take the left-hand road, which becomes unpaved, to reach Josie Bassett's cabin in 10 miles.

THE SUSPECTS: National Park Service, nps .gov/dino.

X MARKS THE SPOT: Download the park-service map from the park website or get one at the entry station. For a topo, try National Geographic Trails Illustrated Topo Map #220, Dinosaur National Monument.

MORE ACTION: An impressive outlaw cave is located across the Green River from the Split Mountain Boat Ramp. Note that you'll need a boat to get across the river, hence exploring the cave is fun to combine with a short 3-mile class II paddling trip from Split Mountain Boat Ramp to the dirt kayak access at Place Point, on the main park road 3.5 miles south of the put-in.

RIDE ONWARD: Several class III whitewater trips on the Green River are very popular, including the multiday Lodore Canyon and a Split Mountain day trip, plus the springtime multiday Yampa River. Check out the park website for more info and a list of guided outfitters.

THE LAW: A permit is required for all river trips within the monument. During the main season, the multiday trips and Split Mountain daily section require obtaining a permit in advance, typically through a lottery. The Split Mountain to Place Point day trip requires obtaining a "play permit." You can get one up to the day of your trip from the visitor center.

THE DIGS: The Utah side of the monument has several campgrounds.

The well-preserved Josie Bassett Morris Cabin in Dinosaur National Monument

THE YARNS: For more on Josie Bassett of Browns Park, see Wild Bunch Stories, Episode 3, On the Outlaw Trail, 1889; and Browns Park Stories, Episode 14, Queen Ann Bassett, 1899–1917.

46

Red Fleet State Park and Dinosaur Trackway

THE LOWDOWN: Named for large red sandstone formations that resemble naval ships, Red Fleet State Park has a 750-acre reservoir, which some call Little Lake Powell, for swimming, paddling, and fishing.

THE ACTION: The **Red Fleet Trail System** is popular for hiking and mountain biking, with about 20 miles of single-track trails ranging from easy to hard.

MORE ACTION: A park highlight is the **Dinosaur Trackway**, a set of three-toed footprints probably belonging to a dilophosaurus, preserved in sandstone on the shore of Red Fleet Reservoir opposite the state park. From the trailhead, follow a somewhat strenuous, hilly path 1.5 miles one-way to the footprints.

THE GIDDYUP: From Vernal, drive north on US 191 for 10 miles and turn right (east) onto the park road to reach Red Fleet. To reach the Dinosaur Trackway, from US 191 about 1 mile north of the park road, turn right (east) onto Donkey Flat Road and continue 2.5 miles to the trailhead.

THE SUSPECTS: Your best bet is to ask for information at the state park entrance, since there's not a lot of info online on the state park website (stateparks.utah.gov/parks/red-fleet).

X MARKS THE SPOT: National Geographic Trails Illustrated Topo Maps #704, Flaming Gorge National Recreation Area, and #220, Dinosaur National Monument.

THE DIGS: Red Fleet State Park has a campground.

47

Flaming Gorge–Uintas Scenic Byway

THE LOWDOWN: Following US 191 and UT 44 over the eastern Uintas for 82 miles from Vernal to Manila on the Wyoming border, the **Flaming Gorge–Uintas Scenic Byway** offers great mountain views and several roadside stops for quick exploration, including a preserved sheepherder cabin and a nature trail.

THE ACTION: The **Aspen Nature Trail** is a stretch-your-legs kind of stop with a 0.5-mile roundtrip walk on pea gravel through aspen forest.

THE LOOT: The **Stringham Cabin** is a well-preserved sheepherders site, with some historical structures that can be entered. The site is just inside the forest, reached by walking about 1,000 feet uphill from the parking area.

THE GIDDYUP: To reach the Aspen Nature Trail, from Vernal drive US 191 north about 24 miles and turn right (east) onto FR 048, which leads into the parking lot. **THE SCENE OF THE CRIME:** GPS 40.7263, –109.4685.

To reach the Stringham Cabin, return to US 191 and continue north for 2 miles. Turn right (east) onto unpaved FR 253 and continue for 0.5 mile, then turn left onto an unnamed dirt road and after about 500 feet, veer right and follow it less than 0.5 mile to a small dirt parking lot. **THE SCENE OF THE CRIME:** GPS 40.7591, –109.4596.

The UT 44 section of the Flaming Gorge–Uintas Scenic Byway

THE SUSPECTS: Ashley National Forest (see Resources). Don't expect a lot of online information, though. For example, at the time of this writing, the Forest Service description of the Stringham site reads only "cabin." Fair. However, both sites can be found on most mapping apps.

RIDE ONWARD: Many hikes are possible in the High Uintas Wilderness. Less than 3 miles up US 191 is the Uinta Highline Trail's eastern trailhead (**THE SCENE OF THE CRIME:** GPS 40.7947, −109.4773); the western trailhead is located on UT 150. This beast of a thru-hike is 104 miles long with about 15,000 feet of elevation gain, depending on which direction you hike. More than half the route is through the High Uintas Wilderness and the rest through national forest, offering high alpine scenery and many mountain lakes. A shorter option popular for weekend backpacking trips is the 27-mile one-way Henry's Fork Trail to Kings Peak, the highest point in Utah.

48

Sheep Creek Geological Loop

THE LOWDOWN: Passing through the stunning uplifted folds of the Uinta Fault, this seasonal 13-mile paved route is off UT 44 just south of the Wyoming state line. Along the way, you'll see colorful geologic layers, spanning hundreds of millions of years of geologic history, that have been twisted and bent. Bonus points for spotting the bighorn sheep that the creek is named for.

THE GIDDYUP: From US 191 just south of Flaming Gorge (35 miles north of Vernal), turn left (west) onto UT 44 and follow it about 14.5 miles to FR 218. Turn left (west) to drive the loop road from its southern starting point.

THE LOOT: Along the loop drive are interpretive sites, including **Sheep Creek Overlook**, **Palisades Memorial Park**, and **Tower Rock**. When FR 218 loops back to UT 44, turn right (south) for 7.5 miles to close the loop, which takes about forty-five minutes to drive.

THE SUSPECTS: US Forest Service (see Resources).

THE YARNS: Sheep Creek Canyon was the location of a ranch owned by early white settler Cleophus Dowd, who was known to assort with outlaws. It's alleged that the Wild Bunch obtained horses from Dowd, and it's possible the Sundance Kid worked on the ranch for a time.

49
Spirit Lake Scenic Backway

THE LOWDOWN: This scenic route meanders through the Uinta Mountains to a shimmering alpine lake. The backway is an unpaved spur off the Sheep Creek Geological Loop (Adventure 48), passable by high-clearance two-wheel-drive vehicles under normal conditions, offering access to the High Uintas from the Flaming Gorge region.

THE GIDDYUP: From about 14 miles west of UT 44 on the southwestern side of Sheep Creek Geological Loop (FR 218), at Hickerson Park–Birch Creek Road, turn south onto

unpaved Spirit Lake Road and continue for about 6.5 miles to the trailhead.

THE SUSPECTS: Ashley National Forest, fs.usda.gov/main/ashley/home; there's also a Forest Service visitor guide to the area (see Resources).

X MARKS THE SPOT: National Geographic Trails Illustrated Topo Maps #711, High Uintas Wilderness, and #704, Flaming Gorge National Recreation Area.

THE ACTION: From the Spirit Lake trailhead, you can day-hike the fairly easy 3.5-mile **Spirit–Tamarack Lake Trail** loop, which passes Jessen and Tamarack Lakes along the way. **THE HARDSHIPS:** The trailhead is at 10,200 feet. Make sure to acclimate and pace yourself.

THE DIGS: The small **Spirit Lake Campground** can be found at the lake, near a private lodge that rents cabins.

Tavaputs Plateau

THE WHOLE KIT AND CABOODLE: The Tavaputs Plateau is an uplifted mountainous region, with elevations topping out around 10,000 feet, that rises between the Uinta Basin to the north and the San Rafael Swell, Robbers Roost, and Canyonlands regions to the south. The Green River runs through the heart of the Tavaputs within colorful Desolation Canyon, which ends at the Roan Cliffs. The river continues through serene Gray Canyon, terminating with the Book Cliffs, which mark the upper boundary of the Green River Basin.

THE GIDDYUP: There are only a few major routes running north to south through the Tavaputs. Today, two are paved highways—CO 139 and US 191—and one is a partially paved backcountry byway through Nine Mile Canyon, all three of which were at one time traveled by outlaws.

50

Nine Mile Canyon

THE LOWDOWN: For starters, the road that passes through Nine Mile Canyon is actually 46 miles long—don't ask, I tried. But that makes sense, given that Nine Mile Canyon has been described as the world's longest art gallery. The artwork, in particular, is Fremont Culture pictographs, with estimates of the total number of rock art sites ranging from the hundreds to over a thousand. This adventure shares just a few of the top sites, which involve short walks to view them.

Originally called the Price-Myton Road, the Nine Mile Canyon Road was constructed in 1886 by the US Ninth Cavalry, a regiment of African American soldiers also called the Buffalo Soldiers. The road was built to bring supplies from the Denver and Rio Grande Railroad to Fort Duchesne in the Uinta Basin, and it soon became a principal route through the Tavaputs Plateau.

THE GIDDYUP: You can start the byway from either the southern end near Wellington or the northern end near Myton. The road is a mix of paved highway (all of the southern side and much of the northern side), plus a well-graded gravel section through Gate Canyon, suitable for most two-wheel-drive vehicles during normal weather conditions. These directions are provided south-to-north and include descriptions to reach the top sites.

From Wellington, head east on US 6/US 191 for about 2.5 miles. Turn left (north) and follow Soldier Creek Road/N. 2200 E. for about 13 miles, continuing onto Nine Mile Canyon Road, which in about 11 miles

passes Nine Mile Ranch (see **THE DIGS** below). Continue on the byway for another 8.5 miles to reach what's called **First Site**, with rock art on the northwest side of the road.

Continue along the byway, past roadside Balance Rock, and in about 6.25 miles you'll reach a three-way junction. For now, continue straight (east) on paved Nine Mile Canyon Road. Keep an eye out for ancestral granaries in the cliffs above the road. After about 5.5 miles the **Daddy Canyon Complex** trailhead is on the north side of the road. Walk the roughly quarter-mile one-way trail to view this site.

Continue driving east another mile, veer right onto Cottonwood Canyon Road, and in 1 mile park along the curve in the road to reach the **Big Buffalo panel** by walking west across the wash.

Continue driving 0.25 mile to the parking area on the west side of the road for a short walk to perhaps the best site of all—the amazing **Great Hunt panel**.

Return to the three-way junction and either retrace your steps south on pavement or complete the byway by turning right (north) onto the unpaved S. Wells Draw Road through scenic Gate Canyon. After about 6.5 miles, the road becomes paved again. After 23 more miles veer left onto Sand Wash Road, which after about 1.5 miles reaches US 191/US 40.

THE ACTION: The original military road has since been widened and straightened, but one original section remains undisturbed near Wells Draw in Gate Canyon, where the road bulges to the west about 6 miles north of the three-way junction. This section of original road can be explored on ATVs or hiked for about 1.5 miles one-way between roughly mile 43 (GPS 39.8709, −110.2466) and mile 47 (GPS 39.8915, −110.2407) from US 6.

THE SUSPECTS: Bureau of Land Management, blm.gov/visit/9-mile-canyon.

X MARKS THE SPOT: Download the BLM road map from the website listed above. A free map and guide is also available at carbonutah.com/attraction/nine-mile-canyon.

THE DIGS: The only place to stay in the canyon is the **Nine Mile Ranch**, a guest ranch with cabins, camping, and bed-and-breakfast rooms. THE SUSPECTS: 9mileranch.com.

THE YARNS: Nine Mile Canyon receives frequent mention in Wild West lore, with author Charles Kelly describing in *The Outlaw Trail* a number of horse thefts and chases through the area. Also see Wild Bunch Stories, Episode 3, On the Outlaw Trail, 1889.

51

Desolation and Gray Canyons River Trip

THE LOWDOWN: Perhaps the best of the few ways to explore the remote Tavaputs Plateau is a trip through the heart of it on the Green River. Along the way, there's some amazing scenery and class II–III whitewater hidden deep inside this mostly inaccessible region. Among the many historic highlights to visit are the ruins of old ranches and Fremont Culture rock art sites.

Paddleboarding the Green River through Desolation Canyon is one of the best ways to explore the remote Tavaputs Plateau.

THE ACTION: The entire trip through Desolation and Gray Canyons is about 85 miles from Sand Wash to Swaseys Beach. Most people join guided raft trips, while experienced boaters run private trips—typically with rafts, and sometimes with a mix of hardshell kayaks, inflatable duckies, and paddleboards. Because of the challenges associated with running a private whitewater trip, you'll need to conduct supplementary research before attempting a DIY adventure here.

THE LAW: A trip through Desolation Canyon requires either winning a permit through a lottery for a DIY trip or joining a commercial outfitter.

THE SUSPECTS: Bureau of Land Management has information about DIY and guided trips (see Resources).

THE YARNS: See Wild Bunch Stories, Episode 9, A Gang by Any Name, 1897–1898.

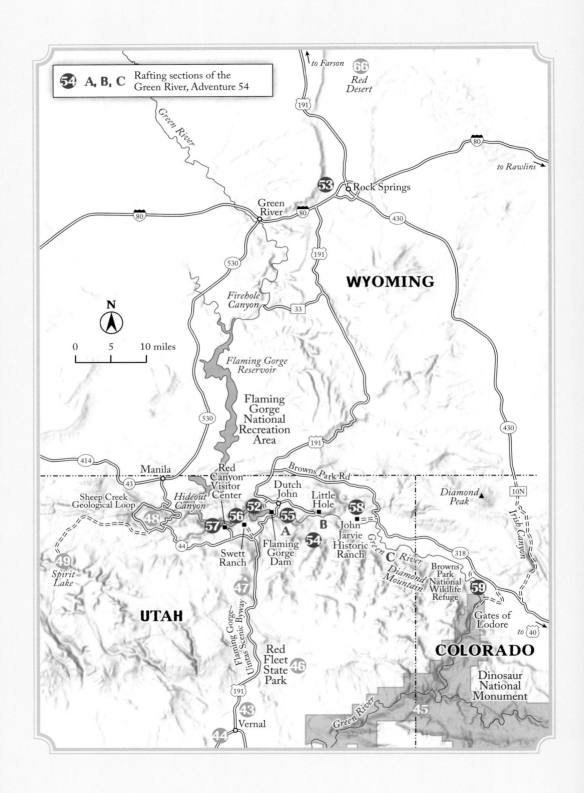

54 A, B, C   Rafting sections of the
Green River, Adventure 54

to Farson

66
Red
Desert

191

80
to Rawlins

Green River

53
Rock Springs

80
Green
River
80
430

530
191

WYOMING

Firehole
Canyon
33

N

0   5   10 miles

Flaming Gorge
Reservoir

Flaming
Gorge
National
Recreation
Area

530
191
430

10N

414
Manila
Red
Canyon
Visitor
Center
Browns Park Rd
Diamond
Peak

43
Dutch
John
Little
Hole
58

Irish Canyon

Sheep Creek
Geological Loop
Hideout
Canyon
52
56
55
B
John
Jarvie
Historic
Ranch
318

48
57
A
54
Browns
Park
National
Wildlife
Refuge
59

49
Spirit
Lake
44
Swett
Ranch
Flaming
Gorge
Dam
Green River
C
Diamond
Mountain
Gates of
Lodore
to 40

47

UTAH

Flaming Gorge–Uintas Scenic Byway

COLORADO

Red
Fleet
State
Park
46

Dinosaur
National
Monument

191

43
Vernal

Green River
45

44

CHAPTER 7
Flaming Gorge and Browns Park

NORTHERN UTAH-SOUTHERN WYOMING

THE WHOLE KIT AND CABOODLE: Perhaps the most-storied hideout along the outlaw trail, the remote Browns Park is little changed from the outlaw era—mostly forgotten, practically empty, and forever haunted by a lawless and secretive past. Being hidden away on the intersecting border of three US Territories—Utah, Colorado, and Wyoming—Browns Hole, as it was originally called, was a jurisdictional nightmare. Thus, it gained a notorious reputation as a haven for livestock rustlers and bank robbers, including Queen Ann Bassett, Butch Cassidy, and the Wild Bunch.

Today the region is mostly known for scenic Flaming Gorge National Recreation Area and the dam-released Green River. The adjacent eastern Uinta Mountains and northern Uinta Basin are increasingly lumped together with the reservoir and marketed as Flaming Gorge–Uintas, with the combined region offering opportunities for paddling, biking, hiking, and visiting many historic sites. Meanwhile, the Browns Park of today continues to fly under the radar of most travelers but offers outlaw enthusiasts and outdoor adventurers several worthy highlights to visit.

X MARKS THE SPOT: One topo map covers the entire reservoir, National Geographic Trails Illustrated Topo Map #704, Flaming Gorge National Recreation Area. Regarding Browns Park, you're SOL.

THE YARNS: The valley appears, or is mentioned, in well over half of the Wild Bunch and Browns Park stories in this book. While some of the stories could be read alone, they're chronologically interwoven to offer a comprehensive retelling about the outlaw trail. Thus, it's recommended to read all seventeen parts in the order numbered. That said, the episodes that significantly include Browns Park are these: Wild Bunch Stories, Episodes 3, On the Outlaw Trail, 1889; 5, Wyoming Rambles, or Becoming Butch Cassidy, 1889–1896; 6, A Most Desperate Plot, 1896; and 7, Desperadoes at Castle Gate, 1896–1897; and Browns Park Stories, Episodes 4, Early Days in Browns Hole, 1878–1884; 12, The Many Battles of Browns Park, 1898; and 14, Queen Ann Bassett, 1899–1917.

52

Flaming Gorge Dam and Reservoir

THE LOWDOWN: The reservoir behind the 502-foot-tall Flaming Gorge Dam serves up a variety of pursuits, some more active than others. The most popular draws among visitors are pleasure cruising or motorboat fishing for trophy-sized lake trout on the reservoir and fly-fishing one of the world's premier blue-ribbon trout streams on the A Section of the Green River (see Adventure 54). But, in recent years, outdoor adventure activities are growing in popularity at **Flaming Gorge National Recreation Area.**

THE ACTION: Paddleboarding and kayaking are increasingly popular on the reservoir in the area near the dam, with a series of suggested paddling routes available from the Flaming Gorge Country website (see **THE SUSPECTS**). One excellent paddling option is to launch from **Sunny Cove**, a small swimming area near Mustang Ridge Campground. Paddle about 0.25 mile west into Dutch John Draw and turn north (left) to explore the arms of this small bay, each of which reach about 0.5 to 1 mile back. **THE HARDSHIPS:** From Sunny Cove, if you turn south (right) you'll venture into the main bay of the southeastern reservoir, which should be done only with caution. When paddling anywhere on this high-elevation reservoir, and especially in the main bay, be wary of motor traffic and rising winds, which typically occur during the afternoon and can create substantial waves. If such conditions arise, paddle another time.

Sheep Creek Bay on Flaming Gorge Reservoir

THE LOOT: Flaming Gorge Dam Visitor Center offers area information and tours of the dam. THE TICKING CLOCK: The visitor center is open from mid-April to mid-October.

RIDE ONWARD: **Firehole Canyon** is a highlight on the far northern end of the reservoir with paddling, motorboating, and fishing opportunities from the boat ramp near Firehole Canyon Campground in the shadows of the Chimney Rocks. This makes a good stop when driving north on US 191 between Dutch John and Green River, Wyoming (see Adventure 53).

THE GIDDYUP: Flaming Gorge Dam Visitor Center is on the north side of US 191 just west of the dam. The town of Dutch John, Utah, is on US 191 about 2.75 miles farther north. To reach Sunny Cove, from Dutch John continue north on US 191 for 2 miles, turn left onto Mustang Ridge Road, and continue about 1.5 miles to the dirt parking lot on the left. To reach Firehole Canyon, from Dutch John continue north on US 191 for 46 miles, turn left (west) onto Flaming Gorge Road/CR 33/FR 106 and follow it for about 10 miles to the campground and boat launch.

THE SUSPECTS: Ashley National Forest, (for info on the National Recreation Area, see Resources); area information can also be found at flaminggorge country.com.

THE DIGS: Most visitors opt to stay at the resorts and lodgings in and around Dutch John, where there are also stores, gas stations, raft rentals, and guided fishing outfitters. Others camp, often with motorboats and RVs, for long weekends at the Utah campgrounds clustered around the reservoir's eastern bays, which offer the vast majority of activities. Near the water, check out **Mustang Ridge Campground**, while two rim-top options are **Red Canyon Campground** and **Canyon Rim Campground**.

THE YARNS: See Browns Park Stories, Episode 4, Early Days in Browns Hole, 1878–1884.

53

Green River and Rock Springs (Wyoming)

THE LOWDOWN: A pair of high-desert towns north of Flaming Gorge Reservoir, Green River and Rock Springs each have a museum that's worth a stop. These towns make for a good side trip from the Flaming Gorge Dam–Browns Park area, especially if you venture north to Firehole Canyon. Or these towns could be a stop on the way to northern adventures like the Wind River Range (chapter 9), Bighorn Mountains and Basin (chapter 10), or Snowy Range (chapter 8).

THE GIDDYUP: Both towns are on I-80—Green River is 9 miles west of US 191 and Rock Springs is 7 miles east of US 191.

THE LOOT: Green River is a river town with two worthy sites. The **Sweetwater County Museum** focuses on events of local significance, including the John Wesley Powell expeditions of 1869 and 1871–72 (for more information, please check out my book *Paddling the John Wesley Powell Route*), coal and trona mining, and the Union Pacific Railroad. The museum publishes a small book called *Browns Park Treks*, with detailed information about the history and sites in the valley. THE TICKING CLOCK: Open Monday–Saturday, mid-March to mid-October; Tuesday–Saturday, mid-October to mid-March. THE SCENE OF THE CRIME: 3 E. Flaming Gorge Way, Green River, WY 82935. THE SUSPECTS: 307-872-6435; sweetwatermuseum.org.

Like a blast from the past, an old-timey fishing dory shoots the rapids in A Section of Red Canyon.

Expedition Island is a park on an island in the Green River, located near the Powell launch site. There's a walking path with informational signs about famous river runners. **THE SCENE OF THE CRIME:** 475 S. Second E. Street, Green River, WY 82935.

MORE LOOT: Rock Springs, 15 miles east on I-80, has many services, restaurants, and stores. Located in the 1894 city hall building, the **Rock Springs Historical Museum** houses the old town jail and outlaw exhibits on Calamity Jane and Butch Cassidy. **THE SCENE OF THE CRIME:** 201 B Street, Rock Springs, WY 82901. **THE SUSPECTS:** 307-362-3138; see Resources for website.

THE SNORT: Downtown Rock Springs has three breweries: Square State, Bad Joker, and Bitter Springs.

THE YARNS: Some historians report that Butch Cassidy worked as a butcher in Rock Springs during one winter in the early 1890s—mentioned in Wild Bunch Stories, Episodes 5, Wyoming Rambles, or Becoming Butch Cassidy, 1889–1896; and 17, Phantoms of the Outlaw Trail, 1922 . . . . Green River and Rock Springs are also mentioned in Browns Park Stories, Episodes 4, Early Days in Browns Hole, 1878–1884; and 12, The Many Battles of Browns Park, 1898.

54

Green River through Red Canyon

THE LOWDOWN: The Green River through Red Canyon is a major highlight in this region for easy class II+ whitewater paddling, rafting, drift-boat fishing, and hiking on the riverside trail (Adventure 55). Three sections of the river below Flaming Gorge Dam—A, B, and C—are commonly boated. The most scenic and popular run is A Section, where you'll see all kinds of watercraft these days, from fishing drift boats and catarafts to paddle rafts, kayaks, and whitewater paddleboards.

THE ACTION: Starting from Spillway Boat Launch, right below the dam, **A Section** offers 7 miles of class II+. Passing through the final miles of sheer-walled Red Canyon, this section has several named rapids and mid-river rocks to negotiate before ending at Little Hole Recreation Area.

B Section continues downstream from Little Hole for 7 miles of class II through low cliffs and foothills of Red Canyon, ending at Indian Crossing near the John Jarvie Ranch in Browns Park (Adventure 58). Overall, this section is less crowded than A Section. THE DIGS: Scattered throughout B Section are seventeen **Green River Float-in Campsites** managed by Ashley National Forest, with most of them first-come, first-serve and some available for reservation. THE SUSPECTS: recreation .gov/camping/campgrounds/250036.

C Section is a class I float for 11.5 slow-moving miles through Browns Park, from Indian Crossing to Swallow Canyon. This section sees far less river traffic than the other two, but with less fishing pressure it is popular among dedicated anglers.

THE JIG: The dam-fed river runs year-round, but most river runners come when it's warmer, typically from late spring (when higher water can increase the difficulty to class III) through early fall. Outfitters mostly operate out of Dutch John. (For options see flaminggorge country.com.)

THE GIDDYUP: The A Section put-in is at Spillway Boat Launch, reached via an access road south of US 191 just east of the dam. Takeout is at Little Hole Recreation Area,

with a fifteen-minute shuttle one-way. Head north on US 191 through Dutch John and in about 3 miles turn right (east) onto Little Hole Road and drive 6 miles.

The B Section put-in is at Little Hole Recreation Area. The takeout is the Indian Crossing boat ramp (fifty-minute shuttle one-way). From Little Hole, head 6 miles west to US 191, turn right (north) and drive 8.5 miles, turn right (east) onto Browns Park Road and drive 20.5 miles, then turn right (south) onto Red Creek Road and drive 2 miles to the put-in.

The C Section put-in is at Indian Crossing. The takeout is at Swallow Canyon boat ramp (twenty-minute shuttle one-way). From Indian Crossing, go east on Red Creek Road for 2 miles, turn right onto UT 1364 and drive about 4.75 miles, then veer right onto Swallow Canyon River Access Road and drive about 2 miles.

THE SUSPECTS: Ashley National Forest, fs.usda.gov/ashley.

55

Little Hole National Scenic Trail

THE LOWDOWN: This 7-mile trail along the Green River offers another way to see the stunning Red Canyon through the A Section.

THE ACTION: **Little Hole National Scenic Trail**, 7 miles one-way, passes through the sheer-walled Red Canyon at river level through the A Section. Damaged by flooding over the years, the trail surface can be spotty in places where segments of boardwalk have washed away, leaving hikers and anglers to cross wire-bound stone stacks. That said, the

Forest Service is working to improve the trail, and it remains passable except during times of high water.

THE GIDDYUP: The upstream trailhead is above the Spillway Boat Launch, reached via an access road south of US 191 just east of the dam. The downstream trailhead is at Little Hole Recreation Area, reached from Dutch John via US 191 northbound about 3 miles, then turning right (east) onto Little Hole Road and driving 6 miles.

THE SUSPECTS: Ashley National Forest (see Resources).

X MARKS THE SPOT: A trail map can be downloaded from the Flaming Gorge Country website (see Resources).

THE YARNS: During the outlaw era, the small river valley around the Little Hole Recreation Area—isolated from Browns Park by cliffs—was used by ranchers to water livestock and ford the Green River. Little Hole was also used by outlaws as an occasional hideout, including a brief stay by Butch Cassidy and Elzy Lay.

56

Swett Ranch Historical Homestead

THE LOWDOWN: This well-preserved turn-of-the-twentieth-century historic ranch has original log structures dating from 1909 and other buildings added throughout the following

Swett Ranch Historical Homestead

decades. At first glance, there appear to be no documented outlaw connections here (see sidebar!), but the ranch offers an excellent look at homesteading as the Wild West era came to an end. High-season tours are available.

THE GIDDYUP: From the junction of UT 44 and US 191, head 0.5 mile north on US 191. Turn left (northeast) onto FR 158. Follow the signs for 1.5 miles to the parking lot at Swett Ranch.

THE SUSPECTS: Ashley National Forest (see Resources).

An Outlaw Tale from Swett Ranch

I was camping at Worthen Meadow Reservoir, high in the Wind River Range above Lander, Wyoming, when a random outlaw connection occurred. I'd made friends with two campers at a nearby site who live in the Bighorn Basin. While talking about the outlaw trail, it came up that one of the guys was a descendant of the Swett family, and he'd often visited the historic ranch near Flaming Gorge Reservoir.

The family story he shared was that one day, long ago, an outlaw came to the ranch and asked—no, demanded—to stay for supper and the night. The family matriarch begrudgingly agreed. When the outlaw teased the woman about whether she could shoot a gun, the matriarch smiled. She asked him to line up some bottles on the fence, then she shot every bottle to bits. When she was done, she told the wide-eyed outlaw that he could stay the night, but afterward he wouldn't be welcome to return. The family never saw the man again.

Local legends and family tales like these are common along the outlaw trail. Just another way that the outlaw era lingers in the memories of those who live along its trails.

57

Canyon Rim Trail

THE LOWDOWN: The upstream end of Red Canyon is now flooded by Flaming Gorge Reservoir. High above on the rim, this scenic trail offers stunning views of the lake below.

THE ACTION: The **Canyon Rim Trail** is 4.5 miles one-way from Red Canyon Visitor Center to Greendale Overlook just off UT 44. The trail is open to hikers and mountain bikers, but most go on foot, starting from the visitor center. The first 1.5 miles closely follow the canyon rim, offering views from about 1,400 feet above the reservoir. Around mile 1.5, a right turn leads to a loop that passes a pair of small lakes and Red Canyon Lodge and returns to the visitor center.

THE LOOT: **Red Canyon Visitor Center** offers regional information, a small bookstore, and a few exhibits about area ecology and history. Outside is the Red Canyon Overlook. THE TICKING CLOCK: Open Memorial Day to Labor Day. THE JIG: Note that the Red Canyon Visitor Center at Flaming Gorge is not to be confused with the Red Canyon Visitor Center of the same name near Bryce Canyon.

THE GIDDYUP: From the junction of US 191 and UT 44, about 9 miles south of Dutch John, head west on UT 44 for 3.5 miles. Turn right (north) onto Red Canyon Road (FR 95) and proceed 2.5 miles to Red Canyon Visitor Center. THE SCENE OF THE CRIME: GPS 40.8915, −109.5607.

THE SUSPECTS: Ashley National Forest (see Resources).

THE DIGS: The seasonal Forest Service **Red Canyon Campground** and **Canyon Rim**

Campground are each just off Red Canyon Road. The **Red Canyon Lodge** offers cabins, tours, and a restaurant.

MORE LOOT: **Hideout Canyon** allegedly was the site of a hideout once used by Butch Cassidy and the Wild Bunch. Since the 1960s, it's been partially flooded by Flaming Gorge Reservoir, and today, there are two ways to visit, with most people motorboating to the Hideout Canyon Boat-in Campground.

MORE ACTION: Another option for exploring Hideout Canyon is hiking or biking from **Dowd Mountain Overlook**, a little-visited scenic viewpoint overlooking the southwestern reservoir. From the overlook trailhead, hike west about three-quarters of a mile along the single-track rim trail. Turn right onto the **Hideout–Carter Creek Trail**, a decommissioned double-track road that drops steadily for 4 miles one-way to the boat-in campground located on the reservoir. From the overlook to the campground, this route descends about 1,500 feet, so don't go down if you can't hike back up! THE GIDDYUP: To reach Dowd Mountain Overlook, on UT 44 at the turnoff to Red Canyon Visitor Center, head west on the highway 10.5 miles, then turn right (northeast) onto Dowd Mountain Road (FR 94) and drive about 4.5 miles to the small parking area and trailhead. Note: Sheep Creek Geological Loop (Adventure 48) starts less than 1 mile north on UT 44 from the turnoff to Dowd Mountain Overlook. THE DIGS: The Forest Service's **Hideout Canyon Boat-in Campground** has eighteen sites reservable at recreation.gov.

There are more elk than people in Browns Park—and everyone seems just fine with it.

Browns Park

THE WHOLE KIT AND CABOODLE: Called Browns Hole during the early outlaw era, **Browns Park** is a remote valley surrounded by mountains on all but its eastern edge. The site of a series of confrontations during the range wars of the Wild West, today the valley is emptier than during the old days. This isolated spot is well worth a visit, especially for outlaw enthusiasts. **THE HARDSHIPS:** Note that because it is so isolated, you need to be self-sufficient out here. Gas up, bring water and food, et cetera.

> "We had been told by one of the friendly hunters we passed to follow the road to the first left and then go down a long canyon. A typical cowboy direction: 'Head out to that juniper, turn left, go west to the Rocky Mountains and may the Good Lord bless your skies.'"
>
> —ROBERT REDFORD, *THE OUTLAW TRAIL*, DESCRIBING HIS VISIT TO BROWNS PARK IN 1975

58

John Jarvie Historic Ranch

THE LOWDOWN: The John Jarvie Historic Ranch is the outlaw highlight in the valley. The ranch, Green River ferry, and general store were established in the early 1880s by Scottish immigrant John Jarvie, who came to know the many outlaws and regulars. In July 1909, after the Wild West's heyday had mostly come to an end, Jarvie was robbed and murdered by two drifters from Rock Springs, Wyoming, who set his body adrift in the Green River.

THE LOOT: Today, the **John Jarvie Historic Ranch** is a restored site—highlights include the original general store (with the safe that was robbed), a waterwheel, blacksmith shop, dugout, and cemetery. The old stone house has exhibits about the Jarvie family and valley icon Queen Ann Bassett.

THE ACTION: Across the river from the Jarvie Ranch is the trailhead for what's called the **Outlaw Trail**, a 3.5-mile single-track for hiking and mountain biking that follows the Green River upstream on its south bank through the pleasant foothills of lower B Section (see Adventure 54).

THE GIDDYUP: To reach the ranch from Dutch John, Utah, head north on US 191 for about 9 miles. Turn right (east) onto Browns Park Road and follow it for 20.5 miles. Turn right onto Red Creek Road and continue 1.5 miles west to the Jarvie Ranch.

To reach the trailhead, from the Jarvie Ranch go east on Red Creek Road for 0.25 mile, turn right onto Taylor Flat Road, and cross the bridge. In 1 mile, turn right onto "Main Street" (quotes added by me, you'll see) and head west. After about a half mile—and don't get all weird with expectations for things like signs—veer off to the right on a dirt road leading toward the river to find the trailhead. **THE SCENE OF THE CRIME:** GPS 40.8997, −109.1773.

THE SUSPECTS: Bureau of Land Management, 435-781-4400 (for ranch website, see Resources). Flaming Gorge Country has a map for the Outlaw Trail at flaminggorge country.com.

THE SNORT: Browns Park has ten breweries. Yes, I'm lying.

THE YARNS: John Jarvie and his ranch are mentioned in two Browns Park Stories in this book: Episodes 4, Early Days in Browns Hole, 1878–1884; and 12, The Many Battles of Browns Park, 1898.

59

Eastern Browns Park

THE LOWDOWN: A driving tour through the mostly empty eastern side of Browns Park leads through Browns Park Wildlife Refuge to several worthy historic sites and a short but dramatic hike to a stunning lookout in the northern corner of Dinosaur National Monument. The Gates of Lodore, on the Colorado side of the monument and the southeastern side of Browns Park, is an impressive geologic feature where the Green River plunges between rising cliffs of the eastern Uinta Mountains. During normal weather and road conditions, the mostly unpaved roads on this driving tour can be navigated by two-wheel-drive vehicles. Highlights are described from west to east.

THE LOOT: Browns Park National Wildlife Refuge has some scenic roads to drive, two primitive campgrounds, a few sites to explore, and some overlooks along the main route described in **THE GIDDYUP.** The Green River moves very sluggishly through this part of Browns Park, so only a few river runners pass through from time to time, usually on multi-day trips involving upstream or downstream

sections. **THE SUSPECTS:** US Fish and Wildlife Service, fws.gov/refuge/browns_park.

MORE LOOT: The **Old Ladore School** operated from 1911 to 1946 and became a social hall (Lodore Hall) after that. It's an impressively restored building rising from the desolate valley floor. The **Lodore Cemetery**, where John Jarvie is buried, is located here. The ruins of the **Two Bar Ranch**, about a half mile north-northwest of the old school, are best reached on foot via a 0.5-mile social trail. A number of rough dirt traces lead to the site, which could be driven by ATVs and possibly four-wheel-drive vehicles, but it's easy to walk there following the trail that winds away from the northwest corner of the old school site. At one time the ranch was the headquarters for one of the largest ranching operations in Colorado and Wyoming.

THE ACTION: The small and lesser-visited Gates of Lodore Campground is near the launch site for three- to five-day class III whitewater river trips through the Canyon of Lodore that end at Split Mountain in the national monument (Adventure 45). Starting from the campground, the **Gates of Lodore Trail** heads 0.75 mile one-way to a very scenic overlook. **THE SUSPECTS:** National Park Service, nps.gov/dino.

THE GIDDYUP: To tour the wildlife refuge on unpaved roads, from Browns Park Road (CO 318) about 1.7 miles past the Colorado state line, turn right (south) on CR 83 and follow it for about 2.5 miles to the river. Turn left (downstream) to stay on Rivers Edge Wildlife Drive (CR 83), which mostly parallels the river along its north side for about 7.5 miles. At CR 164, turn left and in 1 mile return to Browns Park Road (CO 318).

To reach the Old Ladore School and Two Bar Ranch ruins, from the junction of Browns Park Road (CO 318) and CR 164, continue east on Browns Park Road for about 1.75 miles. Turn right onto CR 114 and drive 1 mile to the parking area **THE SCENE OF THE CRIME:** GPS 40.7803, −108.8922.

To reach the Gates of Lodore area, from the junction of Browns Park Road (CO 318) and CR 114, continue southeast on Browns Park Road for about 3 miles, turn right onto CR 34N, and follow it for 1.75 miles. Turn right onto CR 34 and drive 4.5 miles to enter the northern (Colorado) unit of Dinosaur National Monument. The road passes the boat launch and campground and ends at the trailhead. **THE SCENE OF THE CRIME:** GPS 40.7232, −108.8877.

THE DIGS: Small campgrounds can be found near the Jarvie Ranch, in the wildlife refuge, and inside Dinosaur National Monument near the Gates of Lodore.

RIDE ONWARD: For adventurous explorers only, who are willing to do their own research,

it's possible to visit the mysterious Browns Park "diamond field" (see Old West Stories, below). Straddling the Colorado-Wyoming border just north of Diamond Peak, the so-called Diamond Field is listed as such on USGS maps of the area. Specifically, you'll want to study the USGS 7.5-minute quadrangles for Sparks (Colorado) and Scrivener Butte (Wyoming). Don't expect any diamonds. Or interpretation. Or facilities. It's mostly BLM land and high desert (plus a few pockets of private land that must be respected).

As you'll see on the maps, the Diamond Field is near the northern end of Irish Canyon, which unpaved CR 10N passes through—a rough shortcut used by locals between Craig, Colorado, and Rock Springs, Wyoming. To get any closer to the field, you're on your own. **THE HARDSHIPS:** It's all hardships out there.

THE YARNS: The Browns Park area appears in Wild Bunch Stories, Episodes 3, On the

Cabin ruins near the Old Ladore School hint at a more populated past in Browns Park.

Outlaw Trail, 1889; 5, Wyoming Rambles, or Becoming Butch Cassidy, 1889–1896; and 17, Phantoms of the Outlaw Trail, 1922 . . . . Two Bar Ranch and other Browns Park sites are mentioned in Browns Park Stories, Episodes 4, Early Days in Browns Hole, 1878–1884; 12, The Many Battles of Browns Park, 1898; and 14, Queen Ann Bassett, 1899–1917.

OLD WEST STORIES: THE MYSTERIOUS DIAMOND FIELD NEAR BROWNS PARK

Please share our secret, thanks • Tiffany's of New York • Watch out, world gem market! • A chance encounter on a train • Dreams of untold riches • Why no pearls? • A salty retirement

One evening in November 1870, a pair of weather-beaten prospectors named Philip Arnold and John Slack arrived at the office of a San Francisco investor. With them they carried a leather bag containing something valuable. Given it was outside banking hours, the pair of Kentucky natives sought help to deposit the bag somewhere safe. At first, the men were tight-lipped about the contents until one of them let slip the words "rough diamonds."

Reluctantly, they opened the bag, which was filled with uncut diamonds and other gems. The men cryptically explained that they had found them in a vast diamond field, refusing to reveal a more precise location other than somewhere in the Indian territory of the mountain West. They swore the investor to secrecy, so of course he shared the story with several friends, including William Ralston, founder of the Bank of California.

Ralston was enthused and began recruiting other businessmen with the hopes of buying out these simple-minded prospectors, who were clearly in over their heads, and creating a company to mine the mysterious field. During their second visit, Arnold and Slack claimed to have revisited the diamond field and collected sixty pounds of diamonds and gems worth more than half a million dollars. The hesitant prospectors were reluctant to sell out, but Ralston convinced them to create a partnership, offering an initial investment of $50,000.

Arnold and Slack agreed to make a third trip to the diamond field. On their return to San Francisco during the summer of 1871, the two men were disheveled and exhausted. After presenting a sack with thousands of diamonds and gems to partner Asbury Harpending, they told a harrowing story. Supposedly they had obtained two sacks but lost one after flipping a log raft while crossing a flooded river.

Regardless, Ralston and the partners were ecstatic. Soon the collection of diamonds, rubies, emeralds, and sapphires went on public display in San Francisco. This attracted attention from the general public, local newspapers, and more investors. Plans were drawn up for a company valued at $10 million. Ralston and partners had several conditions for Arnold and Slack, including an agreement to take a mining expert to inspect the field.

But first, Harpending took 10 percent of the recently acquired gems to New York for appraisal by esteemed jeweler Charles Tiffany. Quite the high-class crowd assembled for the appraisal, including a *New York Tribune* editor and new investors Civil War general George McClellan and US Congressman Benjamin Butler.

"Gentlemen, these are beyond question precious stones of enormous value," announced Tiffany. His final estimate was $150,000, thereby valuing the entire sack at $1.5 million (about $32 million today).

Due to a cold winter, the trip to the diamond field was delayed until the following summer. The mining expert Henry Janin was hired. In June 1872, the party traveled on the transcontinental railroad to Rawlins, Wyoming. Arnold and Slack led them on a meandering four-day horseback journey through the high desert. The prospectors frequently appeared lost, climbing high points to look for landmarks.

On the fourth evening, they built camp on the gently sloping diamond field. Immediately, they went to work with picks and shovels. One man soon called out, holding up a shimmering gem. During the following two days, they found countless diamonds, plus the occasional colorful gem. Janin was so convinced, he spent much of his time staking out three thousand acres for the company's claim. This new field, he declared, would come to dominate the world gem market.

Slack, who had accepted a buyout for $100,000, and another partner were left behind to guard the field. The remaining men returned to New York, where a final buyout was made to Arnold, whose profits now totaled $550,000, minus expenses. Janin sold his shares for $30,000. News spanned the globe about the lucrative field where diamonds could be found inside ant hills—it almost sounded too good to be true.

That fall, Janin and partners were returning to San Francisco by train when they crossed paths with a geologist from Clarence King's government survey team. The team had recently completed the Fortieth Parallel Survey along a 100-mile-wide corridor following the transcontinental railroad from the Rockies to the Sierra Nevada in California.

Janin and pals bragged about their successful diamond hunt, allowing the surveyors a glimpse of the pretty crystals. The surveyors glanced at each other. From the hints dropped by Janin, this mysterious diamond field was located in northwestern Colorado, not far from the corridor of the Fortieth Parallel Survey. On receiving the news, King realized that the field's discovery would embarrass the efforts of the survey team.

In early November, the survey team rode mules away from Fort Bridger on a freezing ride through Wyoming's high desert. It took five days to travel 150 miles to the region that they deduced Janin had mentioned. After searching, they found the company's claim notices and went to work scouring the field. The first gems found were rubies. Then a diamond was plucked from the ground. The team went to sleep dreaming of untold riches beneath them.

But the next morning, things didn't add up. The gems were found only in disturbed ground. When the team dug a trench, there were no diamonds buried underground. On close inspection, the ant hills yielding gems had more than one hole in them, suggesting the stones had been pushed inside with a stick. The field had been "salted." King hustled back to civilization to inform the world.

It was called the Great Diamond Hoax. A mammoth fraud and fiasco. The greatest swindle ever exposed in America. Most news reports focused on how the supposedly sharpest men in California were so easily duped, losing millions in the process.

For further reading, see Dick Blust Jr.'s "The Diamond Hoax," Asbury Harpending's *The Great Diamond Hoax*, and Robert Wilson's "The Great Diamond Hoax of 1872."

Others pointed out how diamonds, rubies, emeralds, and sapphires aren't even found in the same geologic formations. Observers jokingly wondered why some pearls weren't thrown in for good measure. Were any gems found in nearby trees?

By this point, the two accomplices had disappeared, with Slack never seen again. Slowly the details of their scheme emerged. Two years before, it began with a leather bag of low-grade uncut diamonds obtained by Arnold while working at the Diamond Drill Company in San Francisco. During their claimed second and third visits to the field, they actually traveled to Europe and bought thousands of rough-cut low-grade gems, using these to entice the investors and salt the "diamond" field. Regarding his errant appraisal, it turned out Tiffany of New York was unfamiliar with uncut gems. His estimate was basically a guess.

Arnold returned to rural Kentucky, where his former Confederate neighbors delighted in the story of duped Yankee businessmen

in California. He claimed innocence, saying his counsel was a rifle. Arnold eventually settled out of court with the jilted businessmen for $150,000, using some of the remaining money to open a bank. During a gunfight with another banker, he was shot in the shoulder. While recovering, he died of pneumonia, and the story of America's greatest diamond swindler came to an end.

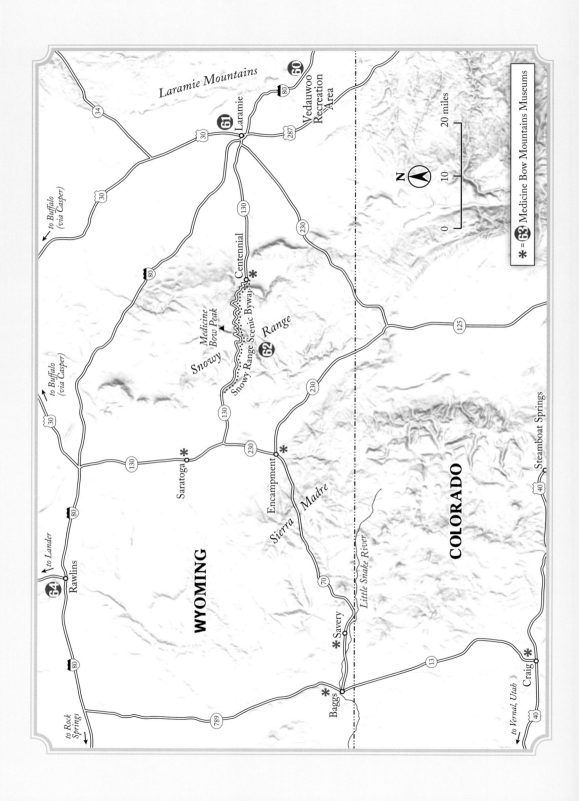

Laramie Mountains

34

30

to Buffalo
(via Casper)

30

80

30

to Buffalo
(via Casper)

80

to Lander

64
Rawlins

80

to Rock
Springs

789

30

130

Saratoga *

130

WYOMING

Medicine
Bow Peak

Snowy

Snowy Range Scenic Byway

Range

230

130

Encampment *

Sierra Madre

70

Savery *

Baggs *

Little Snake River

60

80

Vedauwoo
Recreation
Area

Laramie

61

30

287

130

230

62

230

125

COLORADO

40

Steamboat Springs

13

Craig *

40

to Vernal, Utah

Centennial *

N

0   10   20 miles

* = 60 62 Medicine Bow Mountains Museums

CHAPTER 8

Snowy Range and Laramie Area

SOUTHEASTERN WYOMING

THE WHOLE KIT AND CABOODLE: This lesser-known corner of southeastern Wyoming has a surprising variety of outdoor activities and outlaw-related sites to explore. There are not one but three subranges of the Rocky Mountains: from east to west, the Laramie Mountains, the Snowy Range, and the Sierra Madre. Here's just some of what you'll find within this region: Peaks to ascend. Alpine lakes to fish and paddle—swim at your own ice-cold risk. Wilderness areas to discover. Trails for hiking and roads for biking. Caves to explore where outlaws once hid and now climbers jam roughened hands into cracks. Plus, in the valleys, basins, and towns from Laramie in the east to Rawlins in the west, you'll find quality museums and sites for outlaw enthusiasts and general western-history buffs. Those who visit this area will be pleasantly surprised, and many will stay longer than expected.

60

Vedauwoo Recreation Area

THE LOWDOWN: The Laramie Mountains are a small range composed of 1.4-billion-year-old Sherman Granite, with most elevations ranging between 7,000 and 10,000 feet. The outlaw highlight is Vedauwoo Recreation Area, a 10-square-mile region of dramatic granite rock formations north of Laramie. Native American legends say the rocks were piled by playful spirts. During the 1800s, the caves and ledges were supposedly used as hideouts by bandits.

THE ACTION: Vedauwoo is very popular among area climbers, while most visitors opt to picnic or hike. The main trail is **Turtle**

Rock Loop, which circles the central rock formation in 3 miles. Many hikers go off-trail and scramble upward into the rocks to explore the boulders, cracks, and caves.

THE GIDDYUP: From I-80 about 16 miles east (more like southeast as the crow flies) of Laramie, take exit 329. At the stop sign, turn northeast onto Vedauwoo Road and drive about 1 mile. Turn left into Vedauwoo Recreation Area and continue 0.6 mile to the parking areas near the trail beneath Turtle Rock.

THE SUSPECTS: Medicine Bow National Forest (see Resources).

THE DIGS: The Forest Service **Vedauwoo Campground** near Turtle Rock has twenty-eight sites, all first-come, first-serve, available from roughly May through October.

THE LOOT: Nearby, the **Ames Monument** is a stone pyramid built in the early 1880s to mark the highest point on the first transcontinental railroad. The monument is dedicated to the Ames brothers, who were important Union Pacific investors. THE GIDDYUP: From the Vedauwoo exit off I-80, head southwest from the intersection and turn left onto unpaved Monument Road (CR 234). Head south for about 2 miles and turn right onto the short road leading to the monument.

RIDE ONWARD: Not far from Vedauwoo, **Curt Gowdy State Park** is a popular area known for a wide variety of activities, including reservoir fishing, camping, and 35 miles of trails for hiking, mountain biking, and horseback riding. THE GIDDYUP: From I-80 about 6 miles west (more like northwest) of the Vedauwoo exit, take exit 323 onto WY 210/Happy Jack Road. Head east for about 14 miles and turn right (south) onto Granite Springs Road to enter the park. THE SUSPECTS: Wyoming State Parks (see Resources).

61

Wyoming Territorial Prison

THE LOWDOWN: The outlaw highlight of Laramie is the **Wyoming Territorial Prison**

Legend says outlaws hid among the rocks at Vedauwoo.

State Historic Site. Built in 1872, for thirty years the original territorial prison held violent criminals and infamous outlaws. It also let plenty go free, with the prison being particularly known for escapes. The most famous inmate was Butch Cassidy, who in the mid-1890s served an eighteen-month sentence for buying a stolen horse. THE JIG: Oh, and do you like brooms? If so, the well-restored inmate broom factory will sweep a smile onto your face.

THE LOOT: In addition to touring the prison cell block and warden's home, you can visit a small museum about Butch Cassidy, the outlaw trail, and the Wild West era. A mock frontier town demonstrates the architecture of the period, and a historic ranch and frontier church were relocated to the property.

THE GIDDYUP: From I-80 in Laramie, take the Snowy Range Road/CO 230 exit. Turn east onto Snowy Range Road and drive 0.4 mile. Turn left (west) onto West Garfield Street.

THE SCENE OF THE CRIME: 975 Snowy Range Road, Laramie, WY 82070.

THE SUSPECTS: Wyoming State Parks, 307-745-6161 (see Resources for website).

THE TICKING CLOCK: Open daily May to September; Wednesday–Saturday October to April.

THE TAKE: Modest entry fee.

MORE LOOT: If you're looking for more museums in Laramie, then may I offer this short little list? **American Heritage Center** at the University of Wyoming (at North Ninth and East Lewis Streets), plus the university's **Geological Museum**, **Art Museum**, and **Anthropology Museum**. If you're still looking for museums, then next take a look at the **Wyoming Women's History House**. I'm sorry, you want more?! How about the **Laramie Plains Museum** at the **Historic Ivinson Mansion**? Please, that's enough. I couldn't possibly . . . list . . . any more. Fine: **Laramie Historic Railroad Depot Museum**. THE SUSPECTS: For info on all of these, check out visitlaramie.org.

THE SNORT: This college town has four breweries: Bond's Brewing, Coal Creek TAP, the Library Sports Grill and Brewery, and Altitude Chophouse and Brewery.

THE YARNS: Butch Cassidy's time in prison is described in Wild Bunch Stories, Episodes 5, Wyoming Rambles, or Becoming Butch Cassidy, 1889–1896; and 17, Phantoms of the Outlaw Trail, 1922 . . . .

62

Snowy Range and Scenic Byway

THE LOWDOWN: A dramatic subrange of the Medicine Bow Mountains (which in turn are part of the Rocky Mountains), the Snowies rise sharply to a mile high from the rolling plains below. The range is mostly composed of quartzite. In this case, light-colored sandstone metamorphosed into a hard silicate rock similar to granite. The result is that the range has a year-round white-topped look—from snow cover during fall, winter, and spring and from the grayish-white bedrock and perennial glaciers during summer.

THE LOOT: Extending between the eastern and western boundaries of Medicine Bow National Forest, the **Snowy Range Scenic Byway** offers the best route to explore these mountains. The byway follows an 1870s wagon route, crossing Snowy Range Pass, the

The view from below Medicine Bow Peak

second-highest mountain pass in Wyoming. Looming nearby is Medicine Bow Peak, at 12,018 feet the highest point in the Snowies.

THE GIDDYUP: The Snowy Range Scenic Byway (WY 130) runs for 29 miles from Laramie at I-80 in the east to WY 230 north of Encampment in the west.

THE ACTION: Various trails along the byway lead to adjacent peaks, through forested and tundra-covered meadows, and into the surrounding backcountry. Dozens of alpine lakes are dotted across the glacially carved valley between the highway and mountains. Most visitors choose to day-hike trails around **Mirror Lake Picnic Area** and **Lewis Lake Picnic Area** just east of the pass. The summit of **Medicine Bow Peak** can be reached by two steep trails, each with about 1,600 feet in elevation change, on its north and south flanks. This makes for a challenging loop hike, about 6.5 miles roundtrip, with the Mirror Lake trailhead being common.

You can ascend either side of the mountain, but the switchbacks are slightly more gradual on the north side.

THE HARDSHIPS: This is high-elevation adventuring. Acclimate and stay hydrated. Be wary of high winds, and don't attempt the summit hike if conditions are too gusty.

THE DIGS: On the road to Lewis Lake, the small Sugarloaf Campground is quite popular, while other dispersed options can be found just off the scenic byway.

THE SUSPECTS: Overall, finding information online about the Snowy Range is pretty tough, but Medicine Bow National Forest has a bit (see Resources).

THE SCENE OF THE CRIME: **Centennial Snowy Range Visitor Center** is on WY 130, 1.5 miles west of Centennial; GPS 41.313, −106.1532. Just east of Snowy Range Pass are **Mirror Lake Picnic Area**, GPS 41.3379, −106.3223, and **Lewis Lake Picnic Area**, GPS 41.3584, −106.2946. **Brush Creek/**

Hayden Ranger Station is on WY 130, about 1 mile south of downtown Saratoga; GPS 41.4377, –106.8039.

X MARKS THE SPOT: Your best bet for a map is to stop by either of the two ranger stations listed above. A basic map can be found online at goin2wyo.com/plan-your-visit.

63

Medicine Bow Mountains Museums

THE LOWDOWN: A total of six small museums (count 'em!) can be found around the northern Medicine Bow Mountains. The museums described below are listed in order of outlaw relevance, with some having more Wild West juju than others. Yet all are worth visiting for various reasons. And yes, it does feel like this museum-rich area is trying to show off.

THE GIDDYUP: Should you wish to visit them all, the museums in roughly northeast to southwest order are as follows: Nici Self in Centennial and the Saratoga Museum in Saratoga (both on WY 130); the Grand Encampment Museum in Encampment, the Little Snake River Museum in Savery, and the Outlaw Stop in Baggs (all three on WY 70); finally, the Museum of Northwest Colorado in Craig is on CO 13.

THE TAKE: All are free but accept donations.

THE "LOOTIEST": Of most relevance to the Wild Bunch saga is the **Outlaw Stop**, which preserves two historic buildings. The Mathews-Gaddis House was home to Pearl

Looking down from the summit of Medicine Bow Peak

Mathews Gaddis for seventy years, during which time she ran it as a roadhouse and occasional dance hall. Butch Cassidy and Wild Bunch gang members were said to stop by for food and fun while traveling the outlaw trail. The other building was one of those frontier do-it-all structures—a town hall, fire station, and jail—the insides of which saw plenty of other thorny characters. THE JIG: The Outlaw Stop is managed by the Little Snake River Museum in Savery, so you'll want to check with them for current hours. THE TICKING CLOCK: Typically Saturday and Sunday from late May to midfall. THE SCENE OF THE CRIME: 250 N. Penland Street (WY 789), Baggs, WY 82321. THE SUSPECTS: 307-383-7261; little snakerivermuseum.com/outlaw_stop.

MORE LOOT: The **Museum of Northwest Colorado**, 40 miles south of Baggs, houses one of the largest collections of Old West firearms. There are also some outlaw-relevant exhibits about Browns Park and its famous inhabitants, including the Bassett clan and Isom Dart. THE TICKING CLOCK: Open Monday–Saturday year-round. THE SCENE OF THE CRIME: 590 Yampa Avenue, Craig, CO 81625. THE SUSPECTS: 970-824-6360; muse umnwco.org.

EVEN MORE LOOT: Located 11.5 miles west of the Outlaw Stop in Baggs, just off WY 70, the **Little Snake River Museum** doesn't have many direct outlaw connections itself, but it preserves a small village of restored Old West buildings. These include pioneer cabins, homesteader houses, a schoolhouse, and a picturesque western mercantile, complete with a soda fountain inside. THE TICKING CLOCK: Open daily late May to midfall. THE SCENE OF THE CRIME: 13 County Road 561 N., Savery, WY 82332. THE SUSPECTS: 307-383-7262; littlesnakerivermuseum.com.

HOW 'BOUT SOME MORE LOOT: Just south of Saratoga, between the Snowy Range and the Sierra Madre, the **Grand Encampment Museum** is a nice museum with a grand sense of humor. In addition to a preserved town square of false-front western buildings, with corresponding exhibits inside, there's

The Little Snake River Museum in Savery, Wyoming

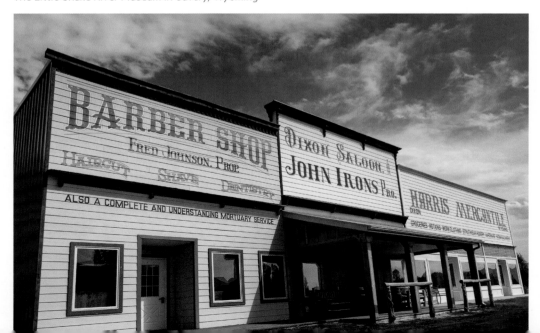

an infamous highlight: a historic *two-story* outhouse, with the vault toilets stacked one atop the other. When snow piled above the first floor, the lower-level seats lifted out of the way. When the snow melted, they cleaned the thing from top to bottom and locked the top to avoid any horrific accidents. Having to use a mountain ranch outhouse like that every day? Could send anybody into a life of crime on the outlaw trail. THE TICKING CLOCK: Open Tuesday–Saturday late May to midfall. THE SCENE OF THE CRIME: 807 Barnett Avenue, Encampment, WY 82325. THE SUSPECTS: 307-327-5308; gemuseum.com.

NEVER CAN HAVE ENOUGH LOOT, HUH?: On the western edge of the Snowy Range, the **Saratoga Museum**, located in a 1915 railroad depot building, has a variety of regional exhibits. THE TICKING CLOCK: Open Tuesday–Saturday year-round. THE SCENE OF THE CRIME: 104 E. Constitution Avenue, Saratoga, WY 82331. THE SUSPECTS: 307-326-5511; saratogamuseumwy.com. RIDE ONWARD: Down the street is the (free) Hobo Hot Springs.

OK, THIS IS A LOT OF LOOT IN ONE REGION!: At the foot of the eastern Snowy Range, the **Nici Self Museum** in Centennial has exhibits focusing on mining, ranching, and railroading history. THE TICKING CLOCK: Open Thursday–Monday Memorial Day to Labor Day. THE SCENE OF THE CRIME: 2734 State Highway 130, Centennial, WY 82055. THE SUSPECTS: niciselfmuseum.com.

THE YARNS: Baggs, Wyoming, is mentioned frequently in Wild West lore, including several stories in this book. See Wild Bunch Stories, Episodes 9, A Gang by Any Name, 1897–1898; 15, The Battle at Roost Canyon, 1899; and 17, Phantoms of the Outlaw Trail, 1922; as well as Browns Park Stories, Episode 14, Queen Ann Bassett, 1899–1917.

The Basset clan is featured in each of the Browns Park Stories. Isom Dart appears in Browns Park Stories, Episode 4, Early Days in Browns Hole 1878–1884, and Episode 14.

64
Rawlins

THE LOWDOWN: If you're craving more outlaw museums and Old West prisons (and who wouldn't be by now, right?), then make a stop in Rawlins while traveling I-80.

THE LOOT: The **Carbon County Museum** has a morbid exhibit about outlaw George "Big Nose" Parrot, including a pair of shoes allegedly made from the criminal's skin. Other exhibits focus on regional history, local women, Western artifacts, and more. THE TICKING CLOCK: Open Tuesday–Saturday year-round. THE TAKE: Donations appreciated. THE SCENE OF THE CRIME: 904 W. Walnut Street, Rawlins, WY 82301. THE SUSPECTS: 307-328-2740; carboncountymuseum.org.

MORE LOOT: Four blocks away is the restored **Wyoming Frontier Prison.** Now a museum, the original prison opened in 1901, during the waning days of the Wild West. THE SCENE OF THE CRIME: 500 W. Walnut Street, Rawlins, WY 82301. THE SUSPECTS: 307-324-4427; wyomingfrontierprison.org.

THE GIDDYUP: From West Spruce Street in downtown Rawlins, head north on Ninth Street for two blocks to West Walnut Street. The Carbon County Museum is at the southwest corner. To reach the Wyoming Frontier Prison, head east for four blocks on West Walnut Street and turn left (north) to enter the parking lot.

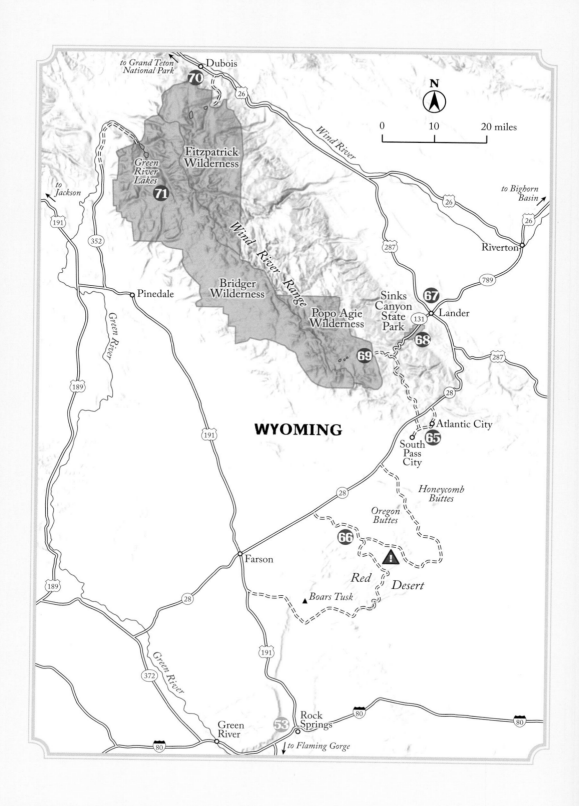

to Grand Teton
National Park

Dubois

70

26

Wind River

to Bighorn
Basin

to Jackson

191

352

Green River Lakes

Fitzpatrick
Wilderness

71

26

26

287

Riverton

Pinedale

Green River

Wind River Range

Bridger
Wilderness

Popo Agie
Wilderness

Sinks
Canyon
State
Park

131

67

Lander

789

68

69

287

189

191

WYOMING

28

Atlantic City

South
Pass
City

65

Honeycomb
Buttes

28

Oregon
Buttes

Farson

66

⚠️

189

28

▲ Boars Tusk

Red   Desert

Green River

372

191

Green
River

53

Rock
Springs

80

80

80

↓ to Flaming Gorge

0   10   20 miles

CHAPTER 9
Wind River Range
WESTERN WYOMING

THE WHOLE KIT AND CABOODLE: The Winds are one of the West's most rugged and remote mountain ranges. When combined with the few surrounding towns, the area is filled with alpine adventures and outlaw history. Many exploits of Butch Cassidy, Matt Warner, and other members of the Wild Bunch often seemed to haphazardly career toward, away from, and occasionally through the Winds. Butch briefly owned a ranch near Dubois, and he got into all kinds of trouble around Lander. He continued to return to the area for years, possibly to see a woman—including long after he died in South America (oh, we'll get to that in Wild Bunch Stories, Episode 16, *Banditos Yanquis en Bolivia*, 1905–1908).

Legends persist to this day about a cache of Cassidy's gold still hidden in the southern Winds, possibly near Lander or South Pass. As the story goes, after one of the Wild Bunch robberies, around the turn of the twentieth century, Cassidy returned to the Winds and filled a cast-iron cookpot with gold pieces. He buried the pot in a familiar area at the center of four equidistant trees, and he nailed mule shoes to each trunk. Before he could return, a forest fire burned through the area and the treasure was lost. Sure, it's possible. But that would be quite a fire to burn up the mule shoes too. Just saying, I'd run a rake through some ash for gold.

Anyway, today the real treasure is exploring the mountains. There are three wilderness areas to hike or backpack: Popo Agie (poh-POH-zhee), Fitzpatrick, and Bridger. Plus there are amazing camping opportunities, paddling and fishing trips, mountain biking and climbing, and plenty of historic sites and museums in the few towns scattered about. The adventures in this chapter start just south of the Winds, not far from I-80, and then work northward along the eastern side of the mountains before skipping west over to near Pinedale.

THE TICKING CLOCK: Due to northern latitude and high elevation, the Winds are best visited from late spring to early fall.

THE SUSPECTS: Info for the entire region can be found at windriver.org.

X MARKS THE SPOT: National Geographic Trails publishes a two-pack of topo maps covering the Winds: #726, Wind River Range North and #727, Wind River Range South.

THE HARDSHIPS: The Wind River Range is bear country—mostly black bears but there are grizzly bears too. While incidents are rare, all wilderness travelers should prepare accordingly. Traveling alone is not recommended.

The larger and louder your group, the better. Recommended safety practices include bear bells, bear spray, even bear songs—where you belt out lyrics to any bear-related songs that come to mind.

THE YARNS: Butch Cassidy and some members of the Wild Bunch spent a fair amount of time in the Wind River Range. Check out Wild Bunch Stories, Episode 5, Wyoming Rambles, or Becoming Butch Cassidy, 1889–1896.

65

South Pass City State Historic Site

THE LOWDOWN: South Pass City is one of the most complete historic townsites from the Old West era. While it doesn't have many explicit connections to outlaw lore, such characters certainly passed through this junction that connects several routes across the West, including the Oregon, California, and Mormon Trails.

THE LOOT: At **South Pass City State Historic Site**, more than thirty structures, originally built between a late-1860s gold rush and the town's abandonment in the early twentieth century, have been restored. Visitors can walk through town and enter more than half of these buildings, which include a stamp mill, hotel, blacksmith shop, and county jail. One historic building houses a small museum about Esther Morris, who became the first female justice of the peace in the US at South Pass City in 1870. Mining tours are also available.

Opposite: The Continental Divide Trail is just one of the ways to explore the Winds.

"The hotelkeeper, the postmaster, the blacksmith, the mayor, the constable, the city marshal and the principal citizen and property holder all came out and greeted us cheerily, and we gave him good day. South Pass City consisted of four log cabins, one of which was unfinished, and the gentleman with all those offices and titles was . . . all condensed into one person and crammed into one skin. . . . And he said that if he were to die as postmaster, or as blacksmith, or as postmaster and blacksmith both, the people might stand it; but if he were to die all over, it would be a frightful loss to the community."

—MARK TWAIN, *ROUGHING IT*, DESCRIBING A VISIT TO SOUTH PASS IN THE 1870S

THE ACTION: There's a 3-mile nature trail and a few shorter walking paths, which are listed on a site map that visitors can pick up on arrival.

THE GIDDYUP: From WY 28, about 43 miles northeast of Farson, turn south onto South Pass City Road and follow this unpaved road for about 2 miles to reach the town.

THE SCENE OF THE CRIME: 125 South Pass Main Street, South Pass City, WY 82520.

THE SUSPECTS: 307-332-3684; southpass city.com.

THE TICKING CLOCK: Open daily May through September.

THE TAKE: Modest entry fee.

MORE LOOT: Nearby, **Atlantic City** was originally a gold-mining camp established during the 1868 boom. Today, the welcome sign reports "about 57 people," while the 2010 census reported exactly thirty-seven, meaning the Pinkertons should probably be searching for about twenty missing persons. The town offers a self-guided historic walking tour, with brochures available outside the **Atlantic City Mercantile**. Originally built as the Giessler Store and Post Office in 1893, the "Merc" has been intermittently operated ever since by a string of proprietors as a store, gas station, and bar. THE GIDDYUP: From South Pass City,

backtrack on South Pass City Road for 0.5 mile to the Y junction. Veer right (northeast) onto South Pass Road and follow for 4 miles to Atlantic City. (You can return to WY 28 by following Atlantic City Road out of town toward the north for about 2.75 miles.)

THE YARNS: Alleged sightings of Butch Cassidy are mentioned in Wild Bunch Stories, Episode 17, Phantoms of the Outlaw Trail, 1922 . . . .

66

Red Desert

THE LOWDOWN: Wyoming's Red Desert isn't a widely known place, but there's plenty of reason to explore the barren and starkly beautiful region north of I-80 between Rock Springs

South Pass City State Historic Site is basically a preserved Old West town.

and Lander. Not only did outlaws use the area as an occasional hideout and travel route but many groups throughout American history also passed through here, including Native Americans, American pioneers, and, today, overlanders.

THE ACTION: There are several recommended loops for driving tours through the northern Red Desert. These loops mostly follow unpaved and minimally maintained Bureau of Land Managment and county roads, plus two sections of paved highway—WY 28 for 33 miles and US 191 for 8 miles. Sites include the Oregon Buttes, the Honeycomb Buttes, the Boars Tusk, the White Mountain Petroglyphs, and more. The northern half-tour loop is about 82 miles. The southern half-tour loop is about 102 miles. The full loop is about 153 miles. Make sure to download, study, and bring the driving map listed below before exploring this rugged region!

THE HARDSHIPS: Given the remote nature and challenging conditions, 4x4 and off-road tires are recommended. Road conditions deteriorate quickly during wet weather. Be wary of side roads, which are often not maintained and much rougher than the main roads. Note that this is a very remote area without services or, for the most part, cell phone coverage. Bring extra everything—water, food, fuel—and be prepared for contingencies. (See Modern Explorations: Mishaps and Injuries at the end of this chapter for how I fully embarrassed myself in the Red Desert.)

THE GIDDYUP: You can start the loop from several spots, and travel in either direction, but the two most common starting points are the western side near Farson or the northernmost corner near Sweetwater Rest Area (on WY 28, about 9 miles west of South Pass City Road).

THE SUSPECTS: Citizens for the Red Desert, reddesert.org/recreation.

X MARKS THE SPOT: The organization has a downloadable detailed travel map for the northern Red Desert.

THE DIGS: Just like the pioneers on wagon crossings, you can pretty much camp anywhere around here.

THE LAW: Uhhh . . . yeah, that's why outlaws hid out here.

THE YARNS: The Red Desert area is an occasional setting in outlaw lore, and the Wild Bunch, which went by many names, was sometimes called the Red Desert Gang.

67

Lander

THE LOWDOWN: Located in the foothills of the southeastern Winds, **Lander** is an adventure-travel gateway to hiking, camping, mountain biking, climbing, and other activities. The town offers restaurants, lodgings, stores, and a microbrewery. Many outlaws passed through Lander over the years, including Butch Cassidy and the Wild Bunch.

THE LOOT: The outlaw highlight, today, is the **Museum of the American West**. Around a dozen restored buildings from 1880 to 1930 are arranged like a frontier village, including a replica livery stable, schoolhouse, and newspaper office from the Old West era. Also in the village is the later home of Sheriff Charles Stough, who arrested Butch Cassidy in the 1890s and took him by train to prison in Laramie. THE SCENE OF THE CRIME: 1445 W. Main Street, Lander, WY 82520. THE SUSPECTS: 307-335-8778; museumoftheamericanwest.com. THE GIDDYUP: In Lander on US 287 (a.k.a. Main Street), head to the north end of town and turn left onto Chisholm Street.

MORE LOOT: Next door, the **Fremont County Pioneer Museum** exhibits regional artifacts from prehistory through the 1920s. The museum also sponsors a self-guided walking tour of Lander's historic district. **THE SUSPECTS:** fremontcountymuseums.com/the-lander-museum.

THE SNORT: The Lander Brewing Company and Cowfish Restaurant. **THE SCENE OF THE CRIME:** 148 Main Street, Lander, WY 82520.

THE YARNS: Butch does a fair bit of partying in Lander in Wild Bunch Stories, Episode 5, Wyoming Rambles, or Becoming Butch Cassidy, 1889–1896; sightings are reported there in Episode 17, Phantoms of the Outlaw Trail, 1922 . . . .

68

Sinks Canyon State Park

THE LOWDOWN: If you're heading into the Winds from Lander, the first highlight is **Sinks Canyon State Park**. This roadside park is named for where the Middle Fork Popo Agie River tumbles inside a cavern, called the Sinks. The river disappears for a quarter mile before emerging in a large clearwater pool, called the Rise, which is filled with massive rainbow and brown trout.

THE ACTION: Most people walk the interesting 0.25-mile paved path along the dewatered riverbed between the Sinks and Rise. There are additional trails along the slopes above the park, but if you're looking for a cool half-day hike, ride onward (see below).

THE DIGS: The park has two roadside campgrounds with sites that must be reserved online.

THE GIDDYUP: From US 287 in Lander, head south on South Fifth Street, which becomes Jerome Street, then Sinks Canyon Road (WY 131). In about 8 miles from town, you'll reach the park visitor center. **THE SCENE OF THE CRIME:** GPS 42.7483, –108.8096.

THE SUSPECTS: 307-332-3077; sinkscanyon statepark.org.

THE TAKE: Day use is free.

RIDE ONWARD: About a mile up the road from Sinks Canyon State Park, near the start of the switchbacks up Fossil Hill, you'll find the trailhead for the **Middle Fork Popo Agie Falls Trail**, which heads gradually uphill for 1.75 miles one-way to the falls. The trail is open to hiking, biking, and horseback riding. If you're looking for a short, easy day hike near Lander, this is the one. **THE GIDDYUP:** From Sinks Canyon State Park, continue driving south on WY 131 for about 3 miles to the trailhead parking lot.

69

Stough Creek Lakes Trail

THE LOWDOWN: The trailheads at Worthen Meadow Reservoir lead to several challenging hikes into the stunning high-alpine Popo Agie Wilderness. Just the scenic drive to the reservoir is a worthy trip, and the unpaved section of road is typically passable for most two-wheel-drive vehicles during normal road conditions.

THE ACTION: The **Stough Creek Lakes Trail** is a popular and very challenging full-day hike or overnight backpack trip. It's 7.5 miles one-way, with 2,500 feet of elevation gain, to reach

Opposite: A boardwalk crosses a soggy meadow on the trail to Stough Creek Lakes.

the open alpine terrain around Stough Creek Lakes.

THE HARDSHIPS: This is rugged wilderness hiking at its finest. Be prepared for wildlife encounters and changing weather.

THE DIGS: There are two small Forest Service campgrounds at Worthen Meadow Reservoir.

THE GIDDYUP: From downtown Lander, take WY 131 south for 10.5 miles (past Sinks Canyon State Park, Adventure 68), then continue onto Louis Lake Road, crossing the Popo Agie River and ascending the impressive Fossil Hill switchbacks. Proceed about 7 miles to a Y junction where the paved highway ends. At this Y, turn right onto FR 302 and continue about 2 miles to the trailhead. THE SCENE OF THE CRIME: GPS 42.6999, −108.932.

THE SUSPECTS: Shoshone National Forest (see Resources).

X MARKS THE SPOT: National Geographic Trails Illustrated Topo Map #727, Wind River Range South.

RIDE ONWARD: From the Y junction described above, continue your scenic drive on the unpaved Louis Lake Road for 20 miles of mountain views and lakes, ending at WY 28 near South Pass City and the Red Desert (see Adventures 65 and 66). A popular driving loop returns to Lander via WY 28 and US 287.

70

Dubois and Lake Louise Trail

THE LOWDOWN: Dubois is located on the upper Wind River amid stunning pink-and-gray badlands in the shadow of the northeastern Winds. This small mountain town offers access to adventures, museums, restaurants, lodgings, and bars—one of which is called the Outlaw Saloon, a nod to the area's Wild West history.

THE LOOT: The **Dubois Museum** focuses on the history of the Upper Wind River valley and includes a small frontier village with restored buildings. THE SCENE OF THE CRIME: 909 W. Ramshorn Street, Dubois, WY 82513. THE SUSPECTS: 307-455-2284; fremontcounty museums.com/dubois. THE TAKE: Modest fee.

MORE LOOT: Next door to the Dubois Museum is the **National Bighorn Sheep Center**. One downtown historic site with an outlaw connection is **Welty's General Store**, established in 1889, which served valley residents during the time Butch Cassidy owned a ranch north of town. THE SCENE OF THE CRIME: 113 W. Ramshorn Street, Dubois, WY 82513.

A few miles south of town is the **National Museum of Military Vehicles**. THE SCENE OF THE CRIME: 6419 US 26, Dubois, WY 82513.

My books *Paddling the Ozarks* and *Paddling the John Wesley Powell Route* can take you to some watery adventures.

THE ACTION: A popular day hike near town is the **Lake Louise Trail**, which climbs to the dramatic granite-basin lake in about 2.5 miles one-way, with 1,000 feet of elevation gain. Departing from the same trailhead, a harder and longer hike reaches **Ross Lake** in about 6 miles one-way, with around 2,500 feet of elevation gain. Using the same trail, turn off toward **Whiskey Mountain**, a route that's several miles shorter one-way, but with an extra 1,000 feet of elevation gain to ascend the summit. THE HARDSHIPS: No joke, these trails are steep, so be in good physical condition.

X MARKS THE SPOT: National Geographic Trails Illustrated Topo Map #726, Wind River Range North.

THE GIDDYUP: Dubois is on US 26/US 287 about 75 miles north of Lander. To get to the trailhead for Lake Louise, from Dubois head southeast on US 26/US 287 for just under 4 miles and turn right (south) onto unpaved Trail Lake Road, which is typically well graded and passable for most two-wheel-drive vehicles during normal conditions. Follow this road for about 9 miles, past several lakes, to Glacier Lake trailhead. THE SCENE OF THE CRIME: GPS 43.4257, −109.5739.

THE DIGS: Along the road to the Glacier Lake trailhead, there are several small campgrounds and dispersed camping sites.

THE SUSPECTS: Dubois Visitor Center (next to Dubois Museum), 307-455-3134; for information on the town and area, see duboiswyoming.org. For the Lake Louise Trail, see Bridger-Teton National Forest, fs.usda.gov/btnf.

RIDE ONWARD: About 60 miles west of Dubois is **Grand Teton National Park**, with some of the most distinctive scenery in the US. Outlaws wisely went around this sharply rising mountain range, but they spent plenty of time in nearby Teton Valley and Jackson Hole—doing their humble best to drive up the cost of living. These days, it's busy as ever but definitely worth a visit

THE YARNS: Butch Cassidy briefly co-owned a ranch near Dubois, discussed in Wild Bunch Stories, Episode 5, Wyoming Rambles, or Becoming Butch Cassidy, 1889–1896.

71

Green River Lakes and Pinedale

THE LOWDOWN: The northwestern Winds don't seem to have many documented outlaw connections, but if you're exploring the range anyway . . . why not check out Pinedale and visit a couple of remote alpine lakes in the Bridger Wilderness?

What better homage to the Wild West than to have a beer at the Outlaw Saloon in Dubois?

THE ACTION: Though they're a bit far to drive to, the two high-alpine **Green River Lakes** offer options for paddling and hiking in the Bridger Wilderness. The **Lakeside** and **Highline Trails** circle the picturesque lower lake in a 7.5-mile loop. Along the way, you'll have stunning views of iconic Squaretop Mountain. THE SUSPECTS: Bridger-Teton National Forest, fs.usda.gov/btnf. X MARKS THE SPOT: National Geographic Trails Illustrated Topo Map #726, Wind River Range North. THE DIGS: There's a campground at the road's end at Lower Green River Lake. THE HARDSHIPS: In addition to being a backcountry wilderness area, which requires self-sufficiency, the mosquitoes and other bugs can get bad here. Black bears and grizzlies are in the area—see THE HARDSHIPS at the beginning of this chapter.

THE GIDDYUP: Pinedale is on US 191 about 60 miles north of Farson. To get to Green River Lakes from Pinedale, take US 191 west 6 miles, then turn right (north) on WY 352 and follow it for about 25 miles. Continue north on unpaved Green River Lakes Road for about 19 miles to Green River Lakes Recreation Area on the lower lake.

THE LOOT: While in Pinedale, visit the **Museum of the Mountain Man**, which exhibits the history of the fur-trapping era in the region. THE SCENE OF THE CRIME: 700 E. Hennick, Pinedale, WY 82941. THE SUSPECTS: Sublette County Historical Society, 307-367-4101; museumofthemountainman.com. THE TICKING CLOCK: Open daily May through October. THE TAKE: Modest fee.

THE SNORT: Check out the Wind River Brewing Company in downtown Pinedale.

Smoke from forest fires gathers around Squaretop Mountain in the Wind River Range.

MODERN EXPLORATIONS: MISHAPS AND INJURIES THAT WOULD MAKE MOST OUTLAWS FORGET MY NUMBER

Who needs fuel in an empty desert? • Nylon tumbleweeds and ghost-town sandals • Remember the brewery, forget everything else • Flat tires to broken faces • Black-eye meetings and bad-haircut goodbyes • A whole-body approach

I was somewhere south of Lander, on my way to the Red Desert, when mistakes began to mount. Rushing to arrive before sunset, I realized I was driving on a third of a tank. Damn. Forgot to fill up.

Was 110 miles' worth of gas enough to explore one of Wyoming's most remote deserts? After some discouraging calculations and failed rationalizations, I turned around and drove 17 miles to the nearest station. It was one of those days when I tried to do too much, and things were about to get a whole lot worse.

· · · · · ·

The night before, a windstorm had hit the shores of Buffalo Bill Reservoir (Adventure 77), just west of Cody. Nylon tarps flew through the campground like tumbleweeds. Tents and shelters collapsed. Neighbors packed up in the darkness and went home. I pulled taut my two-person tent, climbed in with all my water jugs, and spent a sleepless night pondering the aerodynamics of my tent—whether on the ground or in flight. When I left early the next morning, the dumpsters were filled with broken camping equipment.

From Cody, I drove south through Meeteetse and turned onto a dirt road winding up into the Absaroka Range toward Kirwin Ghost Town (Adventure 78). Passing a roadside campground, a twelve-year-old boy flagged me down. He'd left his sandals at the ghost town.

"I know the feeling," I said, agreeing to help him out.

Three moose, seven miles of hiking, twenty historic structures, two smelly sandals, four hours of rough roads, one conversation about bears, and zero grizzly bear encounters later (nailed it), I was back in Meeteetse at the Cowboy Bar, chatting about outlaws who may have passed through—like I had all the time in the world.

Two more highway hours put me in Lander. I congratulated myself for remembering to stop by the brewery, order a pint, *and* thank a server for their camping suggestion the previous month. But I completely forgot about gas! By the time I corrected the error, I'd driven more than seven hours that day, and I didn't reach the Red Desert until dark.

"Are you kidding me?" I rifled through my folders, discovering I must have left the paper map, with my notes, at the brewery. What am I, a twelve-year-old boy? (Don't answer that.)

"Ah-ha!" I had saved a digital version of the map in Dropbox. But of course it was only a 1,000-pixel screen grab. Since I didn't have data service, I backtracked to a rest area on the highway, hoping to download the full PDF. No luck.

Squinting at the blurry low-res version on my phone, I could just make out the road numbers and some place-names. It was after

If you want to visit the places in this story, I've slipped the Adventure numbers into parentheses.

9:00 p.m. Good enough? I wondered. Then I spent the next hour failing to find my intended campsite. So of course it started to rain.

I found some flat ground to park, but my car's sleeping platform was packed with equipment. I was too tired to move everything during a rainstorm, so I moved the gear from behind my seat and reclined. Huh, I wondered, lying at an awkward 45-degree angle, did I eat dinner?

The next morning, I got moving early—stiff and tired—for some sunrise photography. I chased a few wild horses and antelopes, but they just weren't that into portraiture. Still, the area was starkly scenic with plains of sagebrush between desolate badlands. Also, the chaos of the previous day was finally behind me.

While driving through the heart of the northern Red Desert (Adventure 66), my vehicle lurched. A flat tire. My first in the new truck. I reconsidered. Actually, by some stroke of luck, this was my first flat tire in four trucks and almost twenty years of driving. Even though I was alone in the middle of nowhere, I felt pretty confident about the situation. I'd swap out the tire and carefully drive 25 miles to the nearest highway. If I got another flat, I'd have to ride my bike for help.

I unpacked the jack and tire tools. Fit together the extension rods and snapped on the lug wrench perpendicularly, which served as a handle. I slipped the hook end through the access port in the bumper and slid it into the dark shaft. I lay down on the roadway to get a view of the berth, but it was too dark to see much. When the hook hit something hard, I assumed it was in position and cranked on the lug wrench. The tire tool seized up and jammed in place. And when I leaned up to look, my shifting weight freed the whole contraption.

In an instant, the lug wrench swung around and impacted my cheekbone, just below the orbital (eyesocket). I felt a gush of blood and ran to the side mirror to assess the damage.

"Did I just break my face in the Red effing Desert?" I blurted, grabbing a towel to stop the bleeding. "I'm the dumbest adventure writer ever."

For a few minutes, I paced dejectedly, considering better career choices. Maybe a mattress salesman or blanket maker or pillow

Now, how am I getting out of this one?

spokesman like that one guy—basically anything involving softer materials. All the self-pity felt great but didn't do much to fix my flat.

Ignoring my throbbing face, I went to work. This time, I used a flashlight to properly lower the spare. Checked the emergency brake, loosened the lug nuts, jacked up the frame. Due to the angles, the full-size spare wouldn't fit until I used a shovel to dig out several inches of dirt.

Limping back to the highway, I scrutinized the road for sharp rocks. Pushed on my cheekbone, which didn't seem to be broken. In Rock Springs, I went to urgent care, where they closed the wound with glue. Not to brag, but the nurse said I had *perfectly* split it open. Clearly, we each have our talents.

One reason I'd been hurrying in the first place was to visit some museums before the weekend. Since my timeline was delayed by waiting for new tires, I decided to get a haircut. The stylist must have been distracted by my darkening black eye, because she botched the cut. I spent the next week having meetings with western historians and museum curators,

and I never could tell if they were glancing at the shiner or the bizarre cowlicks on the side of my head.

· · · · · ·

I would love to say that such experiences are rare, but it seems that with every project, half the adventure is mishaps and injuries. When exploring the Ozarks, I suffered heat exhaustion, a runaway kayak, and poison ivy on my butt. While paddling the John Wesley Powell Route on the Colorado, I wrecked my hands every way imaginable—heat rash, frostnip, rope burn, bloody cracks.

Over the years following the outlaw trail, I went for a whole-body approach. Ankle sprains and hamstring strains. Heel cracks and sunburned back. I overheated while mountain biking at Red Canyon (Adventure 34) and later wrapped my shoelace around my pedal crank and crashed my bike at Red Fleet (Adventure 46). I got spider bites on my poison ivy scar and dislocated my thumb while lowering my bike off the roof rack.

I began to suspect the wind had a grudge against me, knocking me off my paddleboard in another Red Canyon and off my feet on the trail to Medicine Bow Peak (Adventure 62). In solidarity, occasionally my equipment joined in the fun. While camping at Hole-in-the-Wall (Adventure 75), I returned from a day hike to find my tent collapsed with a broken pole. I didn't even get the opportunity to stumble and fall on it. But believe me, I would have if given the chance.

MONTANA

310

Bighorn Canyon
National Recreation
Area

76

Bighorn
Medicine
Wheel

Bighorn

90

25

Sheridan

Lovell

ALT
14

ALT
14

14

14

16

77 Cody

310

14

ALT
14

20

Mountains

Cloud Peak
Wilderness

72

to Yellowstone
National Park

73

Buffalo

16

90

Bighorn   Basin

78 Meeteetse

120

16

Ten Sleep

25

Bighorn River

WYOMING

Country

Kaycee

Kirwin
Ghost
Town

N

20

Thermopolis

Outlaw Cave
Campground and Trail **74**

Powder River

0   10   20 miles

79

Wind
River
Canyon

Hole-in-the-
Wall Hideout **75**

Middle Fork

TTT Rd

25

Buffalo Creek Rd

Red Wall

Willow Creek Rd

26

26

Wind River

26

Riverton

CHAPTER 10
Bighorn Mountains and Basin
NORTHERN WYOMING

THE WHOLE KIT AND CABOODLE: The region including the Bighorn Mountains and Bighorn Basin is a regular setting for some of the most daring exploits of the outlaw era. A southern offshoot from the mountains—called Red Wall Country—is home to one of the most famous hideouts, and possibly the best named: Hole-in-the-Wall. While the Bighorn Basin, Bighorn Mountains, and Red Wall Country are in some ways part of the same overall region, for this chapter they are separated to aid with trip planning. In the region's towns, you can visit museums, ghost towns, and Old West villages. Outdoor adventures range widely from easy hikes to scenic vistas, plus more rugged adventures like wilderness backpacking.

THE TICKING CLOCK: The typical season to visit is May through October.

THE YARNS: The Bighorn Mountains and Basin are mentioned many times in outlaw lore, including two Wild Bunch Stories in this book: Episodes 5, Wyoming Rambles, or Becoming Butch Cassidy, 1889–1896; and 10, A Seemingly Normal Cowboy Named Jim Lowe, 1899.

72
Buffalo

THE LOWDOWN: On the eastern side of the Bighorn Mountains, the pleasant western town of Buffalo makes a good base for exploring this region, and it has several Wild West connections.

THE GIDDYUP: Buffalo is at the crossroads of I-25 and I-90 and US 16.

THE LOOT: The **Jim Gatchell Museum** presents the region's story with a series of excellent chronological exhibits, from Native Americans to the modern day. Special attention is given to the Johnson County War, the infamous range conflict during the 1890s (see The Real Story of the Johnson County War later in this chapter). THE SCENE OF THE CRIME: 100 Fort Street, Buffalo, WY 82834. THE SUSPECTS: 307-684-9331; jimgatchell.com.

THE DIGS AND A SNORT: A block away, the historic **Occidental Hotel** was visited by many Wild West figures during its heyday, and today you can stop in for a drink in the saloon or stay in a restored room. THE SCENE OF THE CRIME: 10 N. Main Street, Buffalo, WY 82834. THE SUSPECTS: occidentalwyoming .com. THE YARNS: The Occidental Hotel claims Butch Cassidy as a former guest, along with other famous figures, including Calamity Jane, Buffalo Bill, Tom Horn, and Teddy Roosevelt.

MORE DIGS: Fourteen miles south of town on WY 196, the **TA Ranch** of today is an excellent guest ranch where you can stay the night and visit the barn to see actual bullet holes from a standoff during the Johnson County War. THE SCENE OF THE CRIME: 28623 Old Highway 87, Buffalo, WY 82834. THE SUSPECTS: 307-684-5833; taranch.com.

73

Cloud Peak Wilderness

THE LOWDOWN: These days, much of the activity in the Bighorn Mountains centers on outdoor adventures in and around the Cloud Peak Wilderness. One of the more popular places to access this remarkable wilderness is the West Tensleep Lake area. THE JIG: Sightings of moose, along with other wildlife, are common throughout the area. Eyes peeled!

THE ACTION: Several trails begin from the West Tensleep trailhead. For a half-day hike, the **Lost Twin Lakes Trail** #065 reaches Mirror Lake in 3.5 miles one-way, with 500 feet of elevation gain. If you're up for it, continue another 2 miles, with 800 feet of elevation gain, to reach Lost Twin Lakes below Darton Peak.

For a longer day hike or a short backpacking trip, consider the **Misty Moon Trail** #063.

This trail takes about 6.5 miles one-way, with 1,700 feet of elevation gain, to reach Misty Moon Lake nestled in a mountain basin.

RIDE ONWARD: If those hikes aren't enough (you're insatiable!), from the end of the Misty Moon Trail, you can join the **Solitude Loop** #038, which takes 56 miles with a measly 10,000 feet of elevation gain (phew, I'm tired just typing that) to circle around Cloud Peak and Black Tooth Mountain, passing a dozen or more lakes in the Cloud Peak Wilderness just below tree line. Backpackers hike the loop in either direction, with clockwise being considered the slightly easier choice.

THE GIDDYUP: To reach the West Tensleep Lake area, from US 16 about 46 miles west of Buffalo (16 miles east of Ten Sleep), turn north onto Deer Haven Lodge Road/Bower Road/Tyrell Ranger Station Road/Ten Sleep Road (FR 27) and follow it for 7.5 miles to the West Tensleep trailhead. THE SCENE OF THE CRIME: GPS 44.2624, −107.2127.

THE SUSPECTS: Bighorn National Forest (see Resources).

X MARKS THE SPOT: National Geographic Trails Illustrated Topo Map #720, Cloud Peak Wilderness.

THE DIGS: There's no camping allowed at the trailhead, but along Ten Sleep Road are several primitive campgrounds with pit toilets and well-water pumps, including **West Tensleep Campground** near the lake. Additionally, along Ten Sleep Road there are many dispersed primitive camping sites without toilets or water that are intended for self-sufficient and/or RV campers with their own toilets and water supplies.

THE SNORT: On US 16 on the western side of the Bighorn Mountains, the town of Ten Sleep has a nice brewery—plus a pioneer museum.

Backpacking the Solitude Loop near Misty Moon Lake in the Cloud Peak Wilderness

Red Wall Country

THE WHOLE KIT AND CABOODLE: In the foot-hills of the southern Bighorn Mountains, Red Wall Country is a stunningly scenic region with plenty of outlaw history worth explor-ing. The name comes from a series of sheer red sandstone cliffs, part of the Chugwater For-mation, that extend for more than 25 miles south of the Bighorn Mountains. The gateway to the area is Kaycee, where you can obtain more information about the top two sites, Outlaw Cave (Adventure 74) and Hole-in-the-Wall Hideout (Adventure 75).

THE GIDDYUP: Kaycee is off I-25 between Buffalo and Casper, Wyoming.

THE LOOT: The **Hoofprints of the Past Museum** offers exhibits about regional history as well as tours of Johnson County War sites and Hole-in-the-Wall. **THE TICKING CLOCK:** Open Monday–Saturday mid-May through October. **THE SCENE OF THE CRIME:** 344 Nolan Avenue, Kaycee, WY 82639. **THE SUSPECTS:** 307-738-2381; hoofprintsofthepast.org.

74

Outlaw Cave Campground and Trail

THE LOWDOWN: The Outlaw Cave Camp-ground and Trail offer two ways—one above, one below—to experience a dramatic and improbable chasm in the remote Middle Fork

Powder River recreation area. This adventure is a rugged one that's best suited to those who are comfortable with navigating rough roads and exploring wild and empty places.

THE ACTION: Two trails with alleged outlaw significance can be reached from the campground. The main **Outlaw Cave Trail**, which descends steeply—500 feet in 0.5 mile—to the Middle Fork Powder River, is used mostly by fly-fishers to access a 12-mile section of blue-ribbon trout habitat. Several caves can be found in the bluffs near river level. Curiously, the so-called **Outlaw Cave** is not actually a cave but a small alcove with a collapsed ceiling, which seems unlikely to have ever been used as a hideout. Because the fishing paths running up and down the canyon are rough and almost nonexistent in places, most people wade in the riverbed.

A second, lesser-followed trail departs the main trail about a third of the way down and heads upstream on a high terrace on the west side of the canyon. This roughly 1-mile trail (one-way) is very steep and challenging in spots, passing a pair of impressive caves and ending near a small campsite by the river.

THE DIGS: The free campground, located on 500-foot-high bluffs overlooking the narrow river gorge, has twelve first-come, first-serve sites, a vault toilet, and *no* water or trash collection.

THE GIDDYUP: From I-25 in Kaycee, take WY 191 north for 1.5 miles, then turn left onto WY 190 west and follow it for about 16 miles. Turn left onto Bar C Road, following signs for Middle Fork Powder River Management Area, and continue for just under 8 miles to the campground.

THE HARDSHIPS: Much of the route to Outlaw Cave Campground is on unpaved clay-dirt roads, which are impassable when wet but suitable for most two-wheel-drive vehicles during normal conditions. If in doubt, turn around! Also, note that the route to the campground and trail travels through private property belonging to the Hole-in-the-Wall Ranch. Be wary of following routes suggested by navigation apps. Due to private property, it is not permitted to drive directly from Outlaw Cave Campground to Hole-in-the-Wall—you must return to Kaycee and approach the hideout from the southern route described in Adventure 75.

THE SUSPECTS: Bureau of Land Management, blm.gov/visit/outlaw-cave-campground.

75

Hole-in-the-Wall Hideout

THE LOWDOWN: The outlaw highlight of this region is Hole-in-the-Wall, an infamous and isolated hideout in a small valley eroded into the Red Wall. The best part is the emptiness of the area, and just getting there is an adventure. If you don't join a tour (options are available in Buffalo and Kaycee), you'll need a high-clearance four-wheel-drive vehicle for the rough clay-dirt road that's basically a sextuple-track in places and impassable after heavy rains. THE JIG: The hideout itself is on Bureau of Land Management land, but the road passes through private property with about six gates to open—make sure to close them behind you.

THE ACTION: From the trailhead, it's a 3-mile one-way hike into the triangular valley at the base of the Red Wall. Be aware that after crossing the creek and passing through a livestock gate, there are several overlapping and intersecting trails. Luckily, it's easy to navigate if you aim for the notch in the washboard-like

Hiking to Hole-in-the-Wall hideout in Red Wall Country

Red Wall. From the base of the wall, a steep trail leads up to the cliffs and plateau above, where supposedly only a single rider could pass at one time.

RIDE ONWARD: Day hiking is most popular, but you can also backpack and camp on BLM land inside the hideout valley.

THE HARDSHIPS: You'll be on your own out here, just like an outlaw. Come prepared.

THE GIDDYUP: From Kaycee, take I-25 south for 4.5 miles and take the TTT Road exit; follow TTT Road/Lone Bear Road (WY 196) south for about 14 miles. Turn west (right) onto Willow Creek Road (CR 111) and follow this unpaved road for about 18 miles. At the primitive double-track road that bears sharply northeast, turn right on Buffalo Creek Road (CR 105). Follow CR 105 for about 11.5 miles through a series of livestock gates that must be opened and closed. This road ends at the Hole-in-the-Wall parking lot and trailhead. Note: It takes about two hours of driving and opening/closing gates (you'll be a pro by the end) to reach the parking lot. **THE SCENE OF THE CRIME:** GPS 43.5296, −106.8649.

THE SUSPECTS: BLM, blm.gov/visit/hole -wall-foot-trail.

THE YARNS: Hole-in-the-Wall is perhaps the most famous of the Wild Bunch's hideouts, but they seem to have actually spent more time in Browns Park and Robbers Roost. Still, Hole-in-the-Wall receives regular mentions in outlaw lore, including Wild Bunch Stories, Episode 5, Wyoming Rambles, or Becoming Butch Cassidy, 1889–1896.

HELL, *MAYBE* YOU SHOULD WATCH *HEAVEN'S GATE*? (CLEAR A WEEKEND)

"It takes almost as much time to watch this film as it took for them to make this film."

—UNKNOWN OUTLAW

Do you enjoy Westerns with snowcapped mountain vistas, authentic false-front towns set against alpine lakes, and glacially paced stories that bear only passing resemblance to the underlying historical subject matter? Then have I got a half-day event—I mean, movie—for you.

Simultaneously appearing on lists for both the worst and the best films of all time, *Heaven's Gate* is a 1980s epic directed by Michael Cimino. The story very loosely follows the events of the 1890s Johnson County War, with a group of wealthy cattle barons plotting to kill 125 poor settlers who allegedly steal livestock to avoid starvation. The scenes are beautifully shot, and coming in at three hours and thirty-nine minutes, there's plenty of them.

Naturally, the film opens with a seventeen-minute Harvard graduation sequence, with the fortysomething actors playing their drunken twentysomething selves, which has little bearing on the later plot. Finally, we leap forward twenty years to Wyoming—actually shot on location in Montana's Glacier National Park, until the park service kicked out the

The Real Story of the Johnson County War

In early April 1892, a party of about fifty cattle barons and hired guns invaded Johnson County. These representatives of the Wyoming Stock Growers Association came heavily armed, with a list of seventy locals they planned to kill—vigilante justice, they claimed, for alleged cattle theft.

In reality, most of these targeted locals were private ranchers who grazed their smaller herds on the same increasingly overstocked public lands used by the cattle barons, who sought to enforce an illegal monopoly.

One of the invaders' first stops was the KC Ranch, where local rancher Nate Champion was hiding. The year before, Champion had fought off an assassination squad sent by the cattle barons, who now feared his testimony in the court case. The fifty men surrounded the cabin, which Champion defended with gunfire for hours. Finally, the invaders torched the cabin. When Champion

fled from the flames, he was shot down.

By now, the county residents were aware of the invaders and formed a posse. The invaders fled to the TA Ranch (Adventure 72), which was soon surrounded by four hundred regional residents.

On the third day of the siege at the TA Ranch, the posse used hastily constructed go-devils—essentially, log walls on wagon wheels—to approach the ranch. As the posse prepared to hurl dynamite, soldiers from a nearby fort arrived to arrest the invaders.

Due to intervention by political allies, the charges against the barons were eventually dropped.

Tensions between cattle barons and private ranchers, as well as statewide political upheavals, continued in Wyoming for several years, until the Stock Growers Association allowed small private ranchers to join the organization, thus ending one of the greatest range conflicts in US history.

production, which was then shot *near* Glacier National Park.

This film has it all. Plenty of smoky meetings between wealthy businessmen. A five-minute roller-skating scene accompanied by a teenage fiddler. Christopher Walken as a tough hired gun who wears eyeliner and harasses European refugees. A scene where the county marshal reads the names on the kill list—not all 125, but feels like it. Forty minutes of chaotic frontier battles, including a brief ceasefire for some experimental carpentry.

The film can be brutal to watch at times, with graphic depictions of violence, including murder, rape, and suicide. There's a real cockfighting scene. And real cows were slaughtered, with entrails shown onscreen, which led to complaints of animal cruelty and the subsequent creation of the disclaimer "no animals were harmed." It was that, along with other environmental concerns, that led to expulsion by the park service.

> Fun fact! Actor Willem Dafoe was fired from the cast for pretending he spoke Dutch.

On its release, the film was a commercial and critical failure, with much of the blame being pointed at the maniacal director, who some said flew in daily by helicopter. Cimino's obsessive attention to detail created stunning visuals but caused legendary budget overruns and production delays. In one case, he demanded an irrigation system be installed beneath the climactic battlefield to grow emerald-green grass that contrasted the spilled horse blood.

Others claim that, by day six, they were five days behind schedule. One actor became so tired of waiting around, he went off and filmed another movie without much notice, then returned to complete his role in *Heaven's Gate*. A *Washington Post* writer went undercover as an extra, reporting that cast injuries were common, including breaking his own foot during a stampede scene. One extra joked that Cimino interviewed three hundred horses for the film.

Cimino elected to keep the names of real historic figures for wildly inaccurate fictional characters—doing injustice to the real story of the Johnson County War. Yet despite all these controversies, the film's popularity has increased in recent years. For the backstory alone, it's worth a viewing. Oh, also for the roller-skating! The actors spent weeks on skates training for those five minutes.

Bighorn Basin

THE WHOLE KIT AND CABOODLE: This is a massive region of high plains, mesas, valleys, and rivers. Bordered by the Bighorn Mountains to the northeast, the Winds to the southwest, and Yellowstone to the northwest, the interior basin is a lesser-known gem among outdoorsy travelers who often speed through to high points on the periphery. Those who take their time will be pleasantly surprised by a mix of historic towns and adventurous activities.

76

Bighorn Canyon and Medicine Wheel

THE LOWDOWN: On the border of Wyoming and Montana, the southern district of Bighorn Canyon National Recreation Area offers boating and paddling on Bighorn Lake through a dramatic and forgotten canyon.

There are also historic ranches to explore, plus several hiking trails. In general, there's not a lot of information about this recreation area online, so your best bet is to stop by the visitor center in Lovell for up-to-date info.

THE GIDDYUP: US 14 Alt bisects the lake from east to west, just west of the Bighorn Mountains. For the southern district, head west on US 14 Alt to its junction with US 310 at Lovell to get to the Cal Taggart Visitor Center. THE SCENE OF THE CRIME: 20 US 14 Alt, Lovell, WY 82431; GPS 44.8386, −108.3775.

THE LOOT: For Old West enthusiasts, there are four historic ranches to visit in the recreation area, including the Ewing Snell Ranch, the Hillsboro Ranch, and the Mason-Lovell Ranch. Of particular interest is the **Caroline Lockhart Ranch**, which includes more than a dozen intact structures on a spread once owned by this journalist and novelist, also known as Montana's cattle queen. THE GIDDYUP: From US 14 Alt east of Lovell, turn left (north) on WY 37 and follow it north into Montana; the ranch is to the west just north of Barry's Landing Road.

THE ACTION: The recreation area's southern district sees less motor traffic, so this is the side for paddling adventures. Most canoes and kayaks launch from **Barry's Landing** and head upstream or downstream. THE GIDDYUP: From US 14 Alt east of Lovell, turn left (north) on WY 37 and follow it north 22.5 miles, into Montana, then turn right (east) onto Barry's Landing Road to the boat launch.

THE SUSPECTS: National Park Service, 307-548-5406; they have a downloadable Waterway Trail Guide and a hiking trail guide at nps.gov.htm.

Bighorn Canyon National Recreation Area on the border of Wyoming and Montana

MORE ACTION: The recreation area also has 17 miles of hiking trails, with most trailheads on WY/MT 37. The moderate **Barry's Island Trail**, 4 miles roundtrip starting from the Barry's Landing Marina, takes hikers into Chain Canyon, used by cattle rustlers during the Wild West era, before looping around

the mesa top of Barry's Island. A 0.3-mile spur road heading northwest from the neck of Barry's Island leads to Medicine Creek Campground (hike-in/boat-in only), allowing for a short backpacking trip.

THE DIGS: Bighorn Canyon NRA has several medium to large campgrounds, ranging from primitive to fully developed.

RIDE ONWARD: About 33 miles east of Lovell on US 14 Alt is the **Bighorn Medicine Wheel**, a National Historic Landmark that protects a sacred Native American site. The

medicine wheel is a roughly circular arrangement of stones about 82 feet in diameter. Visitors must walk about 1.5 miles each way to the Medicine Wheel and back. THE SUSPECTS: Bighorn National Forest (see Resources).

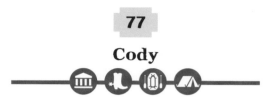

77

Cody

THE LOWDOWN: In the northwest corner of the Bighorn Basin, Cody is a historic Old West town with modern conveniences. Located at the junction of US 14, US 14 Alt, and WY 120, most visitors pass through on their way to Yellowstone National Park. But Cody has plenty of great sites worth visiting in their own right, including several with outlaw connections.

THE LOOT: **Old Trail Town** was established in 1967 when archaeologist Bob Edgar began relocating historic buildings from across Wyoming to the original 1895 Cody townsite. Today there are twenty-six buildings dating from 1871 to 1901, arranged like a Wild West main street, plus wagons and artifacts. The highlight for outlaw adventurers is the original cabin from the Hole-in-the-Wall Hideout (Adventure 75), once visited by Butch Cassidy and other members of the Wild Bunch. THE TICKING CLOCK: Open daily mid-May through September. THE TAKE: Modest fee for ages 6 and up, younger children free. THE SCENE OF THE CRIME: 1831 Demaris Drive, Cody, WY 82414. THE SUSPECTS: 307-587-5302; oldtrailtown.org.

MORE LOOT: The expansive **Buffalo Bill Center of the West** includes five excellent museums in one building: The **Buffalo Bill Museum** documents the life and exploits of

Buffalo Bill Cody and other members of the Wild West Show, including Annie Oakley and Sitting Bull. The **Plains Indian Museum** explores the lives, cultures, and traditions of Native Americans from the Great Plains. The **Whitney Western Art Museum** displays many works from acclaimed Western artists like Albert Bierstadt, Thomas Moran, Frederic Remington, Charlie Russell, and others. The **Draper Natural History Museum** offers a series of kid-friendly exhibits about the plant and animal life of Yellowstone National Park. The **Cody Firearms Museum** houses more than ten thousand firearms that span hundreds of years. THE TICKING CLOCK: Open daily March through November; Thursday–Sunday December through February. THE TAKE: Moderate fee for ages 6 and up, younger children free. THE SCENE OF THE CRIME: 720 Sheridan Avenue, Cody, WY 82414. THE SUSPECTS: 307-587-4771; centerofthewest.org.

EVEN MORE LOOT: Walking tours through the historic downtown are popular among visitors, with stops including the Buffalo Bill Center of the West and the Irma Hotel (see below). The Cody Chamber of Commerce offers a visitor map and walking-tour guide. THE SUSPECTS: codychamber.org/visit-cody.

THE DIGS: Buffalo Bill built the historic **Irma Hotel** in downtown Cody in 1902 and named it for his daughter. Today, the walls are filled with mounted game animals and old photos. THE SCENE OF THE CRIME: 1192 Sheridan Avenue, Cody, WY 82414. THE SUSPECTS: 307-587-4221; irmahotel.com.

THE SNORT: Cody has three breweries: WYOld West, Pat O'Hara, and Cody Craft.

THE ACTION: Other adventures in and around Cody include rafting the East Fork Shoshone River with a guided outfitter, boating on **Buffalo Bill Reservoir**, and camping at

Buffalo Bill State Park. THE SUSPECTS: Park County Travel Council, codyyellowstone.org.

RIDE ONWARD: About 50 miles west of Cody is the east entrance to **Yellowstone National Park**. At just under 3,500 square miles, it's the second-largest national park in the Lower 48. It offers so much to see and do, you'll want to perform your own research before visiting. The park was established in 1872, and it saw a number of daring stagecoach robberies during the Wild West era. In several cases, the victims were park visitors traveling in long caravans of many stagecoaches. Twice, bandits positioned themselves at spots in the road where the drivers couldn't see one another. The outlaws proceeded to hold up the stagecoaches, one after another, before sending the tourists on their way, less their cash and valuables. Some passengers even wondered if it was all part of the tour. Said one enthusiastic victim in 1915, "It was the best fifty dollars I ever spent."

78

Meeteetse and Kirwin Ghost Town

THE LOWDOWN: Meeteetse is a small foothills town with Old West connections that are still discussed at places like the **Cowboy Bar and Outlaw Café**. In addition to having a three-in-one museum, Meeteetse is a gateway to the picturesque Kirwin Ghost Town at the head of the Wood River, high in the Absaroka Mountains.

THE LOOT: The **Meeteetse Museums** include three buildings, with the main museum focusing on local history. There's also the **Charles Belden Museum of Western Photography** and the restored **Bank Museum**,

originally built in 1901. The museum offers free guided tours and a series of self-guided walking tours—including for Kirwin and another historic site, the Double Dee Guest Ranch—via an app that can be downloaded to smartphones (izi.travel/en/3834-meeteetse -museums). THE TICKING CLOCK: Open Tuesday–Sunday February through December. THE SCENE OF THE CRIME: 1947 State Street, Meeteetse, WY 82433. THE SUSPECTS: 307-868-2423; mee teetsemuseums.org.

THE GIDDYUP: Meeteetse is on WY 120 between Cody and Thermopolis, on the western edge of the Bighorn Basin. The museums are clustered in the tiny downtown.

THE ACTION: While **Kirwin Ghost Town** doesn't have any direct outlaw connections, the well-preserved townsite offers an excellent look at gold mining at the turn of the twentieth century, the proceeds from which did invite outlaw activity throughout the Bighorn Basin. Prospecting began in the 1870s, and the Wood River Mining District was formed in 1891. The town was abandoned in 1907 after a massive avalanche swept down from the mountains above. From the Kirwin parking lot, walk on the road a short way upriver and cross on the pedestrian bridge to explore the ghost town. THE GIDDYUP: Driving to Kirwin is a 4x4 adventure itself, or tours can be arranged in Cody and Meeteetse. From Meeteetse follow WY 290 west for about 6.5 miles, turn left (west) onto Wood River Road, and follow it for about 27 miles. As you progress upcanyon to Kirwin, the road becomes increasingly rough, requiring four-wheel drive to navigate rocky sections and to ford the typically shallow Wood River (don't attempt during high water). From Meeteetse, it takes about an hour and forty-five minutes one-way to reach the Kirwin parking lot. THE SCENE OF THE CRIME: GPS 43.8767, −109.2979.

The ghost town of Kirwin in the Absaroka Range near Meeteetse

THE SUSPECTS: Shoshone National Forest (see Resources).

MORE ACTION: In 1934, Amelia Earhart visited the valley and commissioned a cabin to be built near Kirwin, which was never finished after she disappeared in 1937 during her round-the-world flight. To hike to the **Amelia Earhart cabin site**, follow the road, which becomes a rough double-track, upcanyon (southwest) for 1.25 miles one-way.

THE HARDSHIPS: This is bear country, including grizzlies, so be aware. While incidents are rare, all wilderness travelers should prepare accordingly. Traveling alone is not recommended. The larger and louder your group, the better. Recommended safety items include bear bells, bear spray, even bear songs where you take your favorite pop song and substitute the word "baby" with "bear."

79

Thermopolis and Wind River Canyon

THE LOWDOWN: On the southern side of the Bighorn Basin, several sites hold appeal for outlaw adventurers—particularly those traveling between the Wind River Range (chapter 9) and the Bighorn Mountains (chapter 10). The town of Thermopolis has impressive hot springs and a frontier museum. South of town, Wind River Canyon offers a stunning scenic drive and whitewater rafting.

THE LOOT: The outlaw highlight here is the **Hot Springs County Museum**, which displays the original Hole-in-the-Wall Bar, named for the Hole-in-the-Wall Gang, whose members sometimes visited the town. Other exhibits and artifacts span western history, including displays about Native Americans and frontier life. THE TICKING CLOCK: Open Monday–Saturday May through September; Tuesday–Saturday October through April. THE TAKE: Modest fee. THE SCENE OF THE CRIME: 700 Broadway Street, Thermopolis, WY 82443. THE SUSPECTS: 307-864-5183; thermopolismuseum.com.

THE ACTION: Thermopolis is known for the Big Spring, which the town claims is the world's largest mineral hot spring—at the very least, it's up there. Visitors can enjoy the free bathhouse at **Hot Springs State Park**. The park also has about 6 miles of walking paths and hiking trails. The paths and boardwalks along the river near the Swinging Bridge offer excellent views of the colorful travertine terraces where scalding-hot mineral water spills into the Bighorn River.

THE GIDDYUP: Thermopolis is on US 20 at the junction with WY 120. The museum is downtown, and the state park is on the northwest side of town.

THE SUSPECTS: For info on Thermopolis and the surrounding area, see thermopolis.com. For info about the state park, see Resources.

MORE LOOT: The **Wind River Canyon Scenic Byway** (US 20) extends from Thermopolis south for 34 miles to Boysen State Park, near the town of Shoshoni. On your way to or from Thermopolis, the drive through sheer-walled Wind River Canyon is really something. THE JIG: In true Wild West fashion, not even the name of the river that runs through this adventure is simple. Upstream of Thermopolis—and continuing along the eastern flank of the Wind River Range all the way to its headwaters above Dubois (Adventure 70)—it's called the Wind River. But starting just downstream of Wind River Canyon—and then heading north past Thermopolis, across the Bighorn Basin, through Bighorn Canyon (Adventure 76), and into Montana—it's called the Bighorn River. But this is the same river, just with two different names. And why is that, you wonder. Now, now, outlaws never ask too many questions.

MORE ACTION: Various class I–III whitewater rafting and float trips on the Wind River through Wind River Canyon can be arranged with **Wind River Canyon Whitewater and Flyfishing Outfitter**, a business owned by members of the Wind River Indian Reservation. THE SUSPECTS: 307-864-9343; windrivercanyon.com.

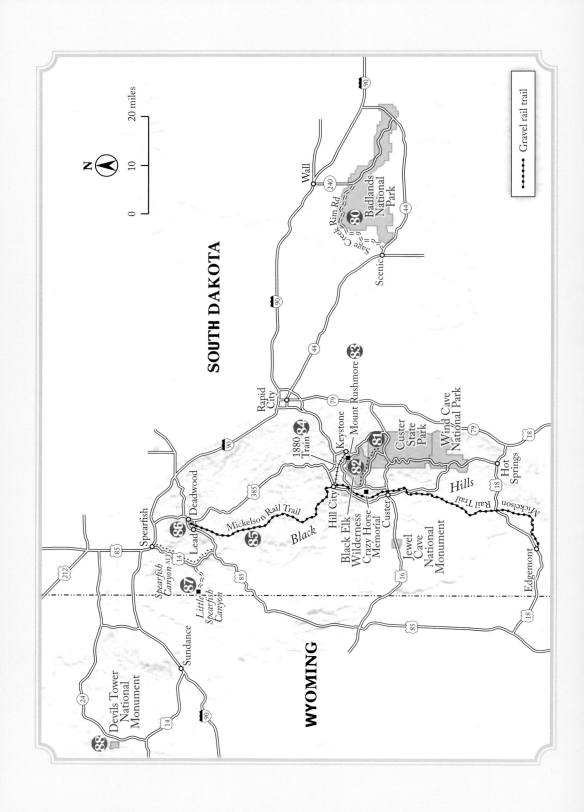

N

0   10   20 miles

Gravel rail trail

SOUTH DAKOTA

WYOMING

Wall

Badlands National Park

Sage Creek Rim Rd

Scenic

80

90

240

44

44

Rapid City

Mount Rushmore

83

79

1880 Train

84

Keystone

Hill City

Mickelson Rail Trail

Black

Hills

82

81

Custer State Park

Wind Cave National Park

79

Hot Springs

18

85

385

90

85

Deadwood

Lead

86

Spearfish

85

212

14

Spearfish Canyon Alt

87

Little Spearfish Canyon

Spearfish Canyon

Sundance

Devils Tower National Monument

88

24

14

90

Black Elk Wilderness

Crazy Horse Memorial

Custer

Jewel Cave National Monument

16

Mickelson Rail Trail

Edgemont

18

18

85

CHAPTER 11
Black Hills and Badlands
WESTERN SOUTH DAKOTA

THE WHOLE KIT AND CABOODLE: The Black Hills of South Dakota are a miniature mountain range rising from the western Great Plains. Filled with Wild West tales, gold rush history, and user-friendly adventures, this is a perfect place for families and outlaw road-trippers. Most visitors to this region focus on driving tours, tourist sites, and short day hikes, while others seek out longer and harder explorations, including hiking or biking a pair of 100-plus-mile trails.

THE TICKING CLOCK: The Black Hills are located between 43 and 45 degrees north latitude, with elevations ranging from 4,000 to 7,000 feet, so typical seasons to visit are late spring through early fall. Temperatures during the summer high season are typically warm but mild (daytime highs in the upper 70s to low 80s), with rainstorms always possible.

X MARKS THE SPOT: National Geographic Trails Illustrated Topo Maps #751, Black Hills North, captures Hill City and everything north; #238, Black Hills South, captures the Black Elk Wilderness and everything south.

THE SNORT: Breweries can be found throughout the Black Hills: Mount Rushmore Brewing Company (Custer), Miner Brewing (Hill City), Sick 'n Twisted (Hill City and Deadwood), Dakota Shivers and Jailhouse Taps (Lead), plus more in the surrounding foothills cities of Spearfish, Sturgis, and Rapid City.

THE YARNS: The Black Hills are mentioned frequently in outlaw lore, including in Wild Bunch Stories, Episode 9, A Gang by Any Name, 1897–1898.

80
Badlands National Park

THE LOWDOWN: There are no explicit outlaw connections in Badlands National Park, but the stark landscape of erosion-carved ridges, hills, and canyons just *feels* like the Wild West. If you're in the neighborhood, why not give it a look?

A striking landscape—the rolling hills of Badlands National Park

THE LOOT: Most visitors to Badlands National Park explore on a driving tour along the **Badlands Loop Road** (about 22 miles one-way, on SD 240), with some continuing onto the unpaved Sage Creek Rim Road near the Pinnacles entrance. Combining the two roads offers about 35 miles of remarkable badlands scenery with many viewpoints along the way, plus chances to spot bison, bighorn sheep, and other wildlife.

THE GIDDYUP: Badlands National Park is between I-90 and SD 44 about 75 miles east of Rapid City. There are several ways to access the popular Badlands Loop Road. Most visitors start from the Northeast or the Interior entrances near the Ben Reifel Visitor Center (from I-90, take exit 131 and head south on SD 240 for about 4 miles). If coming from the west, take exit 110 on I-90 at Wall and head south on SD 240 for about 7 miles to reach the Pinnacles entrance, near the junction of paved Badlands Loop Road and unpaved Sage Creek Rim Road. To tour the entire park from the west, take SD 44 to just past Scenic and turn left (north) onto unpaved Sage Creek Rim Road and continue about 13 miles to join the Badlands Loop Road.

THE ACTION: There are some mostly short trails near the park's eastern entrances and Ben Reifel Visitor Center. One option is the adventurous 1.5-mile one-way **Notch Trail**, which passes through a canyon, up a ladder, and along ledges. **THE GIDDYUP:** From the Ben Reifel Visitor Center, the trailhead is 2 miles east on Badlands Loop Road (SD 240) at the southern end of the parking lot.

RIDE ONWARD: Other cross-country hikes are possible in the Badlands wilderness, but there aren't any official or marked trails, so backcountry navigation is a requirement.

THE DIGS: Badlands isn't really known as a "camping park" but there are two nice campgrounds—one small, one big—worth checking out.

THE SUSPECTS: National Park Service, nps .gov/badl.

THE TAKE: Modest entry fee.

X MARKS THE SPOT: National Geographic Trails Illustrated Topo Map #239, Badlands National Park.

81

Needles Highway and Cathedral Spires Trail

THE LOWDOWN: Custer State Park is the largest state park in South Dakota, offering a mix of rolling prairie, granite mountains, and five lakes for fishing and recreation. The highlight is the **Needles**, a dramatic formation of sharp granite towers popular among hikers and rock climbers.

THE LOOT: The **Needles Highway** is a scenic 14-mile section of SD 87 running through the northwest quarter of Custer State Park. The two-lane road winds beneath granite towers and the Needle's Eye formation and passes through several granite tunnels, with many excellent viewpoints along the way.

THE ACTION: The interior of the Needles formation can be explored on foot from several trailheads along the Needles Highway. In the park's northwest corner, the Sylvan Lake trailhead is the starting point for **Trail #4, Little Devils Tower Trail**, a strenuous

The Needles in Custer State Park

1.4 miles one-way. Near the northeast end of this trail, hikers can connect to the upper end of the Cathedral Spires Trail. The strenuous **Cathedral Spires Trail** is one of the park's best hikes, typically starting from the Cathedral Spires trailhead on the Needles Highway and running for 1.5 miles one-way with about 500 feet of elevation gain on its way through the heart of the Needles.

THE GIDDYUP: From US 385/US 16, about 3.5 miles south of Hill City, head south on SD 87, which becomes the Needles Highway and enters the park after about 4 miles. Other common park entrances are US 16 Alt from the west, SD 36 from the east, and SD 87 from Wind Cave National Park to the south.

THE SUSPECTS: Custer State Park, 605-255-4515; gfp.sd.gov/parks/detail/custer-state-park.

THE TAKE: State park entry fee.

THE DIGS: The park is very popular among families, with nine campgrounds and **Custer State Park Resort**, which offers four lodges and cabin rentals. Camping and lodging reservations are highly recommended, which can be made up to a year in advance.

RIDE ONWARD: From the southern end of the Needles Highway, near the junction with US 16 Alt, you can continue another 19 miles on SD 87 to **Wind Cave National Park**. The park preserves 53 square miles of rolling prairie grasslands in the foothills of the Black Hills, where bison herds are commonly seen. There are several hiking trails and ranger-guided tours into **Wind Cave**, one of the longest caves in the world, with more than 150 miles of passageways in the Pahasapa Limestone having been explored. THE SUSPECTS: National Park Service, nps.gov/wica. THE SCENE OF THE CRIME: Visitor center is at 26611 US 385, Hot Springs, SD 57747. THE TAKE: No entry fee; cave tour fee.

82

Black Elk Peak Trail

THE LOWDOWN: The Black Elk Wilderness is the dramatic core of the Black Hills, with excellent trails winding through rugged mountains blanketed by dense pine forest. This relatively small wilderness area, only 21 square miles, is quite popular among hikers during summer high season, given the easy road access and many trailheads around its periphery. Due to its small size, hikers can cover much of the wilderness area in a long day or two.

THE ACTION: The most popular attraction in the wilderness is hiking up to the stone lookout tower atop granite **Black Elk Peak**. At 7,244 feet in elevation, this is not only the highest point in the Black Hills but also the highest peak in the US east of the Rocky Mountains. The common route to the summit starts in Custer State Park, beginning at Sylvan Lake trailhead and taking the moderate **Trail #9** for 3.5 miles one-way, with 1,100 feet of elevation gain. The trail is wide and mostly gradual, with only a few steep spots. Basically, it's like a highway for the many folks who hike to the summit each day.

THE GIDDYUP: To reach the trailhead, from US 385 south of Hill City, turn south onto SD 87 and continue for about 6 miles. Inside Custer State Park, turn left (north) at the sign for Sylvan Lake and continue 0.25 mile to trailhead parking. THE SCENE OF THE CRIME: GPS 43.8465, −103.5601.

X MARKS THE SPOT: National Geographic Trails Illustrated Topo Map #238, Black Hills South. A free topographic map with trail descriptions from the Black Hills National

Forest is available at info kiosks throughout the area or online (see Resources).

THE TAKE: State park entry fee.

THE JIG: Controversy surrounds the recent name change for this mountain. Prior to 2016, it was officially called Harney Peak, so named in 1855 for a US Army general who fought brutal battles during the Indian Wars yet later advocated for honoring and not breaking past treaties with Native Americans. Prior to conquest by the US, the peak was called Hinhan Kaga in Lakota, meaning "Owl Maker," which referred to the owl-like granite towers surrounding the peak.

MORE ACTION: A longer, more remote, and free-of-charge route is to hike to the summit of Black Elk Peak from the **Horsethief Lake trailhead**, just west of Mount Rushmore. Start this 6.5-mile one-way hike on Horsethief Lake Trail #14, then take Grizzly Bear Creek Trail #7, Norbeck Trail #3, and Black Elk Peak Trail #9. THE GIDDYUP: The Horsethief Lake trailhead is just south of SD 244, about 2 miles west of Mount Rushmore National Memorial (Adventure 83). THE SCENE OF THE CRIME: GPS 43.8892, −103.4823. THE HARDSHIPS: Note that the trails on the north side of the wilderness see less use and can be brushier—watch out for poison ivy!

83

Mount Rushmore and Crazy Horse Memorials

THE LOWDOWN: This adventure visits a pair of controversial monuments, one partially complete, the other in progress, and both worth a visit.

THE LOOT: **Mount Rushmore National Memorial** is quite controversial due to the carvings being on land considered sacred by the Lakota. Only the faces were completed for what was originally intended as a more developed set of sculptures. A promenade leads to the visitor center and viewing area. For a closer look, the **Presidential Trail** is a 0.6-mile loop with 422 stairs that leads along the base of Mount Rushmore. THE GIDDYUP: Mount Rushmore National Memorial is located on SD 244, about 9 miles east of US 385/US 16 and 3.5 miles west of Keystone. THE TAKE: Parking fee—national parks pass doesn't apply. THE SUSPECTS: National Park Service, nps.gov/moru.

THE ACTION: A surreal (and free) alternative to driving the highway to Mount Rushmore is hiking there through the Black Elk Wilderness from the **Horsethief Lake trailhead** (for directions, see MORE ACTION in Adventure 82). The hike is 3.5 miles one-way following Horsethief Lake Trail #14, Centennial Trail #89, and the Blackberry Trail. This moderate route is like an abbreviated stroll through American history, involving hiking through a pristine wilderness, watching as stone-carved faces of American presidents appear between pine trees, and exiting the forest into a parking area filled with RVs.

MORE LOOT: The **Crazy Horse Memorial** is an under-construction stone monument depicting Oglala Lakota warrior Crazy Horse, who defeated US General George Custer at the Battle of Little Bighorn in 1876. Work on the memorial began in 1948, and the face was completed in 1998. Located on private land and managed as a nonprofit organization, the memorial draws controversy similar to nearby Mount Rushmore. THE GIDDYUP: The entrance to the Crazy

Horse Memorial is just east off of US 385/ US 16 about 4 miles north of Custer. **THE TAKE:** Moderate entry fee. **THE SUSPECTS:** crazyhorsememorial.org.

84

The 1880 Train

THE LOWDOWN: The 1880 Train is a restored historic excursion train offering steam engine and diesel trips through the scenic Black Hills between Keystone and Hill City.

THE LOOT: The 20-mile roundtrip **1880 Train ride** is narrated by a tour guide and takes one hour each way. The train follows the original route of the Chicago, Burlington, and Quincy Railroad, which serviced the Black Hills during the 1880s gold rush.

THE GIDDYUP: Depots are located in Keystone, near the intersection of US 16 Alt and SD 40, and in Hill City, a block west of the historic downtown.

THE TICKING CLOCK: The train has two seasons, with many daily departures and returns during the summer high season (mid-May through mid-October). There is a reduced schedule during the winter holiday season (November and December).

THE SCENE OF THE CRIME: 103 Winter Street, Keystone, SD 57751; 222 Railroad Avenue, Hill City, SD 57745.

THE SUSPECTS: 605-574-2222; 1880train.com.

THE TAKE: Moderate fees either one-way or roundtrip, children under 2 free. Reservations recommended at least one week in advance.

Ride the historic 1880 Train for a great Old West experience in the Black Hills.

85

Mickelson Rail Trail and Centennial Trail

THE LOWDOWN: The Black Hills are home to a pair of long-distance trails, each traversing the range from roughly north to south. The more popular one is a gravel rail trail, the Mickelson. The other is a forested single-track trail, the Centennial. Both see primarily day use over shorter lengths, while some adventurous people take on the entire trails for long-distance biking and backpacking adventures.

THE ACTION: The popular **Mickelson Rail Trail** is a dedicated gravel cycling and walking path that runs for 109 miles through the heart of the Black Hills, from Deadwood (Adventure 86) to Edgemont. The trail mostly runs through national forest land, with some areas of private property, and it passes through four old train tunnels and over more than a hundred bridges. There are fifteen trailheads, ranging from 2 to 16 miles apart, with many located in mountain towns along the route. Day riding is most popular, while other riders do overnight bike tours. Completed in 1998 and officially called the George S. Mickelson Trail, it follows the old Burlington Northern grade. The sections north and south of Hill City are particularly scenic. **THE SUSPECTS:** South Dakota Game, Fish, and Parks (see Resources). **X MARKS THE SPOT:** A map and trail guide are available (see Resources). The trail is also on the National Geographic Trails Illustrated Topo Maps #751, Black Hills North, and #238, Black Hills South.

MORE ACTION: Created in 1989 to celebrate the centennial of South Dakota statehood, the **Centennial Trail** is a 111-mile (one-way) single-track trail for hiking, mountain biking, and horseback riding. This long-distance trail heads south from Bear Butte State Park, traversing forests through the Black Hills, to Wind Cave National Park. It is popular for hiking and biking adventures, whether short or long-distance. Along the way, the trail passes through some of the best scenery in the Black Hills, including portions of the Black Elk Wilderness (Adventure 82) and Custer State Park (Adventure 81). One unique hike to Mount Rushmore, involving a portion of the Centennial Trail, is covered in Adventure 83. **THE DIGS:** Long-distance users have a variety of camping options available, including dispersed camping and some developed campgrounds near the trail. **THE LAW:** Note that the 9 miles through Black Elk Wilderness are closed to bikes, requiring a detour on nearby roads and highways. Hiking through the Black Elk Wilderness requires free registration at trailheads. In Custer State Park, no permit is required to hike or bike through, but camping is only allowed in developed campgrounds or the French Creek Natural Area. Wind Cave National Park requires a free permit for backcountry camping. **THE SUSPECTS:** Black Hills National Forest; South Dakota Game, Fish, and Parks; Bureau of Land Management; and National Park Service (for all land managers, see Resources). **X MARKS THE SPOT:** Map and trail guide available on the website listed in Resources. The trail is also included on the National Geographic Trails Illustrated Topo Maps #751, Black Hills North, and #238, Black Hills South.

86

Deadwood and Lead

THE LOWDOWN: Deadwood is a famous gold-rush town known for the colorful Wild West characters who passed through—and the HBO show of the same name. Today, the neighboring towns of Deadwood and Lead are tourist destinations, each with their own Old West vibes. A series of museums and historic sites around Deadwood make for a good one or two days of activities.

THE GIDDYUP: Deadwood is on US 85, 8.5 miles south of I-90. Lead is on US 85 another 3 miles south of Deadwood.

THE LOOT: The **Adams Museum** documents the history of the Black Hills, including housing the mysterious Thoen Stone (see Old West Stories at end of this chapter). THE TICKING CLOCK: Open daily May through September; Tuesday–Saturday October through April. THE TAKE: Donations suggested. THE SCENE OF THE CRIME: 54 Sherman Street, Deadwood, SD 57732.

The **Historic Adams House** is the restored home, originally built in 1892, of Deadwood pioneer W. E. Adams. THE TICKING CLOCK: Open daily May through September; Tuesday–Saturday October and April; closed November through March. THE TAKE: Modest fee for adults and kids 6–12, younger children free. THE SCENE OF THE CRIME: 22 Van Buren Street, Deadwood, SD 57732.

The **Brothel Deadwood** preserves a house of prostitution that operated illegally from 1876 until 1980. THE TICKING CLOCK: Open daily May through September; Wednesday–Saturday October through April. THE TAKE: Moderate fee for ages 16 and up. THE SCENE

OF THE CRIME: 610 Main Street, Deadwood, SD 57732.

The **Days of '76 Museum** displays more than fifty historic vehicles that helped shape the Old West, plus photographs and firearms. THE TICKING CLOCK: Open daily May through September; Tuesday–Saturday October through April. THE TAKE: Modest fee for adults and kids 6–12, younger children free. THE SCENE OF THE CRIME: 18 76th Drive, Deadwood, SD 57732.

THE SUSPECTS: Deadwood History Inc. has info on the Adams Museum, Historic Adams House, Brothel Deadwood, and Days of '76 Museum at deadwoodhistory.com.

MORE LOOT: The historic **Mount Moriah Cemetery** houses the graves of famous Deadwood residents, including Wild Bill Hickok and Calamity Jane. THE TAKE: Small fee. THE SCENE OF THE CRIME: 10 Mount Moriah Drive, Deadwood, SD 57732. THE SUSPECTS: 605-722-0837.

THE ACTION: If you want to stretch your legs in Deadwood, the city offers a historic walking-tour guide (see Resources). The entire town is a National Historic Landmark, and the walking tour covers about a mile in thirty minutes.

MORE ACTION: For a longer hike, check out the **Homestake Trail**, which follows the old grade of the Fremont, Elkhorn, and Missouri Valley Railroad. The trail is roughly 3 miles one-way, with about 800 feet of elevation gain on its way to Lead. Start from the Mickelson Rail Trail trailhead (Adventure 85) and walk it west for less than a quarter mile, then turn sharply right uphill onto a double-track trail. Follow signs to switchback three times up to the ridgeline and follow the trail to Lead, where it ends above the Homestake Mine pit near the edge of town. THE GIDDYUP: The Mickelson Rail Trail trailhead is in Powerhouse Park, on US 85 about 0.25 mile south

The past lives on in Deadwood, South Dakota.

of downtown. THE SCENE OF THE CRIME: GPS 44.3706, −103.7286.

EVEN MORE LOOT: Whether you walk or drive to the small town of **Lead**, make sure to venture in; the Homestake Mine operated here from the late 1870s until 2002, producing about 40 million troy ounces of gold. Learn more at the **Black Hills Mining Museum**, with exhibits about mining in the Black Hills. THE TICKING CLOCK: Open daily May to September. THE TAKE: Modest fee. THE SCENE OF THE CRIME: 323 W. Main Street, Lead, SD 57785. THE SUSPECTS: 605-584-1605; black hillsminingmuseum.com.

THE YARNS: Deadwood is mentioned in Wild Bunch Stories, Episode 9, A Gang by Any Name, 1897–1898.

DEADWOOD: A TOWN AND AN EFFING TV SHOW (BRING EARMUFFS)

"#$%@!"*

—*DEADWOOD* THE TV SHOW

Plenty of folks have never heard of either Deadwood—the Wild West town or the 2004–2006 HBO show. And for those who love curse words—whether spewing forth from TVs or from leather-clad bikers in an old-timey saloon—that's a real effing shame. In all seriousness, while the TV show is clearly NSFW (that's "not safe for work" for you old-timers), the town of today is definitely family friendly.

Some backstory: During August 1874, General George Custer announced the discovery of gold in the Black Hills, which had been recognized by the 1868 Treaty of Fort Laramie as being part of the Great Sioux Reservation. Under the treaty terms, half of South Dakota Territory—everything west of the Missouri River—belonged to the Teton Sioux, a.k.a. the Lakota.

Before the month was over, white American and European prospectors and businessmen flocked to the Black Hills, establishing illegal settlements like the infamously lawless camp of Deadwood.

"Bleeeeeeeeppp."

—(ALSO) *DEADWOOD* THE TV SHOW

Blending fact with a healthy amount of fiction, the HBO show begins six months after the camp's establishment. Over three seasons and thirty-six episodes, the show follows the evolution of Deadwood into an established mining town, including its annexation into Dakota Territory and the discovery of the Homestake Mine.

*"G***** *********ING *********!"*

—(YEP) *DEADWOOD* THE TV SHOW

Throughout the series, several well-known figures from the Wild West (mostly fictionalized characters with real names) converge in Deadwood and proceed to drink, murder, and swear their bloody heads off. Viewers witness the assassination of Wild Bill Hickok. The drunken adventures of Calamity Jane. The devious plots of brothel owner Al Swearengen

(swear engine? Mind blown!). The inner turmoil of former US Marshal Seth Bullock. The ruthless dealings of George Hearst. Plus about a thousand other characters—just saying, it's an ensemble show.

Deadwood is regularly placed on lists of the best TV shows of all time as well as shows that were cancelled too soon. Plenty of praise was offered for the acting and the writing, noting that much of the dialogue was written in Shakespearean iambic pentameter—if Shakespeare had sworn like an effing sailor in a saloon.

Responding to demand, a long-awaited feature film followed in 2019, which included plenty of fan service. The story involves the characters reuniting in 1889 to celebrate South Dakota statehood. This naturally leads to a murder—and plenty of cursing, of course.

"Welcome the f*** back."

—*DEADWOOD: THE MOVIE*

87

Spearfish Canyon

THE LOWDOWN: Spearfish Canyon is a deep, forested gorge with cliffs of Pahasapa Limestone rising above Spearfish Creek. There are many resorts and lodges throughout the canyon, and the scenic drive is popular with families, road trippers, motorcyclists, and cyclists. Along the way, you'll find waterfalls, short hikes, and even a film site from a famous Western. The driving directions below include descriptions of sites and hikes from north to south.

THE GIDDYUP: The **Spearfish Canyon Scenic Byway** (US 14 Alt) runs south from the town of Spearfish for 20 miles to Cheyenne's Crossing, at US 85 about 8 miles southwest of Lead.

THE LOOT: Most of the highlights are roadside. Bridal Veil Falls is on the east side, about 6 miles south of Spearfish. Spearfish Falls is about 7 miles farther south, on the northeast side of the road across from Spearfish Canyon Lodge.

THE ACTION: There are several hikes into side canyons, with one popular option being the short but steep **76 Trail**. This challenging, 1.25-mile one-way trail climbs about 700 feet to a lookout with stunning views back up the canyon. THE GIDDYUP: The trailhead is 13 miles south of Spearfish on the west side of Roughlock Falls Road (CR 22) across from Spearfish Canyon Lodge.

For an easier hike, explore the less-developed Little Spearfish Canyon. From Spearfish Canyon Lodge, drive south about 0.25 mile on unpaved Roughlock Falls Road. From the parking lot on the left (south side), you can walk the mostly flat, 2-mile roundtrip trail to picturesque **Roughlock Falls**.

MORE LOOT: The next roadside highlight is a film site from the final winter scene in 1990's *Dances with Wolves*. From Spearfish Canyon Lodge, the film site is 2.75 miles south on Roughlock Falls Road.

Other highlights of Little Spearfish Canyon include a few longer hikes, like the moderate 6-mile **Little Spearfish Loop Trail**, which starts at Timon Campground (see below).

THE DIGS: There are two campgrounds in Little Spearfish Canyon. From Spearfish Canyon Lodge, drive 3 miles on Roughlock Falls Road to Rod and Gun Campground; Timon Campground is another 1.5 miles beyond.

THE SUSPECTS: Online info is a bit spotty, but check out visitspearfish.com/things-to-do /spearfish-canyon.

RIDE ONWARD: Spearfish, South Dakota, is a larger town at the northern (downstream) end of Spearfish Canyon. It's a mountain biking hub for the northern Black Hills' Forest Service roads, with several trails in town and easy highway access to other nearby trails. THE SUSPECTS: visitspearfish.com/things-to -do/mountain-biking. For outlaw enthusiasts, a highlight in town is the short hike to the **Thoen Stone Monument** (see Old West Stories at end of this chapter).

88
Wyoming Black Hills

THE LOWDOWN: The Wyoming Black Hills are located just over the state line northwest of the South Dakota Black Hills. This lower-elevation region offers rolling hills, several towns and campgrounds to explore, and Devils Tower National Monument. A small town with outlaw significance, Sundance is the place where Harry Longabaugh was imprisoned in his early twenties and thus became the Sundance Kid. Can you imagine if he'd instead been imprisoned in, say, Ding Dong, Texas? Lucky kid.

THE GIDDYUP: Sundance, Wyoming, is on I-90 33 miles west of Spearfish, South Dakota. THE LOOT: Learn more about the story of the Sundance Kid and the region's history at the **Crook County Museum**, which displays the jail-room furniture from the Kid's trial, among other exhibits. THE SCENE OF THE CRIME: 108 N. Fourth Street, Sundance, WY

82729. THE SUSPECTS: crookcountymuseum district.org.

THE ACTION: The area is home to **Devils Tower National Monument** (a.k.a. Bear Lodge Butte to Native Americans), an igneous rock tower composed of many hexagonal columns of porphyritic phonolite—uhhh, OK, enough mineralogic mumbo-jumbo— rising about 1,000 feet from the surrounding terrain. You can hike around it on the 1.3-mile **Tower Trail** loop. Four other trails range from 0.6-mile one-way connecting trails to the 2.8-mile **Red Beds Trail** loop. The tower is a famous rock-climbing location, but the butte is sacred to Native American tribes, who ask that it not be climbed during their holy month of June. There are a million prairie dogs on the surrounding plains. What else? The tower was in that movie *Close Encounters of the Third Kind*. But, hey, what are the first two kinds? Is there a fourth kind? Will there be a reboot? I have so many questions. THE GIDDYUP: To reach Devils Tower, from Sundance drive US 14 west for 20 miles, turn right (north) onto WY 24, and in 6 miles turn left (west) onto Main Park Road (WY 110), which leads to a campground, many pullouts, and a visitor center at the road's end. THE SUSPECTS: National Park Service, nps.gov/deto/index.htm. THE TAKE: Entry fee.

THE YARNS: The Black Hills appear in Wild Bunch Stories, Episode 7, Desperadoes at Castle Gate, 1896–1897.

OLD WEST STORIES: MYSTERY OF THE THOEN STONE

In March 1887, a pair of Norwegian immigrant brothers, Louis and Ivan Thoen, were collecting sandstone for a building project at the base of Lookout Mountain—near Spearfish, South Dakota. During their search, Louis spotted a small sandstone slab roughly nine inches square and three inches wide. Despite being covered in dirt, the stone appeared to have writing carved into it.

After cleaning the stone at home, Louis discovered a cryptic message. On one side it said, "Came to these hills in 1833. Seven of us: DeLacompt, Ezra Kind, G. W. Wood, T. Brown, R. Kent, Wm. King, Indian Crow. All ded but me, Ezra Kind. Killed by Ind. Beyond the high hill. Got our gold. June 1834." On the other side, it said, "Got all of the gold we could carry. Our ponys all got by the Indians. I hav lost my gun and nothing to eat and Indians hunting me."

Visit!

The original Thoen Stone is on display at the **Adams Museum** in Deadwood, South Dakota (Adventure 86). You can hike a 0.25-mile one-way trail up to the **Thoen Stone Monument** from the end of Thoen Stone Road/Saint Joe Street via the East Jackson Street exit off I-90 in Spearfish, South Dakota. THE SCENE OF THE CRIME: Thoen Stone Road, Spearfish, SD 57783. THE SUSPECTS: blackhillsthehike.com/thoen-stone.

Louis quickly spread word around town about the stone, which became a hot topic. He invited a future mayor of Spearfish to visit the site where the stone was found. Next, he brought the stone to the *Spearfish Register* office. Within a day, Louis put it on display at a local store, where he and the owner, John Cashner, sold postcards with pictures of the stone.

If the message proved true, it would mean that a party of white Americans had discovered gold in the Black Hills forty years before

The Thoen Stone Monument in Spearfish, South Dakota

Custer's expedition led to the infamous 1870s gold rush. Others claimed the stone was a hoax, pointing out that Louis was a stonemason who easily could have carved the message himself.

In 1888, Cashner traveled to Michigan and sold the story to the *Detroit Free Press*. Louis died of the Spanish flu in 1919, insisting until his death that the stone was authentic. In the 1950s, historian Frank Thomson traveled to the East Coast to investigate the names listed on the stone and wrote about the search in his 1966 book *The Thoen Stone: A Saga of the Black Hills*. Thomson describes locating several families with similar last names who claimed to have ancestors who vanished in the American West.

In the 2000s, a handwriting expert compared the writing on the stone with that on the postcards once sold by Thoen and Cashner. The expert claimed the writing did not match that of either of the Thoen brothers or of Cashner. Today the debate continues, and the mystery of the Thoen Stone lingers.

CHAPTER 12

Spurs of the Outlaw Trail

IDAHO, SOUTHERN ARIZONA, NEW MEXICO, KANSAS, AND ARKANSAS

THE WHOLE KIT AND CABOODLE: The Wild West was much more than just the stunning mesas and sheer canyons of the high desert often depicted in movies and dime novels. In a figurative sense, what came to be called the outlaw trail extended far beyond the central region of the Colorado Plateau and Rocky Mountains mostly covered in this book.

During much of the nineteenth century, the vast area from the Mississippi River to the West Coast, known as the American Frontier, was wild, lawless, and crisscrossed by faint trails used by desperate and villainous bandits. In the Ozarks of Missouri and Arkansas, the infamous Jesse James was robbing trains and banks while young Bob Parker was just a boy dreaming of making his mark on the world. Elsewhere, in Northern California, the eccentric bandit Black Bart was robbing stagecoaches and leaving behind poems. Gunfighting lawmen like Bass Reeves were patrolling thousands of square miles in the Indian Territory of modern-day Oklahoma. Ramshackle frontier mining camps were springing up from Montana to Mexico.

Today, the remnants of this wild era can be found all across the country—even in the East. Below are just a few spurs of the outlaw trail, working from west to east. Two of these spur adventures have Wild Bunch significance (Adventures 89 and 91), offering a taste of what else is out there. **THE GIDDYUP:** Pick any direction . . . and go.

89

Butch Cassidy Bank Robbery Museum, Montpelier, Idaho

THE LOWDOWN: This spur of the outlaw trail visits the original bank building in southeastern Idaho that Butch Cassidy robbed on August 13, 1896.

THE LOOT: The **Butch Cassidy Bank Robbery Museum** bills itself as the last standing

bank in the world that was robbed by Butch Cassidy (along with Elzy Lay and Bub Meeks). Called the Bank of Montpelier at the time, it was robbed of $7,142 in gold, silver, and currency.

THE GIDDYUP: Montpelier is located in southeastern Idaho, at the junction of US 89 and US 30. The nearest adventures in this book are found in the Wind River Range (chapter 9), Flaming Gorge and Browns Park (chapter 7), and the Uinta Basin and Eastern Uinta Mountains (chapter 6)

THE TICKING CLOCK: Open seasonally Memorial Day to around Labor Day.

THE SUSPECTS: butchcassidymuseum.com.

THE YARNS: The bank robbery in Montpelier is featured in Wild Bunch Stories, Episode 6, A Most Desperate Plot, 1896.

90

Tombstone, Arizona

THE LOWDOWN: Billed as "the town too tough to die," Tombstone is a historic Wild West boomtown best known for the gunfight at the O.K. Corral, which saw the Earp brothers and Doc Holliday facing off against the Clanton Gang. Established in 1879 as an Arizona silver-mining town 25 miles north of the Mexican border, today Tombstone is less rough and tumble and more touristic meets historic. Now it's a family-friendly destination similar to Deadwood, South Dakota.

THE LOOT: Highlights include a walking tour of several fun pedestrian-only blocks on Allen Street, with restored and mock Old West buildings. The **O.K. Corral** site has been re-created for daily reenactments. The **Bird Cage Theater**, opened in 1881, claims to be home to twenty-six alleged murders, 140-plus bullet holes, and countless ghosts of former cowboys and prostitutes. (Ghosts and tours are kid friendly.) A few blocks away, the **Tombstone Courthouse State Historic Park** preserves the original structure as a museum. Other sites include the **Boothill Graveyard**, the **Gunfighter Hall of Fame**, the *Epitaph* **Museum** (local newspaper), and the **Western Heritage Museum**.

THE GIDDYUP: Tombstone is located on AZ 80, about 25 miles south of I-10 at Benson, Arizona. It's about a 75-minute drive from the city of Tucson, or a measly 150-hour horse ride (only 7 hours by automobile) from the Paria River area and South Lake Powell near Page, Arizona (chapter 5).

THE SUSPECTS: Tombstone Chamber of Commerce (see Resources).

MORE LOOT: Outside of Tombstone, the **Ghost Town Trail** follows rural highways and roads for about 35 miles through three historic townsites. In addition to abandoned structures, **Gleeson** now has a restored jail. **Courtland** was even larger in its day, but only ruins remain. **Pearce**, where the Alvord-Stiles Gang operated, survives to this day with about two thousand residents plus some stores and restaurants. THE GIDDYUP: From downtown Tombstone, drive east on AZ 80 for a few blocks. Turn left (north) onto Camino San Rafael. Drive about 1 mile to Gleeson Road and turn right. After about 14 miles, you'll reach the intersection with unpaved North High Lonesome Road. Gleeson is just north of

the intersection. To reach Courtland, continue west on Gleeson Road for about 1.25 miles. Turn left onto unpaved North Ghost Tower Trail and proceed about 2.75 miles. At the Y turn left and drive about 1 mile. The Courtland ruins are on the right. To reach Pearce, continue north on North Ghost Tower Trail/North Pearce Road for just under 12 miles. Turn left onto (old friend!) US 191 and drive north for about a mile. The town of Pearce is on the left, where you'll find several historic buildings. THE SUSPECTS: Arizona Highways, arizonahighways.com/ghost-town-trail.

91

Wild Bunch Sites and Billy the Kid Scenic Byway, New Mexico

THE LOWDOWN: Not much is left of this southern spur of the outlaw trail, but diehard Wild Bunch enthusiasts may still want to take in the scenery and see some ghost-town remains from the Wild West.

THE LOOT: There are two ghost towns in the area. **Alma** was the closest to WS Ranch headquarters, and today the old cemetery remains. About 9.5 miles east of Alma on NM 159 is the former mining town of **Mogollon**, which has some remaining structures from its Old West days. THE GIDDYUP: Alma is located in west-central New Mexico on US 180, about 120 miles north of I-10 at Deming. It's about as far from everywhere as anywhere in this book. Call it a 3.5-hour drive from Tombstone, and roughly 4.25 light-years from Proxima Centauri. THE YARNS: Butch Cassidy and other members of the Wild Bunch worked on the WS Ranch and frequented Alma in Wild Bunch Stories, Episode 10, A Seemingly Normal Cowboy Named Jim Lowe, 1899.

MORE LOOT: In central New Mexico, the roughly 75-mile **Billy the Kid Scenic Byway** loop takes in a variety of excellent Old West sites. THE GIDDYUP: From Alma, head northeast on NM 12 to US 60 at Datil, then drive east 145 miles to Capitan to start the loop. There are a few common places to start the loop. Coming from the east, Hondo is located at the junction of US 380 and US 70. From the southwest, Ruidoso Downs is at the junction of US 70 and NM 48. From the northwest, Capitan is located at US 380 and NM 48, which is used as the starting point below. THE SUSPECTS: New Mexico Tourism Department (see Resources).

From Capitan, head east on US 380. In about 4 miles, turn south (right) onto NM 220 and proceed 2.5 miles to reach **Fort Stanton–Snowy River Cave National Conservation Area**. The historic fort is one of the best-preserved nineteenth-century military outposts in the US. THE SUSPECTS: fortstanton.org.

Return to US 380 and continue west for 8 miles to Lincoln. The **Lincoln Historic Site** offers roughly ten preserved historical buildings, including a frontier store and old courthouse. Exhibits span regional history to the bloody Lincoln County War and its most famous combatant, Billy the Kid. THE SUSPECTS: nmhistoricsites.org/lincoln.

Continue east on US 380 for 10 miles to Hondo and turn right (west) onto US 70. After about 24 miles you'll reach Ruidoso Downs and the **Hubbard Museum of the American West**, with Old West artifacts, wagons, Native American art, and more. THE SUSPECTS: facebook.com/hubbardmuseum.

Continue west on US 70 for 3 miles and turn north (right) onto NM 48, proceeding 20 miles back to US 60 and Capitan to complete the loop. Know there are more sites to explore along the byway.

92

Dodge City, Kansas

THE LOWDOWN: Founded in southwest Kansas in 1872, Dodge City was known as a wild frontier town during the heyday of the Old West. Wyatt Earp was an assistant marshal here in the mid-1870s, but the city is best known for its role in Wild West legend and fiction. The beloved TV western *Gunsmoke*, which ran for twenty seasons from 1955 to 1975, was set in the town. In the process, the catchphrase of the show's town marshal, Matt Dillon, became a ubiquitous American idiom: "Get out of Dodge." These days, another saying around town is that Dodge City is known all around the world, less for the things that did happen here and more for the things that didn't.

THE LOOT: Modern Dodge City has several outlaw-themed museums and attractions that make a good stop during a cross-country road trip, particularly when combined with places in southwestern Colorado (chapter 1). The highlight is **Boot Hill Museum**, a replica frontier town with false-front buildings, period shops, and private homes filled with thousands of artifacts, including authentic furniture, clothing, and guns. Visitors can enter reconstructions of a bank, stable, newspaper office, jail, church, an operating saloon, and more. The museum, which also offers variety shows, reenactment gunfights, and dinner events, is named for the onsite Boot Hill Cemetery, a common term for Wild West burial grounds where gunfighters were said to be buried "with their boots on." THE SUSPECTS: boothill.org. THE TAKE: Moderate entry fee; more for shows and events.

THE GIDDYUP: Dodge City is located in southwestern Kansas, about 90 miles south of I-70 as the crow flies. Depending on where you're headed, several cross-state routes will allow you to plan a more efficient detour.

THE SUSPECTS: Dodge City Convention and Visitors Bureau, visitdodgecity.org.

MORE LOOT: There's plenty more to do here, including a historic walking tour that leads to many sites around Dodge City like the **Gunfighters Wax Museum**. Nine miles west of town on US 400, the **Santa Fe Trail Rut Site** preserves wagon tracks from the nineteenth century.

THE SNORT: You'll find Dodge City Brewing downtown.

RIDE ONWARD: An hour northeast of Dodge City, the **Fort Larned National Historic Site** preserves a complete authentic military outpost that operated from 1858 to 1878. Visitors can explore barracks, officer quarters, warehouses, shops, and more. Located on the **Santa Fe Trail**, the fort protected trade and wagon traffic during westward migration and the Indian Wars. THE GIDDYUP: From Dodge City take US 50 east 34 miles, turn right (east) onto US 56 and continue 9 miles, turn left (north) onto US 183 and proceed 12 miles to KS 156, and turn right (east), then turn right to enter the site. THE SUSPECTS: National Park Service, nps.gov/fols.

93

Fort Smith, Arkansas

THE LOWDOWN: The farthest-east adventure in this book is a little-known city on the Arkansas River just south of I-40. Located near the eastern edge of what was once called Indian Territory (later renamed Oklahoma), the region was the end point for Native American tribes forcefully relocated on the Trail of Tears. During the nineteenth century, this increasingly lawless region became home to many settlers and fleeing outlaws—including Native Americans, whites, and Blacks recently freed from slavery. In 1875, President Ulysses S. Grant sent Federal Judge Isaac C. Parker to an abandoned Civil War installation named Fort Smith to clean up the territory. A gallows was constructed that would soon give Parker the nickname the Hanging Judge. To patrol the 75,000-square-mile territory, about two hundred deputy US Marshals were hired, the most famous of whom was Bass Reeves, an African American lawman and gunfighter who may have provided real-life inspiration for the fictional Lone Ranger. Today, a national historic site and two museums make for great stops when passing through.

THE GIDDYUP: Fort Smith is located in far western Arkansas, a few miles south of I-40. From the west, take I-40 to US 64. From the east, take I-40 to US 71 Business.

THE LOOT: The highlight is the preserved **Fort Smith National Historic Site**. Visitors can enter the restored courtroom of Judge Parker, as well as a replica gallows that stands outside. THE GIDDYUP: From US 71 Business near downtown, turn northwest onto Garrison

Visiting historic Fort Smith on the Arkansas River is a great way to extend your adventures on the outlaw trail.

Avenue (US 64). After about five or six blocks, turn left, then right on Parker Avenue and follow it to the parking lot. THE SUSPECTS: National Park Service, nps.gov/fosm.

THE ACTION: A series of walking paths allow visitors to explore the 11-acre site, including the 1.5-mile **River Trail**, which loops around Belle Point, a bluff overlooking the confluence of the Poteau and Arkansas Rivers. You can extend your walking tour by continuing into downtown, where a series of impressive building murals called **The Unexpected** have been created by international artists. There are also statues of Bass Reeves in Pendergraft Park and Judge Parker in Gateway Park.

MORE LOOT: Next to the historic site, the **Fort Smith Museum of History** has exhibits about the people of the city and region. Opening perhaps by 2023 but maybe later, the under-construction **US Marshals Museum** will present the more than two-hundred-year history of the US Marshals Service, including the exploits of Wild West legend Bass Reeves.

THE SNORT: One block from the historic site you'll find Bricktown Brewery.

RIDE ONWARD: Located a 1.5 hours' drive from Fort Smith, amid the rugged hills and cliffs of eastern Oklahoma, **Robbers Cave State Park** is named for a nearby outlaw cave that allegedly was used by Jesse James and Belle Starr. There are hiking and mountain biking trails, a recreational lake, a campground, and more. THE SUSPECTS: Oklahoma State Parks (see Resources).

The cracks of the Joint Trail, in the Needles District of Canyonlands National Park (Adventure 16), sure feel like an outlaw hideout if there ever was one.

PART IV

★ THE ENDS OF THE ★

OUTLAW TRAIL

Stories Conclude

WILD BUNCH STORIES

From Manhattan to Patagonia, 1901–1903

Frozen in place • The pampas of Cholila • The return of Butch and Sundance in Illinois? • A letter home • The Pinkerton plans • A close call

IN FEBRUARY 1901, Harry and Ethel Place, with her brother, James Ryan, checked into a boardinghouse in the West Village of Manhattan. They spent the next three weeks enjoying city nightlife: Vaudeville and music shows. Bars and taverns. They stopped by Tiffany's, where James bought a watch for Ethel, and Harry bought a diamond stickpin for himself. The young couple even had their portrait taken at DeYoung Photography Studio on Broadway.

The winter weather was often in the teens, with strong winds and snow, but these visitors were accustomed to harsh conditions. Midway through their visit, people went out to the Battery to witness quite a scene. Dense flows of floating ice blocks came down the Hudson and East Rivers, meeting in the harbor where dozens of boats—steamships, side-wheelers, tugs, scows, and barges—became stuck. This ice blockade lasted for hours, with the entire harbor locked amid a sea of shifting ice.

A week later, the trio boarded the steamship *Herminius*, bound for Argentina. They arrived in Buenos Aires on March 23, under the same names, and registered at a fancy hotel. When depositing $12,000 at a reputable bank, Harry asked how secure it was. Wouldn't want any bandits, he joked.

Their goal was the Argentinian Patagonia, a land of opportunity confirmed by an American ambassador they befriended named George Newbury. The trio traveled by train to Bahia Blanca and onward to Neuquén. There they purchased horses and a wagon and continued southwest toward the base of the Andes Mountains. In western Chubut Province, not far from the Chilean border, they found what they sought in the valley of Cho-

The famous portrait taken in NYC of the Sundance Kid and Etta Place (Library of Congress)

lila: *pampas*, rolling grassy foothills perfect for grazing cattle on a sprawling ranch. Four hundred miles from the nearest railroad. Not a law officer in sight. It was perfect.

They put up some canvas tents and got to work building a four-room cabin, barn, and stable. They acquired sheep, cattle, and horses, eventually registering several brands with the territorial government. They became friends with their few neighbors, some of whom noticed their intense gazes and nervous demeanors. Ethel spoke a little Spanish, rode horses with a man's saddle, and kept two pistols holstered on her waist.

In spring 1902, the trio returned to Buenos Aires to petition for title to their 25,000-acre ranch. While James Ryan visited with George Newbury to seek guidance about filing the paperwork, Harry and Ethel returned to the US. Part of the trip was to visit Harry's family in Pennsylvania, where he mentioned his new digs in Cholila. Another reason was seeking medical treatment, possibly for old wounds or maybe even venereal diseases. Back in South America, the man once known as Butch would soon come down with his own bad case of the "town disease." As members of the Wild Bunch, the outlaws had rarely shown restraint. Meanwhile, the history of the mysterious Etta Place often pointed to her being a prostitute before falling in with the gang and going north via the outlaw trail to become a teacher.

While readying to return to Argentina, Harry read in the newspaper that, a few days before, Butch and Sundance had been identified as robbing a train in Illinois. The more things changed, the more they stayed the same. Harry and Ethel boarded a steamship and settled in for the monthlong trip.

. . . .

Back at the Cholila ranch, James Ryan found himself alone and decided to write a letter to a friend in Vernal, the former mother-in-law of Elzy Lay. Feeling it was safe, he even indicated his exact location in Argentina so that the recipient could write back.

> *"My Dear friend . . . I am still alive . . . [the] US was too small for me . . . I was restless, I wanted to see more of the world. . . . Another of my Uncles died and left $30,000 . . . to our little family of 3 so I took my $10,000 . . . I visited the best Cities and best parts on the countrys of South A. till I got here . . . and I think for good. For I like the place better every day. . . . The only thing lacking is a cook. For I am still living in Single Cussidness and I sometimes feel very lonely . . . but I am at the foot of the Andes Mountains, and all the land east of here is prairie and Deserts . . . the Chilian Gov. had cut a road almost across so that next summer we will be able to go to Port Mont, Chile, in about 4 days. . . . The climate is a great deal milder than Ashley Valley. . . . "*

When Harry and Ethel returned, the three expats continued their ranching life. They raised cattle on the open range until they doubled their stock. They grazed sheep and planted grain and vegetables. Back home in the US, reports began to circulate that the infamous bandits had finally gone straight. The *Wyoming Press* reported in November 1902 that Butch was no longer wanted in that state, provided he stayed away. That winter, Sheriff Pope of Uintah County claimed he'd been in touch with Butch, who had given up his wild outlaw days and now lived a quiet life that would continue if he were left alone.

Explore the Outlaw Trail!

We're pretty far from home now, folks, but how about **Adventure (#TBD): Argentina**?

But the Pinkertons had other plans. The detective agency recognized the publicity bonanza they'd receive for capturing the West's most infamous outlaws. Their army of operatives across the US continued to hunt for clues to Butch and Sundance's whereabouts. In February 1903, they got their break. The Pinkertons intercepted a letter written by Harry to his sister in Pennsylvania, which listed the location of their ranch.

Robert Pinkerton wrote to the Union Pacific Railroad and the American Bankers Association, seeking funding for a mission to Argentina to capture the outlaws. But the banks and railroads balked. Why bring their two biggest nemeses back to US soil, where they might very well escape and renew their reign of terror? Better to leave them where they were.

On their own dime, the Pinkertons sent agent Frank Dimaio to Buenos Aires a month later. The detective interviewed George Newbury, who identified James Ryan and Harry Place as the outlaws Butch Cassidy and the Sundance Kid. But Newbury discouraged Dimaio from trying to immediately arrest them. March in the southern hemisphere, with the rainy season about to begin, was a dangerous time to be trekking for weeks through impenetrable jungles. A far better approach was for Newbury to lure the men to Buenos Aires on the pretense of paperwork related to their land. Dimaio agreed to the plan, and before returning to the US to inform Robert Pinkerton, he sent wanted posters for Butch and Sundance to authorities across southern Argentina.

Once Dimaio was gone, Newbury probably realized it was only a matter of time before the Pinkertons returned. Especially if they discovered there were no jungles on the road to Cholila.

BROWNS PARK STORIES

Queen Ann Bassett, 1899–1917

An impulsive plan • A mysterious assassin • Drunken confessions • The war escalates • The trials of Queen Ann • A bittersweet end

THE BROWNS PARK range wars were in full effect during the summer of 1899 when a herd of twenty-one cattle with an unfamiliar brand crossed the divide, the ridge halfway between Browns Park and the Little Snake River. Learning about the cattle's arrival, Ann Bassett was furious at the incursion. Whether they were a breach of the divide by the cattle companies or a herd stolen and moved into the area by rustlers was unclear. Regardless, she wanted them out. Hatching a plan, she and some friends herded the cattle into the Green River, which was swollen with spring runoff. Those that made it across wandered into Utah, disappearing into the mountains south, never to be seen again.

Soon the owner inquired with the Browns Park Cattle Association about the missing herd. He was an independent owner unaffiliated with the Snake River Stock Growers Association, and they'd been stolen from his ranch near Baggs, Wyoming. Matt Rash recognized a precarious situation during a tense time and began searching. The twenty-one-year-old Ann, embarrassed at her impulsiveness, kept quiet.

Without realizing it, Ann had fallen for a trap set by Tom Horn, the mysterious agent of the stock growers. Claiming to find hides branded with VD at the homes of several Browns Park ranchers, including Matt Rash, Horn presented his evidence to the cattle barons. Clearly, Browns Park was a den of thieves, and they authorized his ruthless plan.

In early July 1900, Matt stopped by the Bassett Ranch to visit with fiancée Ann. Afterward, he rode up to a summer cabin on Cold Springs Mountain. He was eating lunch in the cabin when he was shot in the back through the open door. Turning around, he was shot again in the chest. He dragged himself to bed, where he was found dead a few days later.

Ann was devastated and filled with vengeful rage toward Ora Haley and Two Bar Ranch. She went to the sheriff, convinced the shooter was Tom Hicks, who had left the valley a few days before Matt was murdered. But then a letter came from Hicks, postmarked in Denver on the day of Matt's murder, saying the cook would be returning soon. Ann didn't buy this alibi, but no one seemed inclined to arrest Hicks when he returned to the valley as the letter had said. Hicks pointed blame at Matt's friend Isom Dart, claiming he'd seen the two friends get into a fight not long back. Then Hicks left the valley again.

Months later, Isom Dart was walking with George Bassett at the Cold Springs Ranch. A rifle shot caught Isom in the back, and he fell dead. George fled inside and hid with his siblings for hours, until they finally ventured out for help. The assassin had shot from behind a tree at a distance of 120 yards. Everyone in the valley liked Isom tremendously, agreeing that, like most ranchers, he came about the majority of his cattle honestly.

The ruins of Two Bar Ranch in Browns Park (Adventure 59) speak to the valley's past.

These murders worked as desired. The fight went out of the Browns Park ranchers, who stopped patrolling the divide. Only Ann Bassett resumed the campaign, riding by herself atop her horse with a rifle, shooting the occasional Two Bar livestock that came her way.

The reply was swift. In November 1900, Ann received a letter saying she should leave Browns Park within thirty days or she would be killed. A month later, two bullets came through the front door of her home and impacted the opposite wall. The family extinguished the lamps and fired guns out the window, hiding in the dark until morning.

The threatening letter had been postmarked in Cheyenne, where that same month Horn gave a sensational interview. He claimed he was a colonel from the Indian Wars, and he slandered Rash and Dart as two of the most notorious outlaws ever seen in the Rocky Mountains. Furthermore, he said, the men were drunks who harbored the West's worst criminals. The papers printed such lies as facts, but Horn's pathological ways would soon be his undoing.

Known for bragging about his many murders, Horn was entrapped by the Pinkerton agent Joe Lefors through a drunken confession for the murder of a fifteen-year-old boy named Willie Nickels. Though Horn had killed many innocent people in his time, he was found guilty for the one murder he may not have committed. In November 1903, Horn fell through the gallows, a noose snapping his neck. One of the West's most notorious assassins had outlived his usefulness to the nefarious cattle barons. They had done what they felt necessary to intimidate the independent ranchers, and only a few of them continued to fight against the odds.

Back in Browns Park, Ann was just as determined as ever to win her war against Ora Haley, the owner of Two Bar Ranch. Things had quieted down since the attempt on her life, with the *Denver Post* informing readers about a tasteless "War on a Woman," according to Grace McClure in *The Bassett Women*. In 1904 Ann made her next move. Summoning Hi Bernard from Two Bar, she presented him with a surprising offer: manage an expansion of the Bassett family cattle holdings. Bernard countered Ann's offer with one of his own: a proposal of marriage. Why wouldn't he fall in love with the voluptuous and feisty Ann, who never backed down, he later said. For her part, he admitted, it was mostly about the cattle, and Ann looked the other way regarding Bernard's part in hiring Tom Horn and sanctioning the murder of her former love, Matt Rash.

Josie couldn't believe it when Ann announced the engagement, though Josie understood the challenging nature of relationships in the mountains.

Regardless, Ann saw in Hi a capable manager who followed orders, a rugged cowboy even if he was twenty-four years her senior. For six years, Ann and Hi expanded the Bassett Ranch, while at the same time Ora Haley expanded his. In 1909 Haley made his final strikes, buying the Hoy Bottoms and

Josie Bassett's Later Life

After divorcing Jim McKnight and moving to Rock Springs, Wyoming, Josie Bassett's life took a series of turns. She married and divorced four more times, during an era when divorce was almost unheard of. Josie was accused of poisoning the fourth husband, a violent alcoholic, but she denied it. In 1913 she established a homestead and ranch at Cub Creek in what is now Dinosaur National Monument. During Prohibition, she made chokecherry wine and apricot brandy, hiding her still in nearby Box Canyon. In her sixties, she was tried for cattle rustling. But Josie ditched her ranch pants for a typical grandma's dress and charmed her way to a not-guilty verdict. She spent the final fifty years of her life at Cub Creek and died in 1963 at the age of ninety.

Ann's Final Days

In 1928 Ann married Frank Willis and they relocated to a small town near Saint George, Utah, where they operated a ranch. She died in 1956 at the age of seventy-seven. Her final request was to be cremated and her ashes spread at her longtime home in Browns Park.

moving his headquarters into Browns Park, practically within sight of the Bassett lands.

Then Haley sent an undercover stock detective who posed as a visiting rancher. While staying at the Bassett Ranch, the man found a hanging beef as evidence. There wasn't just one trial of the century in nearby Craig, Colorado, but three. The first two ended in hung juries. Ora Haley testified that Ann had butchered a Two Bar cow, cutting away the brand but leaving a unique spay mark. The defense countered that the cow was from her brother's 7L ranch and that the trial was a charade to obtain access to the spring on Bassett land.

During the first trial, a witness testified he overheard Two Bar employees discussing how to get Ann out of the way. Then, before the second trial, this witness was killed by hired stock detective Bob Meldrum. Fearing for her life, Ann fled to Mexico and refused to appear at the second trial. But she returned for the third and this time earned an acquittal. As the verdict was read, the audience applauded.

Not long after the trial, Ann and Hi divorced, though he stayed on as an unofficial manager of the Bassett lands, which now were surrounded on all sides by Two Bar. And then one day in 1917, Ora Haley became ill. After two decades of conflicts with Ann Bassett, he quietly sold his ranch. Haley's parting statements to the buyer were that the only good rustler was a dead rustler. Then he tossed out three cashed checks, implying they'd been written for the murders of Matt Rash, Isom Dart, and the trial witness.

The war was over, and though Queen Ann had won her battle, it was a bittersweet victory. Most of the other residents and ranchers from the Browns Park of her youth were gone. Only a few holdouts, like Ann, remained. The West that she had known as a child, where Native Americans and homesteaders mingled in an idyllic valley called Browns Park, was gone for good.

Explore the Outlaw Trail!

Frequently mentioned Baggs is in **Adventure 63: Medicine Bow Mountains Museums.** See the cabin and homestead where Josie Bassett lived out her days in **Adventure 45: Dinosaur National Monument (Utah Side)**. And the remains of Two Bar Ranch can be explored in **Adventure 59: Eastern Browns Park.**

The Battle at Roost Canyon, 1899

The safety of Robbers Roost • A posse assembles • A trio of friends • A starlit night • The posse arrives • The end of an era

THE FINAL RUSTLE by the outlaws known as Blue John Griffith, Indian Ed Newcomb, and Silver Tip happened in southeastern Utah during February 1899. A few weeks before, they'd stolen horses near Baggs, Wyoming, and were chased by a gun-toting rancher. After selling the horses in Colorado, the three men turned west on the outlaw trail. Along the way, they began collecting a new herd: Nabbing one from a ranch near Monticello, Utah. A mule from the Courthouse Rock stagecoach station. A gray racehorse, plus others, from around Moab.

The trio crossed the Colorado and Green Rivers, turning south toward Robbers Roost, where they figured they'd be safe from pursuit. They reached Roost Spring on a sunny but cold afternoon in late February. After watering their stock from the trough, they proceeded up the dry creek bed to the cabin above the spring.

This was a time when livestock rustling around Utah was at an all-time high. Despite Robbers Roost's reputation for harboring known outlaws, no sheriff had ever entered the Roost. In part, this was because no one paid them enough to take the risk. Back then, Utah sheriffs were paid $500 a year. To encourage lawmen to go after these brazen outlaws, Governor Wells offered $500 rewards for each of twelve well-known outlaws who frequented the Roost. Two of the names on the list were Blue John and Silver Tip.

When three outlaws stole horses from the Moab area, Sheriff Jesse Tyler wasn't pleased. He suspected two of the robbers were Blue John and Silver Tip. So Sheriff Tyler decided it was time to a pay a visit to the Roost. He gathered a posse of five deputies and citizens, setting off in a southwesterly direction toward their quarry.

All three outlaws were minor members of the Wild Bunch, known mostly for lending a hand when needed: Delivering supplies. Transporting people. Assisting with robberies. The trio had been friends for ten years, ever since they'd met at White Canyon town, near Dandy Crossing on the Colorado River, during the winter of 1889. When the spring of 1890 had arrived, the trio of new friends rode up Trachtye Canyon toward the Henry Mountains and soon discovered the Roost. They were still riding the same trails together ten years later.

Silver Tip was the oldest, about forty by the turn of the twentieth century, with dark hair that was turning gray around the temples. Indian Ed was in his late twenties, a tall, somber man who was half Cherokee, known for sketching doodles, including images of the people he was speaking with, in the sand with a twig while talking. Blue John was thirty-five years old, with one brown eye and one blue. A small-time rustling equivalent of a renaissance man, Blue John was a cook, errand boy, and experienced boatman along the Colorado River.

Visiting the so-called Butch Cassidy cabin in Robbers Roost (Adventure 20) makes for an excellent outlaw adventure.

In late February 1899, when they reached the cabin near the head of Roost Canyon with the stolen horseflesh from Moab, Blue John threw open the cabin door and was greeted by the stench of a rat's nest.

"Why don't we go on up and camp at the cave spring?" mused Silver Tip.

The three men rode east a few hundred yards and turned north up a creek bed filled with rabbitbrush. After a short way, they entered a narrow canyon with steep walls of sunburnt sandstone. The spring was just a trickle coming from a grotto at the tapering head of this side canyon. Tucked into the western cliffs were a pair of small caves. In one cave, Silver Tip had hidden firewood. He and Blue John went to work unloading the saddle packs. Indian Ed took the stolen horses to a grassy area in the main wash and tied each pair of front legs together to hobble them.

From an article in the Tacoma Times *in 1913 (Library of Congress)*

For supper that evening, the trio had steaks from an antelope they'd shot. They baked biscuits in a dutch oven on the open fire. In the narrow gap between canyon walls, thousands of stars dotted the sky like raindrops frozen midfall.

"Guess I'll have to haul down another load of wood," mused Blue John.

"I don't think we'll ever need it," said Silver Tip. "Looks to me like the old days are about gone."

"I bet you're right," said Indian Ed, wiping away the image he had made in the sand.

The three men soon settled in their bedrolls on flat ground cleared inside the shallow caves. When the moon rose over the cliffs, it shined a milky light, with a dim iridescence like a cloudy day.

The next morning, Indian Ed was going for the horses when a blast of rifle fire broke the dawn silence. The shot ricocheted off the sandstone walls and embedded just above Indian Ed's knee. He fell to the ground and crawled back to the cave.

Silver Tip and Blue John grabbed their rifles and returned fire in the direction of the main wash. Given the commotion, it was hard to tell where Sheriff Tyler's posse was located. But Silver Tip thought he spotted them about a hundred yards down from the caves, behind some brush and rocks. Indian Ed dressed his bleeding wound before joining in the fracas.

A horrendous firefight continued, with bullets flying in both directions yet all missing their targets. Eventually, Blue John pinpointed the posse and resumed firing. Soon the posse withdrew and rode south past Roost Spring and out from Robbers Roost toward Hanksville. The battle at Robbers Roost was over.

The reactions back in town were mixed. On one hand, the law had finally come to the Roost. On the other, the outlaws got away yet again.

"As far as I can see, this is it," said Silver Tip, after they were sure the posse had gone. "I'm getting out while I can still travel."

"Me too," agreed Blue John. "And I think we better split up right here."

"I'm plumb through with this kind of life," said Indian Ed, grimacing from his throbbing leg. "And if I can get out of this scrape, this finishes my outlaw days."

The three men split up the camping equipment and horses. Indian Ed and Silver Tip went partway to Hanksville before going their own directions. Indian Ed stayed with some sheepherders for two weeks, letting his leg heal, before a mysterious ally brought him a horse and he rode off. Some said he returned to Oklahoma, but no one could say for sure.

Silver Tip went overland between the steps of the Grand Staircase and the western shore of the Colorado River. At a cabin in upper Paria River canyon, he was surprised by a three-man posse that had trailed him. They caught him at the cabin door, and there wasn't much to do but surrender. Silver Tip was put in leg irons and taken to the courthouse in Beaver, Utah. He was sentenced to ten years in the Utah State Penitentiary but was released after two. He drifted through Browns Park and into Wyoming, where he spent the rest of his life.

The fate of Blue John was the most mysterious of the three. After leaving Robbers Roost, he picked up a trail that led him through a maze-like region of multicolored rock spires, then he dropped down a steep cliff to Spanish Bottom and crossed the Colorado River. That fall he was spotted at Hite, where ten years earlier his adventure on the outlaw trail had begun.

From Hite, Blue John departed by boat for Lees Ferry. But he never arrived. The last he was seen, Blue John was rowing on the Colorado River through the confines of Glen Canyon.

Explore the Outlaw Trail!

Whoa, more excuses to visit Utah? Well, shucks. The battle took place at **Adventure 20: Robbers Roost Spring, Cabin, and Caves**. The trio met near **Adventure 29: Hite Marina**; they went up Trachyte, which is adjacent to **Adventure 28: North Wash**, and passed the Henry Mountains (**Adventure 27: Mount Ellen Summit Hike**). Silver Tip was caught somewhere up around **Adventure 39: Paria Townsite and Paria Box**. Blue John's steep hike to Spanish Bottom is found in **Adventure 21: The Maze District**, but the trail is most commonly used by rafters during **Adventure 30: Cataract Canyon River Trip**.

WILD BUNCH STORIES

EPISODE 16

Banditos Yanquis en Bolivia, 1905–1908

Enter Grice and Hood • On the outlaw trail again • Old habits die hard • The Concordia Tin Mine • A friend named Percy Seibert • The Aramayo Payroll robbery • A shootout in San Vincente • All contact ceases • A 1930s article • A 1960s screenplay • Lula lights a match

ON FEBRUARY 14, 1905, a pair of Yankee bandits walked inside the Banco de Londres y Tarapacá in Rio Gallegos, a town on the coast of southern Argentina. They had come to make a withdrawal, presenting long-barreled revolvers in lieu of identification. They rode away with 70,000 pesos, using a series of horse relays to outdistance pursuing law enforcement, cutting telegraph wires as they went.

The outlaw who did the talking was described as stout and shorter, with light-brown hair and green eyes. The other one was taller and quieter, with blond hair and a skinny face. Both were between twenty-five and thirty years old. Early suspects included a pair of American outlaws named Grice and Hood, who had allegedly spent time visiting a ranch in Cholila. But when reviewing the details supplied by the Pinkertons, the authorities became

Storm clouds rise over buttes near Hanksville, Utah.

convinced these *bandidos yanquis* were none other than the infamous Butch Cassidy and the Sundance Kid.

Except there were a few problems. James Ryan and Harry Place were 700 miles away on their ranch in Cholila when the robbery occurred. Plus they were thirty-nine and thirty-eight, respectively. But when word came that they were the top suspects in the robbery, Butch and Sundance knew exactly what to do. By late spring, they had their affairs in order and beat a trail high into the Andes Mountains, heading for Chile. Sometime that summer, Etta decided to sail aboard a steamship for New York.

In December of that year, four American men robbed the Banco de la Nacion in Villa Mercedes, Argentina. After a close chase and shootout, the bandits got away with 12,000 pesos, aided by a string of horse and supply stations along a route leading across the pampas, over the Andes, and into Chile. The suspects were Butch and Sundance, along with Grice and Hood. If you can't beat them, join them, was possibly the theory.

It had been five years since their last robbery, in Winnemucca, Nevada. But old habits die hard. Soon after the Villa Mercedes robbery, Butch and Sundance returned to a familiar pattern. They rode north and took jobs at the Concordia Tin Mine, about 75 miles southeast of La Paz in the Bolivian

Andes. The two outlaws became couriers for the mine, transporting supplies and payroll from La Paz. Often they carried six figures in cash, and none ever went missing.

Back home, the latest exploits of Butch and Sundance made the *New York Herald*. "Yankee Desperadoes Hold Up Argentine Republic," read the headline. The rest of the article was less accurate, including an appearance at the bank by the deceased Harvey Logan. The *Herald* spiced things up with the murder of the manager, and during an invented stagecoach robbery, the Wild Bunch made a triumphant return by shoving two innocent victims into a bottomless abyss. Regardless, the word was out.

One day, Butch and Sundance stopped into a sheriff's office in the Bolivian town of Santa Cruz and spotted their photos on wanted posters. By now, Butch wore a thick beard and Sundance had gained enough weight that neither was recognizable. Butch joked with the sheriff that they'd keep an eye out for the men so they could split the reward money.

While at the Concordia mine, Butch became friends with the manager, Percy Seibert. The two outlaws would often join the Seibert family for Sunday dinner. Butch would always sit at the table with a view out the window at the road leading up to the house. Seibert soon learned about their true identities, but given that they kept the company safe, he never said a word.

Butch often talked with Percy about his continuing interest to go straight and lead a quiet life. Butch was in his forties now, and life on the run was getting old. Every time they tried to disappear, he explained, someone—bounty hunters, Pinkertons, lawmen—always showed up. Butch told Percy about the old days. Harvey Logan was the most fearless of the Wild Bunch. But the bravest man Butch had ever encountered was an express-car agent who refused to open the door for the gang. They had to use dynamite. A fella named Woodcock.

In the spring of 1908, Sundance slipped up while drunk and bragged to fellow mine employees about their former lives. Soon after, the two outlaws left the company. Over the coming months, Percy tried to keep tabs on his friends. At one point, he thought they took jobs at a stagecoach company run by a Scotsman named James Hutcheon. Then a string of robberies occurred, attributed to a pair of *bandidos yanquis*, which seemed like the work of Butch and Sundance. The payroll of the Santo Domingo Mine. A train near the town of Eucalyptus. A construction company.

In November 1908, two well-armed outlaws wearing bandanas robbed a pack train from the Aramayo and Francke Mining Company. They took the payroll—15,000 bolivianos—and a single mule. Heading southeast, they passed through the village of Tupiza, where they learned that news of the robbery had already spread. Some named the suspects as two *yanquis*, while others said one *yanqui* and a *chileno*. Concerned, the outlaws hustled out of town, heading back toward the northwest, possibly making a run for Peru.

In the village of San Vincente, these bandits made their first of two mistakes. They rode into the village center and rented a room for the night from a resident, who they sent out with money for beer and food. Suspicious of the visitors' weapons and possibly noticing the branded mule, the resident informed the local constable. A small army patrol was stationed nearby, and soon officers and several soldiers approached the rented room.

Through the open doorway, the shorter, slender outlaw fired his revolver, killing one of the soldiers. A horrific gun battle erupted between the parties. Foolishly, the outlaws had left their rifles and extra ammunition in the courtyard, near their horses—their second mistake. In a desperate attempt, the taller, heavier outlaw ran for the weapons, but he was struck by bullets. The smaller outlaw ran out and dragged his friend inside. As night descended, the gun battle slowed, but the standoff lingered, with occasional shots from both sides. Around 10:00 p.m., two shots came from inside the house and then silence. The besiegers, believing it was a ruse to draw them into the open, waited until daylight.

When the soldiers approached the room in the morning, all was quiet. Inside, they found the two *bandidos yanquis* dead. The shorter, slender bandit had shot his injured friend and then turned the gun on himself. Searching their belongings, the soldiers found the stolen payroll from the Aramayo mine, plus gold and silver from the train near Eucalyptus. During an inventory of their possessions, the smaller bandit was found to carry business cards under two names, Enrique B. Hutcheon and Edward Graydon. The larger bandit carried an English dictionary. In their baggage, the soldiers found a map of Bolivia, with a northwesterly route marked. The investigation seemed pretty straightforward, and the two bodies were buried in unnamed graves in a nearby Indian graveyard.

Around this time, back in the US, all letters from Butch and Sundance ceased. When friends heard rumors that they'd been killed in a shootout in Bolivia, most dismissed these tales as yet another fanciful report of their demise. Both had died plenty of times already. But as the years passed, without a word from the two men, people began to wonder. Sure, the occasional article still came out describing Butch and Sundance's latest dramatic capers, but with the Wild Bunch there had always been sensationalized fiction masquerading as fact. Maybe they had died in South America after all?

In 1930, almost twenty-two years after the gunfight in San Vicente, an article titled "'Butch' Cassidy" by Arthur Chapman was published in *Elks Magazine*. The article laid out the dramatic last stand of Butch and the Sundance Kid in South America. After robbing the Aramayo payroll, they had ridden into San Vincente, where they were confronted by dozens of Bolivian solders. After a horrific gunfight and siege lasting for hours, the two outlaws found themselves mortally wounded and running dangerously low on ammunition. Butch reserved the final two bullets for Sundance and himself.

Chapman's main source for the article was the former manager at the Concordia Tin Mine, Butch's friend Percy Seibert, who claimed to have identified the outlaws from San Vincente as his old friends. So dramatic and authoritative was the 1930 account that, within a few years of its publication, friends like Matt Warner were repeating variations of this story as fact.

Later, in the 1960s, a screenwriter named William Goldman used Chapman's story as the basis for a remarkable screenplay, and the acclaimed performances by Paul Newman and Robert Redford solidified the version of events in viewers' minds for generations.

Even Butch's little sister, Lula Parker Betenson, joined the fun by offering her own version of Butch's story. Her book *Butch Cassidy, My Brother* was published in 1975, based on stories their father, Maxi, had told long after Butch had left home.

Then Lula lit a stick of dynamite and tossed it, offering information that would blow up Chapman's tale. Butch didn't die in South America, she claimed. Percy Seibert only said they had died so that Butch and Sundance could escape one last time. Not long after the shootout in Bolivia, Butch had departed South America heading north.

And then he had come home.

WILD BUNCH STORIES

EPISODE 17

Phantoms of the Outlaw Trail, 1922 . . .

A Model T with a camping trailer • Sightings of a phantom • Throwing rattlesnakes • Enter Charles Kelly • Quite a homecoming on the outlaw trail • The story after South America • The adventures of William T. Phillips • Sightings continue • Parting words

IN ROCK SPRINGS, Wyoming, during 1922, a Ford Model T towing a trailer filled with camping equipment pulled into an auto shop owned by John Taylor. While the mechanics went to work on the vehicle, the driver asked Taylor about old-timers who used to frequent the area. Though the driver never gave his name, there was something familiar about him. From a while back, maybe even thirty years. As the Model T drove away, Taylor felt a jolt when he realized who it was.

Two years later, Tom Welch was working on his ranch near Henrys Fork, south of Green River, Wyoming, when a Model T towing a trailer with camping gear lurched to a halt.

"Tom, b'gawd," yelled the driver. "I come back to visit my old friends. You hop in with me and we're goin' to make all the rounds!"

Recognizing the phantom of a friend from long ago, Tom climbed aboard, and off they went on a familiar circuit—South Pass, Lander, Rock Springs, Vernal, and Browns Park.

There were other sightings too.

Stencil Riders of the San Rafael Swell (chapter 3) could be a great title for some Zane Grey fan fiction.

A resident of Circleville came home from a trip to California, claiming he saw a familiar face getting on a train in Los Angeles. The mystery man waved before the train pulled away.

A cousin of the Parker family said a long-gone family member stopped for fuel in a motorboat on the Colorado River.

A seventeen-year-old boy was hunting sage grouse with a friend of his father, who was camped on their family ranch near Jackson, Wyoming. The boy later overheard his dad call the mysterious visitor by the name of a famous Wild West outlaw.

A fella by the name of Fred Hilman was no longer a kid but a married man when a stranger approached him one day.

"Anyone throw a rattlesnake at you lately?" asked the grinning man.

Fred stared at the vaguely familiar face for a moment. A look of realization spread across Fred's face as he remembered a day long past. He'd been a thirteen-year-old boy, standing atop the haystack. A live rattlesnake landing at his feet. The man who threw it stood below, laughing.

Butch Cassidy?

Josie Bassett said Butch visited her twice. The first was in Rock Springs during 1929, when Josie was managing a boardinghouse owned by Tom Vernon.

"Killed in South America—hell!" said Tom after the two of them shared a round of drinks with a supposed dead man.

The second meeting between Josie and Butch happened in Baggs, Wyoming, three years later. Butch brought along a mutual friend.

In 1899, Elzy Lay had been sentenced to life in the New Mexico Territorial Penitentiary, and soon Maude Davis had divorced him. Seven years into his sentence, a riot broke out and Elzy had negotiated the release of the warden's wife and daughter. For his efforts, Elzy received a pardon from the New Mexico governor in 1906. On his release, he'd gone straight and moved to Los Angeles, where he oversaw construction of the All American Canal through Imperial Valley. Apparently, civilian life had been all too kind to Elzy.

"Out of condition," observed Josie about her old friends, Butch and Elzy. "Carried too much weight."

Josie's daughter-in-law, Edith, described a trip in the late 1920s that she took with her aunt, Ann Bassett Willis, to a mining camp in Nevada. One day a man came into camp and began asking Ann about the old days in Browns Park. Did she remember Thanksgiving back in '96? A bank robber who was terrified by serving coffee?

Ann narrowed her eyes at the man. Who was this guy?

"When we were young, I knew you well," said Butch. "I had many a meal at the Bassett cabin."

"If you ever got a close look at his eyes," said Edith, "you'd never forget those eyes."

In the 1930s, Charles Kelly began researching his book *The Outlaw Trail: A History of Butch Cassidy and His Wild Bunch*. Kelly interviewed or corresponded with many people who had lived through the Wild West era and were still alive, including Ann Bassett and Matt Warner.

Folks told Kelly about these stories: Butch Cassidy was still alive and had been seen throughout the West. But Kelly dismissed these claims as fanciful rumors. If Butch were alive, Kelly reasoned, it seemed strange that he'd never returned to the family ranch in Circleville, Utah, to visit his aging father, Maximillian.

. . . .

It was fall 1925 when a black Model T parked in front of the Parker family ranch in Circleville, according to Lula Parker Betenson. Mark Parker, the tenth child, was fixing a fence when he looked up and thought he saw his cousin hopping out. The driver walking across the field wasn't a cousin, but curiously his face displayed that characteristic Parker grin.

Maximillian Parker was eighty-one years old when his son Bob finally came home. Maxi's hair and mustache were white now, and he was sitting in the shade on the kitchen doorstep.

Bob's face was solemn, uncertain how he'd be greeted after forty-one years away. Then he tossed his hat through the open door, and it landed on a post of the rocking chair inside.

"I'll bet you don't know who this is," said Maxi, smiling.

Inside the kitchen, Lula glanced at the stranger with a familiar face. Lula's jaw dropped and her knees felt like rubber. Any lingering resentment toward her outlaw brother, who'd left home when she was two months old, melted away.

"I'm no ghost—no angel either."

—BUTCH CASSIDY, ACCORDING TO LULA PARKER BETENSON,
BUTCH CASSIDY, MY BROTHER

Dinner was an energetic feast. Lamb chops. Mashed potatoes. Garden vegetables. Homemade bread. And bullberry pie for dessert.

"Lula, your bread is as good as Ma's," said Butch. Then he became somber. "Bullberries always have made me homesick. They remind me of Ma."

"We just couldn't understand why you didn't come," said Maxi.

"I can just see her standing," said Butch, describing the day he'd left in 1884.

The family talked into the early morning hours, often about Annie Parker, who had passed away in 1905. Butch said he knew he'd broken his mother's heart. He'd been too ashamed to come home.

When his father asked if he'd killed anyone, Butch said, no, thank God. But some of his boys had itchy trigger fingers, and Butch felt real bad about some posse men who got shot.

Had Butch pulled all the jobs attributed to him?

"Horses were too slow to be in Alaska one day and New Mexico the next," said Butch.

The former outlaw explained his movements over the preceding twenty years. He and Sundance had gone to South America with the intention of going straight, but they'd come to realize they'd always be on the run. When the names of Butch Cassidy and the Sundance Kid were on wanted posters across the continent, they decided to leave South America. But while readying to depart, Butch's leg became swollen from a scorpion bite, and he was unable to travel to meet Sundance at the agreed place and time.

On his own, Butch had drifted up into Mexico City. He was sitting at a bar one day when someone grabbed his shoulder from behind. He tensed

Absolutely no evidence suggests that this is Butch Cassidy's car—but who's to say it isn't?

up, fearing the Pinkertons. Instead, it was Etta Place. She and Sundance got an apartment in the city. Butch visited with them for a few days, including watching a bullfight, before he parted ways. That was the last he ever saw them.

From there, Butch traveled to Alaska but only stayed a year, finding it too cold. Next he went to Europe, traveling around Spain and Italy. He had a little money left, and he wasn't afraid to work along the way.

After listening to his son's story, Maxi invited Butch to stay in Circleville with the Parker family, but his son said it wouldn't be right after all this time. He didn't belong anymore. Plus, he still had some people to look up.

Maxi nodded before turning to Lula and the rest of the family.

"This is our secret," said Maxi. "You are never to mention it to anyone."

According to Lula, a letter came in 1937 claiming Butch had died of pneumonia in the Northwest. And that might have been the end of the story of Robert Leroy Parker.

If not for a man named William T. Phillips.

Starting in the late 1970s, Lula's revelation stirred up the community of outlaw historians. Most dismissed Lula's claims as fabricated to sell books. But a few set about trying to figure out where Butch, had he truly survived, might have lived out his life.

> "No conclusive evidence proves that Butch Cassidy died in the shootout at San Vincente. . . . Some have speculated that if Lula Betenson had been a middle-aged man in a business suit rather than a spry ninety-one-year-old woman, her book would have gotten more respect."
>
> —BILL BETENSON, *BUTCH CASSIDY, MY UNCLE*

In 1977, historian Larry Pointer published *In Search of Butch Cassidy*, a book claiming that Butch Cassidy had returned to the US and lived under the alias William T. Phillips, dying in Spokane, Washington, in 1937.

The evidence linking the two men was substantial. Photos of Phillips, taken later in his life, bore a striking resemblance to photos of Butch, including his Laramie mug shot and the Fort Worth Five portrait.

During the 1930s, Phillips had traveled along the outlaw trail, searching for lost caches of robbery loot and visiting old friends of Butch and the Wild Bunch. Phillips carried on an affair with Butch's former girlfriend, Mary Boyd, in Lander, Wyoming, giving her a ring inscribed from "Geo. C. to Mary B.," recalling Butch's brief alias George Cassidy.

When Phillips walked the streets of Lander, old acquaintances walked up and called him George. Phillips even wrote an unpublished biography of Butch called "The Bandit Invincible," which painted Butch as a turn-of-the-twentieth-century Robin Hood and offered plenty of insider information that few outside the Wild Bunch would have known. For years, Phillips tried to sell his story in Hollywood. When that didn't work, he tried magazines. But the writing was clumsy and filled with clichés, and Phillips met with only rejection.

Phillips even met with Butch's brother, Dan Parker, who seemed satisfied he was his long-lost brother. But other observers remained unconvinced, including Lula, who declared that Phillips was definitely not Butch. The Bassett sisters were similarly unconvinced. Others said they recalled Phillips from the old days, perhaps someone who was associated with Butch.

Then in 2012, Larry Pointer found a mug shot from the Wyoming Territorial Prison in Laramie of an inmate named William T. Wilcox. The mug shot was clearly a young Phillips. His hoax was revealed. The imposter Phillips was several inches taller and as much as fifty pounds heavier than Butch. But of course observers were left to wonder. Were some, if not all, of the sightings of Butch Cassidy actually Phillips all along?

Until the end of her life, Lula maintained that Phillips was not Butch. That the two men died in the same year was simply a coincidence—but one that is hard to believe. Meanwhile, the sightings of Butch continued to be reported.

A doctor in Lander claimed that Butch had his face altered with plastic surgery in Paris.

In 1941 a police officer in Kanab, Utah, pulled over an old man with a California license plate who'd sailed through a stop sign. After giving the old man a warning, the officer went home to his in-laws' place. He was shocked to find the same old man in their living room, chatting about the old days. "This here's an old friend of the family," said the officer's father-in-law. "Bob Parker."

Joyce Warner, daughter of Matt Warner, claimed a man came to her door in November 1939 asking for her father. When the stranger learned Matt had died the previous year, he asked if her father had ever mentioned Butch Cassidy. Joyce explained that Matt had never believed the stories that Butch had died in South America. The man admitted he was Butch and later wrote letters, which stopped coming in 1941.

A twelve-year-old girl stopped by the Parker home in Circleville around 1925 to collect money for a magazine subscription. She recalled a man with piercing eyes who grinned when he spoke. She later overheard the name Bob.

GEORGE CASSADY, ALIAS "BUTCH."

A sketch from an 1896 article in the Salt Lake Herald *(Library of Congress)*

"As absurd as some of the claims of Butch's reappearance seem to be, and many are indeed absurd, should the entire list of sightings be so quickly swept aside? Some of these persons— maybe even just one—could have really met him."

—Richard Patterson, *Butch Cassidy: A Biography*

Sometime in the early 1920s, 50 miles west of Grand Junction, Colorado, between entrenched meanders of the Colorado River through Horsethief Canyon and the rising line of the Book Cliffs, where the trio of outlaws Butch Cassidy, Matt Warner, and Tom McCarty had once made their dramatic escape from Telluride, a Model T Ford filled with camping gear pulled to a halt in the open desert.

Ray Merrick was six years old, milling around while his father and another man fixed a culvert.

Two men climbed out of the Model T. They grabbed shovels and began digging nearby. After a while, they pulled from the ground a cache of ten-dollar gold pieces. The man with the square face gave one to the boy and two each to the working men. Later, Ray and his father would look at wanted posters from the Old West and realize the square-faced man was the infamous outlaw, Butch Cassidy.

"Remember," the man said with a grin. "You never saw a thing."

Explore the Outlaw Trail!

We've reached the end of the story, but the legend of Butch Cassidy gives us a parting romp across the Old West. The sightings began in **Adventure 53: Green River and Rock Springs (Wyoming)**, with mentions spanning **Adventure 65: South Pass City State Historic Site**, **Adventure 67: Lander**, **Adventure 43: Vernal**, and **Adventure 59: Eastern Browns Park**. The famous outlaw allegedly returned to his family at **Adventure 33: Butch Cassidy's Boyhood Home**. Imposter Wilcox apparently met Butch in Laramie at **Adventure 61: Wyoming Territorial Prison**. And the final sighting described happened near **Adventure 15: Colorado River Trips**.

EPILOGUE

Who Were the Outlaws and Why Do We Celebrate Them?

ONE DAY, Butch Cassidy and members of the Wild Bunch were riding across the open desert when they came to an isolated shack. The boys were hungry, according to Charles Kelly in *The Outlaw Trail,* so they asked the old woman inside if they could get something to eat. All she had were a few milk cows and some hens for laying eggs.

The old woman was too frightened to protest, so she went inside the cabin to find something to cook. While tending the fire, she startled as shots came from the front yard. Looking out the window, she saw Butch Cassidy shooting the heads off her chickens.

"Good Lord!" the old woman cried out, explaining the hens were all she had to live on. "You ought to be ashamed of yourself."

"We wanted a chicken dinner," said Cassidy, laughing. "And we've got the money to pay for it."

Cassidy dropped into her hand one ten-dollar golden eagle coin for each chicken he'd shot. Tears welled in the old woman's eyes as she stared at more money than she'd ever seen. Then she went to work preparing the chickens.

Stories like this, involving roughened outlaws demonstrating surprising generosity toward regular folk, even if their requests weren't negotiable, are quite common in Wild West lore. In fact, an almost identical story is told around the Ozarks about another famous outlaw from the Wild West, Jesse James.

Supposedly, one evening Jesse James and his gang came to a cabin owned by an old woman. They asked her to cook up every chicken on her farm. She was worried her family would go hungry, but she didn't dare refuse. After the gang ate, they thanked her politely and left. While clearing the table, the old woman found a gold piece under each plate.

Granted, it's certainly possible that both events could have happened. Such generosity toward common citizens was, in part, good public relations. Outlaws needed assistance during their many treks across remote and inhospitable landscapes. They also wanted to keep witnesses from speaking up when eventual posses came through, asking, "Which way did they go?"

But there are so many romanticized stories about outlaw generosity, it seems reasonable to ask why. Regardless of whether these stories of kindness are true, perhaps the insistence on the continual telling of the outlaws' positive qualities reveals something else. Not about the outlaws themselves, but about the enthusiastic observers who celebrate and glamorize them.

Here's another outlaw generosity story, as told by Matt Warner. During one rough winter in Star Valley, Wyoming, the poor settlers were running low on supplies, but the local shopkeeper refused to sell on credit. So Tom and Bill McCarty held him up, telling the hungry settlers to help themselves to whatever they needed. Then the McCarty brothers paid the shopkeeper half the retail price of the goods, totaling $1,150. An amount worth around $33,000 today—which casts the story in a somewhat dubious light. Still, it might have happened.

So before we discuss the celebrants of the Wild West, let's ponder who these outlaws were. Selfish criminals? Selfless Robin Hoods? Or something in between?

Most biographies place the typical outlaw as growing up in poverty. Often they were rural farmers and hired cowboys who, like Butch Cassidy, watched the American West spring up around them. Occasionally, they were urban poor from cities or towns back East who came west for adventure, like the Sundance Kid.

With the arrival of the railroads came an influx of newcomers and wealth to the West. Prices rose, rents increased, and debts grew. Meanwhile, farming and ranching in the arid mountain environment didn't get any easier. Railroads and cattle barons gobbled up lands, resources, and water rights. It became increasingly challenging to make an honest buck and keep pace, socially, with the wealthier newcomers. So some folks turned to livestock rustling and robbery. But the need for money wasn't their only reason. Another pull was the corresponding notoriety that came with a life on the outlaw trail.

When they were young, many future outlaws no doubt read news stories and dime novels about the bandits who'd gone before them, noticing the fascination and reverence that their exploits received from the general public. Jesse James was one of the first Wild West outlaws, but before him, there had been a long lineage of famous bad men. Pirates, conquistadors, Vikings, crusaders.

So why do we romanticize the stories of bad men like outlaws? What do we gain by glamorizing bank robberies? After all, the outlaws were criminals—thieves and, often, murderers. And yet, to this day, our culture remains fascinated by their law breaking.

Perhaps the reason we glamorize outlaws and continue to turn them into nineteenth-century Robin Hoods has more to do with the people telling the stories than it does with the outlaws who lived them. Maybe we make them into antiheroes because we know what they did is bad and that's precisely what thrills us. Their robberies and escapes, gunfights and murders, captivate our attention. Their casual disregard for the law. Their lack of fear. Their ability to stare death in the face. All of it fascinates the observer who is too cautious to ever go down that path themselves. Even though we know we shouldn't celebrate such behaviors, we can't help ourselves. So we search for reasons why it's OK to look in the first place. The idea of the gentleman outlaw offers a sneaky way around the thorny issue of celebrating criminals.

Though we share the good parts of their story, we do so because we're really interested in the bad parts. Our cultural obsession with violence guarantees that we will keep telling the stories of outlaws and mobsters. But we know that their actions are wrong, so in our attempts to divert criticism for our fascination, we soften the stories. We embellish. We add little positive flourishes about their generosity. Whether these positive features were real or not, we'll probably never know.

If all of this is true, then perhaps Butch Cassidy is the outlaw most appropriate for our modern sensibilities. One who, as far as we know, never killed another person except during his final stand—if that Bolivian gunfight ending his life is accepted as true. Butch seems to have had plenty of fights, of course. He carried a gun and pointed it at people during robberies. And he rode with ruthless murderers. But Butch also seems to have been a friendly and well-liked individual, an outlaw whose generosity seems a bit more believable than others'.

Sure, it's worth asking if he ever was the lone leader of the Wild Bunch that the press made him out to be. It seems debatable that there even was a military-like leader to begin with. It seems possible that the Wild Bunch was just a loose affiliation of bandits and friends, each supplying the skills they best could offer.

My own interest in the outlaw trail has long related to the physical exploits of the outlaws who rode it—specifically the getaways, the travel between hideouts, and the hiding in places that are now considered must-see destinations. Regarding the question of who the outlaws were, I come back to the realization that we'll probably never fully know. For good reason, they kept much of their true selves hidden within their hideouts. Away from the watchful eyes of the general public.

They certainly welcomed such mixed views of themselves, as evidenced by one last anecdote from the annals of Butch Cassidy. This one, also reported by Charles Kelly in *The Outlaw Trail*, was allegedly told by the outlaw himself to Mr. Webster, an old resident of Hanksville:

I'm not as bad as I've been painted. I done a poor feller and his wife a good turn this trip. As I was cutting across the hills, I came to a run-down-looking outfit, but I stopped to see if I could get something to eat. There was an old man and an old woman there. They had tried to make a home, but old age hit quicker'n they imagined, and the fact is they were just about to be run off the place by a feller who had a note again' em. I asked 'em who this gent was and they said they looked to see him show up any minute.

"Which way will he come in?" I asks, and the old woman pointed at an old trail.

I made the old lady take $500, the amount due, and I told her to give it to the feller. I said goodbye and left. I hid out along the trail, and along comes a feller on a horse. He has on black clothes and I had a hunch this was the collector, so I watched him and he went to the old log cabin and the old lady let him in. Maybe five minutes later he come out. When he came up the trail I stopped him, took the $500—and here I am!

Acknowledgments

A big thank-you to everyone who helped out during the creation of this book, including the many insightful museum folks, the fellow adventurers along the trail, and the whole team at Mountaineers Books. *See you out there!*

Resources

ONLINE MAPS AND INFO

Sometimes, the most helpful online materials are found at the longest of unwieldy URLs. The items below are presented by chapter and adventure in the order they appear in the book. In the event of kindling emergency, feel free to burn this page first.

Chapter 1: San Juan Mountains, Southwestern Colorado

Adventure 1. San Juan Skyway
Colorado Department of Transportation, San Juan Skyway, www.codot.gov/travel/scenic-byways/southwest/san-juan-skyway
Durango Area Tourism Office, San Juan Skyway map, www.durango.org/things-to-do/scenic-drives/san-juan-skyway

Adventures 2 & 3. Telluride
Historic district map, www.telluride.com/play/activities/walking-tours
Telluride Via Ferrata, www.telluride.com/activity/via-ferrata

Adventure 4. Escape from Telluride Unofficial Outlaw Byway
Canyons of the Ancients, Sand Canyon and Rock Creek Trails, www.blm.gov/sites/blm.gov/files/SC%20Newspaper%202018.pdf
Montezuma Canyon, www.blm.gov/visit/montezuma-canyon

Adventure 5. Ouray and Perimeter Trail
Box Cañon Falls Park, www.ci.ouray.co.us/city_offices/city_resources/box_canon_waterfalls_vs2.php
Ouray Trail Group, Perimeter Trail map, https://ouraytrails.org/city-ouray-trails/perimeter-trail

Adventure 8. Alpine Loop 4x4 Trail
Colorado Department of Transportation, www.codot.gov/travel/scenic-byways/southwest/alpine-loop
Colorado Tourism, www.colorado.com/byways/alpine-loop
US Forest Service, www.fs.usda.gov/Internet/FSE_DOCUMENTS/stelprdb5286478.pdf

Adventure 9. Durango
Durango Area Tourism Office, www.durango.org/press-room/fact-sheets/historic-walking-tour-facts
Durango Business Improvement District, www.downtowndurango.org/historic-walking-tour

Adventure 11. Upper Arkansas River Valley
Leadville walking tour, https://leadville.com/historic-leadville-walking-tour

Chapter 2: Canyonlands and Moab, Southeastern Utah

Adventure 15. Colorado River Trips
Canyonlands National Park, Cataract Canyon and Meander Canyon, www.nps.gov/cany/planyourvisit/guidedtrips.htm
Moab Daily, www.blm.gov/programs/recreation/recreation-activities/utah (see the "river running" tab)
Ruby-Horsethief, www.blm.gov/visit/ruby-horsethief-canyon-permits
Westwater Canyon, www.blm.gov/programs/recreation/passes-and-permits/lotteries/utah/westwatercanyon

Adventure 17. Blue Mountains
Abajo Loop State Scenic Backway, www.fs.usda.gov/recarea/mantilasal/recarea/?recid=73228
"Abajo Mountains Guide," www.fs.usda.gov/Internet/FSE_DOCUMENTS/fseprd690572.pdf

Chapter 3: Robbers Roost and San Rafael Swell, South-Central Utah

Robbers Roost
Robbers Roost map, www.blm.gov/sites/blm.gov/files/uploads/BLMRobbersRoostMap.pdf

Adventure 18. Green River, Utah
Desolation and Gray Canyons, www.blm.gov/programs/recreation/passes-and-permits/lotteries/utah/desolationgray

Adventure 19: Horseshoe Canyon
Canyonlands National Park, www.nps.gov/cany/planyourvisit/horseshoecanyon.htm

Adventure 21: The Maze District
Canyonlands National Park, www.nps.gov/cany/planyourvisit/maze.htm

San Rafael Swell
San Rafael Swell Recreation Area, www.blm.gov/visit/san-rafael-swell-recreation-area

Adventure 22. Little Grand Canyon
Fullers Bottom put-in, www.blm.gov/visit/fullers-bottom-trailhead
Good Water Rim Trail map, www.alltrails.com/trail/us/utah/the-wedge-and-goodwater-canyon-rim-trail?u=m

Adventure 24. Goblin Valley State Park
Utah State Parks, https://stateparks.utah.gov/parks/goblin-valley

Adventure 25. San Rafael Reef
BLM map, www.blm.gov/sites/blm.gov/files/uploads/BLMUtahTempleMtRec.pdf

Adventure 26. Capitol Reef National Park
Roads, www.nps.gov/care/planyourvisit/roads.htm
Scenic drive, www.nps.gov/care/planyourvisit/scenicdrive.htm

Chapter 4: Henry Mountains and North Lake Powell, Southern Utah

Adventure 30. Cataract Canyon River Trip
Canyonlands National Park, www.nps.gov/cany/planyourvisit/guidedtrips.htm
River permits, www.nps.gov/cany/planyourvisit/riverpermits.htm

Adventure 31. Sundance Trail, Dark Canyon
Dark Canyon trail guide, www.fs.usda.gov/Internet/FSE_DOCUMENTS/stelprdb5316023.pdf
Sundance Trail conditions, www.blm.gov/office/monticello-field-office

Chapter 5: Grand Staircase and South Lake Powell, Southwestern Utah–Northern Arizona

Grand Staircase–Escalante National Monument
General information, www.blm.gov/programs /national-conservation-lands/utah/ grand-staircase-escalante-national-monument

Adventure 34. Red Canyon and Thunder Mountain Trail
Red Canyon Bicycle Trail, www.nps.gov/brca/ planyourvisit/shared-use-path.htm

Adventure 36. Million Dollar Highway and Calf Creek
Box–Death Hollow Wilderness, www.fs.usda .gov/recarea/dixie/recarea/?recid=70912

Adventure 37. Hole-in-the-Rock Road and Coyote Gulch
Glen Canyon National Recreation Area, www.nps.gov/glca/planyourvisit/driving-the-hole-in-the-rock-road.htm

Adventure 38. Cottonwood Canyon Road
BLM map, www.blm.gov/sites/blm.gov/files/ uploads/BLMUtahCottonwoodRoad.pdf

Adventure 41. Southern Lake Powell
Lake Powell paddling trips, www.nps.gov/ glca/learn/management/guidedservices.htm

Adventure 42. Lees Ferry and Glen Canyon
Wilderness River Adventures, www.river adventures.com/horseshoe-bend-rafting-trips/ backhauling-services

Chapter 6: Uinta Basin and Eastern Uinta Mountains, North-Central Utah

Adventure 47. Flaming Gorge–Uintas Scenic Byway
Ashley National Forest, www.fs.usda.gov/ recarea/ashley/recarea/?recid=72355

Adventure 48. Sheep Creek Geological Loop
US Forest Service, www.fs.usda.gov/detail/r4/ learning/nature-science/?cid=stelprdb5166699

Adventure 49. Spirit Lake Scenic Backway
US Forest Service, www.fs.usda.gov/Internet/ FSE_DOCUMENTS/stelprdb5177114.pdf

Adventure 51. Desolation and Gray Canyons River Trip
BLM, www.blm.gov/programs/recreation /passes-and-permits/lotteries/utah/ desolationgray

Chapter 7: Flaming Gorge and Browns Park, Northern Utah–Southern Wyoming

Adventure 52: Flaming Gorge Dam and Reservoir
Ashley National Forest, Flaming Gorge National Recreation Area, www.fs.usda.gov/detail/ashley/ specialplaces/?cid=stelprdb5212203

Adventure 53. Green River and Rock Springs (Wyoming)
Rock Springs Historical Museum, www.rswy .net/department/index.php?structureid=15

Adventure 55. Little Hole National Scenic Trail
Ashley National Forest, www.fs.usda.gov /recarea/ashley/recreation/hiking/ recarea/?recid=72675&actid=50
Flaming Gorge Country, www.flaminggorge country.com/Little-Hole-National-Scenic-Trail

Adventure 56. Swett Ranch Historical Homestead
Ashley National Forest, www.fs.usda.gov /detail/ashley/learning/history-culture/?cid =stelprdb5274691

Adventure 57. Canyon Rim Trail
Ashley National Forest, www.fs.usda.gov/ recarea/ashley/recarea/?recid=72377

Adventure 58. John Jarvie Historic Ranch
BLM, www.blm.gov/visit/john-jarvie-historic
-site

Chapter 8: Snowy Range and Laramie Area, Southeastern Wyoming

Adventure 60. Vedauwoo Recreation Area
Curt Gowdy State Park, https://wyoparks
.wyo.gov/index.php/places-to-go/curt-gowdy
Vedauwoo Recreation Area, www.fs.usda
.gov/wildflowers/regions/Rocky_Mountain/
VedauwooRecAreaPoleMtn/index.shtml

Adventure 61. Wyoming Territorial Prison
Wyoming State Parks, https://wyoparks
.wyo.gov/index.php/places-to-go/wyoming
-territorial-prison

Adventure 62. Snowy Range and Scenic Byway
Medicine Bow National Forest, www.fs.usda
.gov/recarea/mbr/recarea/?recid=81614

Chapter 9: Wind River Range, Western Wyoming

Adventure 69. Stough Creek Lakes Trail
Shoshone National Forest, www.fs.usda.gov/
recarea/shoshone/recarea/?recid=36391

Chapter 10: Bighorn Mountains and Basin, Northern Wyoming

Adventure 73. Cloud Peak Wilderness
**Bighorn National Forest, West Tensleep
trailhead**, www.fs.usda.gov/recarea/bighorn/
recarea/?recid=30656

Adventure 76. Bighorn Canyon and Medicine Wheel
**Bighorn National Forest, Bighorn Medicine
Wheel**, www.fs.usda.gov/detail/bighorn/
home/?cid=fseprd521531

Adventure 78. Meeteetse and Kirwin Ghost Town
Shoshone National Forest, www.fs.usda
.gov/recarea/shoshone/recreation/fishing/
recarea/?recid=35991&actid=43

Adventure 79. Thermopolis and Wind River Canyon
Hot Springs State Park, https://wyoparks.wyo
.gov/index.php/places-to-go/hot-springs

Chapter 11: Black Hills and Badlands, Western South Dakota

Adventure 82. Black Elk Peak Trail
Black Elk Wilderness, www.fs.usda.gov/
recarea/blackhills/recarea/?recid=80906

Adventure 85. Mickelson Rail Trail and Centennial Trail
Black Hills National Forest, www.fs.usda.gov/
recmain/blackhills/recreation
Centennial Trail, https://gfp.sd.gov/userdocs/
centennial-trail-brochure.pdf
Mickelson Rail Trail map, https://gfp.sd.gov/
userdocs/mickelson-trail-map.pdf
South Dakota Game, Fish, and Parks, https://
gfp.sd.gov
Wind Cave National Park, Centennial Trail,
www.nps.gov/places/centennial-trail.htm

Adventure 86. Deadwood and Lead
Deadwood walking-tour guide, www
.cityofdeadwood.com/sites/default/files/file
attachments/historic_preservation_office/
page/4011/downtown_walking_tour
_brochure.pdf

Chapter 12: Spurs of the Outlaw Trail: Idaho, Southern Arizona, New Mexico, Kansas, and Arkansas

Adventure 90. Tombstone, Arizona
Tombstone Chamber of Commerce,
https://tombstonechamber.com/directory/
museums-galleries-and-historic-attractions
-in-tombstone-az

Adventure 91. Wild Bunch Sites and Billy the Kid Scenic Byway, New Mexico
New Mexico Tourism Department, www.newmexico.org/places-to-visit/scenic-byways/billy-the-kid

Adventure 93. Fort Smith, Arkansas
Oklahoma State Parks, www.travelok.com/state-parks/robbers-cave-state-park

(Let's Get) Physical Maps & Guides

Belknap, Buzz. *Belknap's Waterproof Canyonlands River Guide All New Edition*. www.westwater books.com.

Bezemek, Mike. *Paddling the John Wesley Powell Route*. Lanham, MD: Falcon, 2018.

Kelsey, Michael. *Hiking and Exploring Utah's Henry Mountains and Robbers Roost*. Self-published, 2009.

———. *Hiking and Exploring Utah's San Rafael Swell*. Self-published, 2014.

Latitude 40° Recreation Topo Maps. *Moab Singletrack Utah; Salida Buena Vista; Southwest Colorado Trails*. www.latitude 40maps.com.

Martin, Tom, and Duwain Whitis. *RiverMaps Guide to the Colorado and Green Rivers in the Canyonlands of Utah and Colorado*. www.vishnutemplepress.com.

National Geographic Trails Illustrated Topographic Maps series. www.natgeo maps.com/trail-maps/trails-illustrated -maps.

US Forest Service, *Bridger-Teton National Forest, Pinedale Ranger District and Bridger Wilderness*. https://store.usgs.gov/fsmaps.

Bibliography

Most of these listings are the sources I used when writing this book, and I quote from many of them throughout the text. A few are recommended reading for those interested in knowing more about the outlaw trail.

Baker, Pearl. *The Wild Bunch at Robbers Roost.* Los Angeles: Westernlore Press, 1965. Reprinted. Lincoln: University of Nebraska Press, 1989.

Betenson, Bill. *Butch Cassidy, My Uncle: A Family Portrait.* Rev. ed. Glendo, WY: High Plains Press, 2017.

Betenson, Lula Parker. *Butch Cassidy, My Brother.* Provo, UT: Brigham Young University Press, 1975.

Blewer, Mac. "Butch Cassidy in Wyoming." WyoHistory.org. November 8, 2014. www.wyohistory.org/encyclopedia/butch-cassidy-wyoming.

———. *Wyoming's Outlaw Trail.* Mount Pleasant, SC: Arcadia Publishing, 2013.

Blust, Dick, Jr. "The Diamond Hoax: A Bonanza That Never Was." WyoHistory.org. March 9, 2020. www.wyohistory.org/encyclopedia/diamond-hoax-bonanza-never-was.

Burroughs, John Rolfe. *Where the Old West Stayed Young.* New York: William Morrow and Co., 1962.

Carlson, Chip. *Tom Horn: Blood on the Moon: Dark History of the Murderous Cattle Detective.* Glendo, WY: High Plains Press, 2001.

Chapman, Arthur. "'Butch' Cassidy." *Elks Magazine.* April 1930.

Deseret Evening News. "Butch Cassidy to Surrender." June 29, 1900.

Fifer, Barbara, and Martin Kidston. *Wanted Posters of the Old West: Stories Behind the Crimes.* Helena, MT: Far Country Press, 2003.

Harpending, Asbury. *The Great Diamond Hoax: And Other Stirring Episodes in the Life of Asbury Harpending.* San Francisco, CA: James H. Barry Co., 1913.

Horan, James D. *Desperate Men: The James Gang and the Wild Bunch.* Lincoln: University of Nebraska Press, 1997.

Kelly, Charles. *The Outlaw Trail: A History of Butch Cassidy and His Wild Bunch.* Self-published, 1938. Reprinted. Lincoln: University of Nebraska Press, 1959.

Kouris, Diana Allen. *Nighthawk Rising: A Biography of the Accused Cattle Rustler Ann Bassett of Browns Park.* Glendo, WY: High Plains Press, 2019.

———. *Riding the Edge of an Era: Growing Up Cowboy on the Outlaw Trail.* Greybull, WY: Wolverine Gallery, 2009.

———. *The Romantic and Notorious History of Browns Park.* Greybull, WY: Wolverine Gallery, 1988.

McCarty, Tom. *Tom McCarty's Own Story: Autobiography of an Outlaw.* Hamilton, MT: Rocky Mountain House Press, 1986.

McClure, Grace. *The Bassett Women.* Athens, OH: Swallow Press, 1985.

Meadows, Anne. *Digging up Butch and Sundance.* Lincoln: University of Nebraska Press, 2003.

Patterson, Richard. *Butch Cassidy: A Biography.* Lincoln: University of Nebraska Press, 1998.

———. *Historical Atlas of the Outlaw West.* Chicago: Johnson Publishing Co., 1985.

———. *Train Robbery: The Birth, Flowering, and Decline of a Notorious Western Enterprise.* Chicago: Johnson Publishing Co., 1981.

Phillips, William T. "The Bandit Invincible." Unpublished manuscript.

Pointer, Larry. *In Search of Butch Cassidy.* Norman: University of Oklahoma Press, 1977.

Redford, Robert. *The Outlaw Trail: A Journey Through Time*. New York: Grosset and Dunlap, 1976.

Reilly, P. T. *Lees Ferry: From Mormon Crossing to National Park*. Logan: Utah State University Press, 1999.

Rutter, Michael. *Wild Bunch Women*. Lanham, MD: Globe Pequot/TwoDot Books, 2003.

Salt Lake Herald. "Desperadoes at Castle Gate." April 22, 1897.

——. "Most Desperate Plot Unearthed." September 9, 1896.

——. "Outlaws Are in the South." September 17, 1896.

San Francisco Call. "Rounding Up Outlaws in the Colorado Basin." April 3, 1898.

Siringo, Charles A. *A Cowboy Detective: A True Story of Twenty-Two Years with a World-Famous Detective Agency*. Chicago: W. B. Conkey Co., 1912.

Stockbridge, Frank Parker. "'Easy Money' Didn't Pay." *Tacoma Times*. September 2, 1913.

Sun, The. "Cassidy's Outlaw Band." April 29, 1900.

Thomson, Frank. *The Thoen Stone: A Saga of the Black Hills*. Detroit, MI: Harlo Press, 1969.

Turner, Erin H., ed. *Outlaw Tales of the Old West*. Lanham, MD: Globe Pequot/TwoDot Books, 2016.

Warner, Matt, as told to Murray E. King. *The Last of the Bandit Riders*. New York: Bonanza Books, 1938.

Washington Bee. "Bloodthirsty Outlaws." May 27, 1899.

Wellman, Paul I. *A Dynasty of Western Outlaws*. Lincoln: University of Nebraska Press, 1961.

Wilson, Robert. "The Great Diamond Hoax of 1872." *Smithsonian Magazine*. June 2004. www.smithsonianmag.com/history/the-great-diamond-hoax-of-1872-2630188.

Wommack, Linda. *Ann Bassett: Colorado's Cattle Queen*. Glendo, WY: High Plains Press, 2018.

Index

About the Author

MIKE BEZEMEK is the author and photographer of six books, including several that combine stories with trip guides such as *Paddling the John Wesley Powell Route: Exploring the Green and Colorado Rivers* and *Space Age Adventures: Over 100 Terrestrial Sites and Out of This World Stories*. He has written for a variety of publications, including *Outside, Men's Journal, National Parks Magazine, Adventure Cyclist, Blue Ridge Outdoors, Duct Tape Diaries*, and *Terrain Magazine*. Connect with him at mikebezemek.com.

MOUNTAINEERS BOOKS including its two imprints, Skipstone and Braided River, is a leading publisher of quality outdoor recreation, sustainability, and conservation titles. As a 501(c)(3) nonprofit, we are committed to supporting the environmental and educational goals of our organization by providing expert information on human-powered adventure, sustainable practices at home and on the trail, and preservation of wilderness.

Our publications are made possible through the generosity of donors, and through sales of 700 titles on outdoor recreation, sustainable lifestyle, and conservation. To donate, purchase books, or learn more, visit us online:

MOUNTAINEERS BOOKS

1001 SW Klickitat Way, Suite 201 • Seattle, WA 98134

800-553-4453 • mbooks@mountaineersbooks.org • www.mountaineersbooks.org

An independent nonprofit publisher since 1960

Mountaineers Books is proud to support the Leave No Trace Center for Outdoor Ethics, whose mission is to promote and inspire responsible outdoor recreation through education, research, and partnerships. The Leave No Trace program is focused specifically on human-powered (non-motorized) recreation. For more information, visit www.lnt.org.

YOU MAY ALSO LIKE